Lutheran Identity and Political Theology

CHURCH OF SWEDEN

Research Series

❦

Göran Gunner, editor
Vulnerability, Churches, and HIV (2009)

Kajsa Ahlstrand and Göran Gunner, editors
Non-Muslims in Muslim Majority Societies (2009)

Jonas Ideström, editor
For the Sake of the World (2010)

Göran Gunner and Kjell-Åke Nordquist
An Unlikely Dilemma (2011)

Anne-Louise Eriksson, Göran Gunner, and Niclas Blåder, editors
Exploring a Heritage (2012)

Kjell-Åke Nordquist, editor
Gods and Arms (2012)

Harald Hegstad
The Real Church (2013)

Carl-Henric Grenholm and Göran Gunner, editors
Justification in a Post-Christian Society (2014)

Carl-Henric Grenholm and Göran Gunner, editors
Lutheran Identity and Political Theology (2014)

Lutheran Identity and Political Theology

Edited by
CARL-HENRIC GRENHOLM
AND GÖRAN GUNNER

⸲PICKWICK *Publications* · Eugene, Oregon

LUTHERAN IDENTITY AND POLITICAL THEOLOGY
Church of Sweden Research Series 9

Copyright © 2014 Trossamfundet Svenska Kyrkan (Church of Sweden). All rights reserved. Except for brief quotations in critical publications or reviews, no part of this book may be reproduced in any manner without prior written permission from the publisher. Write: Permissions, Wipf and Stock Publishers, 199 W. 8th Ave., Suite 3, Eugene, OR 97401.

In cooperation with the Department of Theology, Uppsala University, Sweden

Pickwick Publications
An imprint of Wipf and Stock Publishers
199 W. 8th Ave., Suite 3
Eugene, OR 97401

www.wipfandstock.com

ISBN 13: 978-1-62564-890-7

Cataloging-in-Publication data:

    Lutheran identity and political theology / edited by Carl-Henric Grenholm and Göran Gunner.

    xii + 242 p. ; 23 cm. Includes bibliographical references.

    Church of Sweden Research Series 9

    ISBN 13: 978-1-62564-890-7

    1. Lutheran Church—Doctrines. 2. Political Theology. I. Title. II. Series.

BX8065.2 L853 2014

Manufactured in the U.S.A.

New Revised Standard Version Bible, copyright 1989, Division of Christian Education of the National Council of the Churches of Christ in the United States of America. Used by permission. All rights reserved.

Contents

Contributors | vii
Abbreviations | xi

1 Introduction: Lutheran Tradition in Transition—*Carl-Henric Grenholm and Göran Gunner* | 1

PART ONE: Lutheran Identity in a Global World

2 Planet Luther: Challenges and Promises for a Lutheran Global Identity —*Vítor Westhelle* | 15
3 Burning Issues—*Göran Gunner* | 30
4 Lutheran Perspectives on the Right to Health in a Global World —*Ville Päivänsalo* | 49
5 "There's an App for That!": A Post-Christian Lutheran Response —*Michael R. Trice* | 67

PART TWO: Lutheran Tradition and Gender

6 For the Sake of the Future: Rekindling Lutheran Theology on Spirituality, Equality, and Inclusivity—*Kirsi Stjerna* | 83
7 Liberating Aspects in Lutheran Theology for a Post-Gender Politics —*Else Marie Wiberg Pedersen* | 101
8 Re-Embracing the Body of Jesus Christ: A Queer, Lutheran Theology of the Body of Christ—*Mary Elise Lowe* | 117
9 Idolatry-Critical Justification and the Foreclosed Gendered Life *Mary J. Streufert* | 134

PART THREE: Lutheran Theology and Politics

10 Luther, Wittgenstein, and Political Theology—*Tage Kurtén* | 155
11 The "Communitarian" Critique of Luther's Ethics—*Leif Svensson* | 172
12 Reconfiguring Church-State Relations: Toward a Rwandan Political Theology—*Victor Thasiah* | 190
13 Transforming Domination Then and Now—*Karen L. Bloomquist* | 208
14 Eros, Ethics, and Politics: Nuptial Imagery in Luther Read as a Challenge to Traditional Power Structures—*Elisabeth Gerle* | 222

Contributors

KAREN L. BLOOMQUIST is the Dean of Pacific Lutheran Theological Seminary of California Lutheran University in Berkeley, USA. Previously she directed the theology and studies unit in the Lutheran World Federation, and before then, in the Evangelical Lutheran Church in America. She has also been on the faculty of ELCA seminaries in Chicago, Dubuque, and Philadelphia, and has also served as a parish pastor. Among her publications are *The Dream Betrayed: Religion Challenge of the Working Class* (1990) and *The Promise of Lutheran Ethics* (1998). She has edited a number of LWF publications, among them the six-book Theology in the Life of the Church series (2007–2009).

ELISABETH GERLE is Adjunct Professor in Ethics, especially Human Rights at Uppsala University and Researcher at Church of Sweden Research Unit, Uppsala. She has worked on religion and politics, and written on neo-atheism and neo-nationalism, on racism, and xenophobia. Within a broad research project on Lutheran theology today she has written on marriage and sexuality from a Lutheran perspective. Among her publications are *Farlig förenkling* (Dangerous Simplification 2010), *Luther som utmaning: Om frihet och ansvar* (Luther as Challenge: On Freedom and Responsibility, 2008), and *Mänskliga rättigheter för Guds skull* (Human Rights for God's Sake, 2006).

CARL-HENRIC GRENHOLM is Senior Professor of Ethics at the Department of Theology, Uppsala University, Sweden. His main research areas are ethical theory, Christian social ethics, work ethics, ethics and economics, and theological ethics. He is the leader of a research project on Lutheran Theology and Ethics—in a Post-Christian Society. Among his publications are *Protestant Work Ethics* (1993), *Teologisk etik* (Theological Ethics, 1997), *Bortom Humanismen* (Beyond Humanism, 2003), *Sustainable Development and Global Ethics* (2007), and *Etisk teori: Kritik av moralen* (Ethical Theory, 2014).

GÖRAN GUNNER is Associate Professor in Mission Studies, Uppsala University, and Researcher at Church of Sweden Research Unit, Uppsala. Dr. Gunner is also Senior Lecturer at Stockholm School of Theology, Stockholm, Sweden. His research areas include religious minority situations in the Middle East and issues related to human rights. He is also the editor of Church of Sweden Research Series. Among his publications are *An Unlikely Dilemma: Constructing a Partnership between Human Rights and Peace-Building* (co-authored with Kjell-Åke Nordquist, 2011) and *Genocide of Armenians: Through Swedish Eyes* (2013).

TAGE KURTÉN is Professor in Theological Ethics and Philosophy of Religion, Åbo Akademi University, Finland. His main interest is in contemporary theology with an emphasis on presuppositions taken for granted in secular views of life, in morality, and in religious beliefs. He took part in a large Nordic network on Religion, Ethics and Law (2003–2008), and has been in charge of three interdisciplinary projects on Ethics, law and late modernity (2000–2011). He is editor of the anthologies *Homo moralis. Människan och rättssamhället* (Human Being and the Rule of Law, 2005), *Legitimacy: The Treasure of Politics* (2011), and *Crisis and Change: Religion, Ethics and Theology under Late Modern Conditions* (2012).

MARY ELISE LOWE is Associate Professor of Religion at Augsburg College in Minneapolis, USA. Her main areas of research and teaching are in the field of contemporary theology, with specialities in theological anthropology, feminist theologies, queer theologies, the doctrine of sin, and disability theologies. Among her publications are "'Rabbi, Who Sinned?' Disability Theologies and Sin" (2012), "Queering Kenosis: Luther and Foucault on Power and Identity" (2011), "Sin from a Queer, Lutheran Perspective" (2010), and *The Human Subject and Sin: The Anthropology of Pannenberg, Ruether, and Fulkerson* (2010).

VILLE PÄIVÄNSALO is Assistant Professor in global theology, world views, and ideologies on the Faculty of Theology, the University of Helsinki, Finland. He has also served as an acting university lecturer in theological and social ethics in Helsinki. His main research areas are theories and theologies of justice and health. He is the author of *Balancing Reasonable Justice: John Rawls and Crucial Steps Beyond* (2007).

KIRSI STJERNA is Professor of Reformation Church History and Director of the Institute for Luther Studies at the Lutheran Theological Seminary at Gettysburg, PA, USA and a docent at the Faculty of Theology at the University of Helsinki, Finland. Her research areas include Luther and Lutheran theology, Reformation and gender studies, contemporary issues of justice. Among her publications are *Martin Luther, the Bible and the Jewish People* (co-authored with Brooks Schramm, 2012), *No Greater Jewel: Thinking about Baptism with Luther* (2010), and *Women and the Reformation* (2009). She is one of the general editors, and a volume editor, for *The Essential Luther* (six volumes, forthcoming by 2016).

MARY J. STREUFERT is Director for Justice for Women in the Evangelical Lutheran Church in America. Her research includes Christology, soteriology, ethics, gender, and feminist and Lutheran theology. She assists in developing a social message on gender-based violence and a social statement on gender justice in the ELCA and serves as the Lutheran World Federation Women in Church and Society North American regional coordinator. Publications include *Transformative Lutheran Theologies: Feminist, Womanist, and Mujerista Perspectives*, editor (2010) and "Philosophical Kinship: Luther, Schleiermacher, and Feminists on Reason" (2011).

LEIF SVENSSON is Doctor of Philosophy student at the Department of Historical, Philosophical, and Religious Studies, Umeå University, Sweden. His main field of research is Lutheran ethics. In his dissertation, he is discussing the relationship between, on the one hand, interpretations of Luther's ethics in Wilhelmine Germany and, on the other hand, modern German culture and philosophy, with special attention to Albrecht Ritschl and Karl Holl.

VICTOR THASIAH is Assistant Professor of Religion at California Lutheran University, Thousand Oaks, USA. His main research areas include contemporary political theology, the history of religion and political thought, and Christian ethics. Among his interests are critical theory and human rights. He is currently working on a book on political theology in post-genocide Rwanda, based on ethnographic research.

MICAEL R. TRICE is Assistant Dean of Ecumenical and Interreligious Dialogue at the School of Theology and Ministry, Seattle University, USA. He has previously served as the Associate Executive of Ecumenical and Inter-Religious Relations for the Evangelical Lutheran Church in America. As Assistant Professor of Practical Theology he continues his research interest on the theological practicalities of reconciliation when trespass and trauma defy language. His recent book, *Encountering Cruelty: A Fracture in the Human Heart* (2011) won the distinguished best original dissertation award for Loyola Jesuit University, Chicago.

VÍTOR WESTHELLE is Professor of Systematic Theology at the Lutheran School of Theology at Chicago and the chair of Luther Research at FACULDADES-EST, São Leopoldo, Brazil. Born in Brazil and ordained in IECLB, his research areas include Luther, liberation, creation, the apocalyptic, eschatology, and post-colonialism. Among his publications are *The Scandalous God: The Use and Abuse of the Cross* (2006), *After Heresy: Colonial Practices and Post-Colonial Theologies* (2010), and *Eschatology and Space: The Lost Dimension in Theology Past and Present* (2012).

ELSE MARIE WIBERG PEDERSEN is Associate Professor of Systematic Theology in the Department of Culture and Society, Aarhus University, Denmark. Her research areas are medieval and Reformation theology as well as contemporary systematic theology, and include ecumenism and a gender perspective. Among her publications are *Bernhard af Clairvaux: Teolog eller mystiker?* (Bernard of Clairvaux: Theologian or Mystic?, 2008) currently being translated into English and *Gudstankens aktualitet* (The Relevance of the Concept of God, 2010).

Abbreviations

FBO	Faith-based organization
LGBT	Lesbian, Gay, Bisexual, and Transgender
LGBTQI	Lesbian, Gay, Bisexual, Transgender, Queer, Questioning, and Intersex
LW	Luther, Martin. *Luther's Work's*. 55 vols. Philadelphia: Fortress Press; St. Louis: Corcordia, 1955–1986.
LWF	Lutheran World Federation
NGO	Non-govermental organization
N-T	Natal-Transvaal
RPT	Religion in Philosophy and Theology
TBT	Theologische Bibliothek Töpelmann
VLASR	Veröffentlichungen der Luther-Akademie Sondershausen-Ratzeburg
WA	Luther, Martin. *Werke: Kritische Gesamtausgabe*. 65 vols. Weimar: Hermann Böhlau Nachfolger, 1883–1993.
WABr	Luther, Martin. *Luthers Werke: Kritische Gesamtausgabe. Briefwechsel.* Weimar: Verlag Hermann Böhlaus Nachfolger, 1930–1985.
WA TR	Luther, Martin. *Werke. Kritische Gesamtausgabe. Tischreden.* Weimar: Hermann Böhlaus Nachfolger, 1912–2000.

1

Introduction

Lutheran Tradition in Transition

CARL-HENRIC GRENHOLM & GÖRAN GUNNER

With the Reformation Jubilee in 2017 in mind, there is a need for critical evaluation of the Lutheran tradition, which has been of great importance not just within the churches but also for society and culture in general. Lutheran tradition has in various ways influenced attitudes to work, the economy, the state, education, and health care. How should this tradition be evaluated in the contemporary multicultural and post-Christian society? What can be learned from this tradition today and what should be criticized? What are the characteristics of Lutheran identity five hundred years after the Reformation?

Lutheran tradition has never been uniform. Of course, there are some basic theological positions that are summarized in *Confessio Augustana* and developed in the writings of Martin Luther and Philip Melanchthon. Some of these are the doctrine of justification by grace alone, the conviction that the Bible is a primary source of the content of theology, and the sharp distinction between law and gospel. However, these positions have been interpreted in different ways in later Lutheran tradition. Some of the positions of the Luther orthodoxy in the seventeenth century were questioned by pietism, in search of an interpretation of faith that made experiences and piety more important than rational considerations. The Luther renaissance in the beginning of the twentieth century was to a high degree influenced by neo-Kantianism, which later on was criticized by neo-orthodoxy.

One reason that Lutheran theology has been interpreted in various ways is that it is always influenced by the surrounding social and cultural context. Questions that need to be dealt with in theological reflection are of different kinds depending on the particular social context in which they are raised. Experiences, perspectives, and concepts are often related to particular cultures, and the result is that theological positions are interpreted in many various ways. From feminist theology and postcolonial theory we can learn that differences is social positions and inequalities related to power structures have a great impact also on the understanding of theological conceptions.

The Lutheran tradition was originally formed in Northern Europe. In Germany, Denmark, Norway, Sweden, Finland, and Iceland Lutheran churches have had a strong position in society, often with a close relationship between state and church. Later on, Lutheran churches became rather strong also in the USA, even if they are not majority churches. Mainstream Lutheran theologies have developed in Northern Europe and the USA, as a response to issues raised in this particular cultural and social context. Therefore Lutheran theology has often been formed by perspectives and experiences within Western culture.

However, migration and missionary activities have led to the formation of many Lutheran churches also in the Global South. These churches are often minority churches, living in societies quite different from Northern Europe and the USA. Many of these Lutheran churches are growing rapidly, and soon their members will be the majority of Lutherans in the world. They are struggling with issues that are different from those that are regarded to be important in Western societies. Since they are minority churches one urgent issue is how they should relate to other religions. Since they are living in societies with great social problems and economic inequalities they need to reflect upon their political role and their possibilities to contribute to the liberation from oppression and poverty.

How should we understand Lutheran identity in this global world? Do minority churches in the global South understand their identity in a different way than majority churches in Northern Europe and the USA? What are the new theological perspectives that are developed within Lutheran churches in Africa, Asia, and Latin America? Is it possible to develop a Lutheran political theology that gives adequate contributions to issues concerning social and economic justice? What is the role of women in church and society around the world? Is it possible to interpret Lutheran theology in such a way that it includes liberating perspectives?

These questions were discussed at an international conference in Uppsala during October 8–10, 2013, on the theme "Remembering the

Past—Living the Future. Lutheran Tradition in Transition." The conference was hosted by the Church of Sweden Research Unit and the Department of Theology at Uppsala University. During the conference almost two hundred participants from all parts of the world discussed issues concerning Lutheran identity and different interpretations of Lutheran theology. Lectures were given and papers presented on eight different themes: (1) Lutheran theology and ethics in a post-Christian society, (2) the Bible in Lutheran tradition, (3) Lutheran identity in a global world, (4) Reformation as a model for interpretation of the present, (5) Lutheran theology and politics, (6) atonement, reconciliation, and forgiveness, (7) Lutheran tradition and tolerance, and (8) Lutheran tradition and gender.

The question of Lutheran identity is raised in two different contexts. It is raised in Western societies that can be characterized as being post-Christian and multicultural. In a society where the church has lost a great deal of its cultural impact and authority, and where there is a plurality of religious convictions, it is urgent to find out what is the Lutheran identity. However, this question is also raised in the Global South where Lutheran churches need to find their identity in a relationship with several other religions. Here this relationship is developed from a minority perspective.

In the Global South the question concerning Lutheran identity is closely related to the question regarding the role of the church in society and politics. Lutheran churches in Africa, Asia, and Latin America are not always living in liberal societies, where the state is said to be secular. Instead they are living in societies where religion usually has a great impact on political issues. How should Lutherans in these societies understand their role in society and the public arena? Is it possible to develop a distinct Lutheran social doctrine that can give interesting contributions to urgent political issues? And how should Lutheran churches in Europe and USA understand their political role in a post-secular society that is often said to be characterized by the return of religion?

Finally the question concerning Lutheran political theology is closely related to the question of Lutheran tradition and gender. The patriarchal principle in Lutheran ethics has meant not only that Lutheran churches often have supported those in political power. It has also meant a defense of male superiority over women. Mainstream theology in Lutheran theology has most often been developed by men, who did not criticize these patriarchal power structures. Therefore it is urgent to develop a Lutheran feminist theology that articulate those liberating perspectives that can be found also in the theology of Martin Luther.

The conference in Uppsala on "Lutheran Tradition in Transition" has resulted in two volumes based upon some of the lectures and papers presented. The volume on *Justification in a Post-Christian Society* deals with the issues of justification and atonement, Lutheran theology and ethics in a post-Christian society, and Reformation as a model for interpretation of the present. In this volume on *Lutheran Identity and Political Theology* three main problems are discussed. How should we understand Lutheran identity in the contemporary global world? Are there perspectives in Lutheran theology that can contribute to the liberation of women and a critique of traditional patriarchal power structures? Is it possible to develop a Lutheran political theology that does not support existing authorities?

LUTHERAN IDENTITY IN A GLOBAL WORLD

The first theme of this book is Lutheran identity in a global world. The changes in the religious arena in the world today mean serious challenges for Lutheran churches. Traditionally, Lutheran identity has been formed in Northern Europe, where the churches have been in majority and where they often have had a close relation with the state. However, today the Lutheran churches are growing in the Global South. Most of the Lutheran churches are today minority churches in Africa, Asia, and Latin America. Some of them have been established by immigration or as a result of missionary activity, and today they are independent churches working in contexts that are quite different from the societies in Northern Europe and the USA.

What are the new challenges facing Lutheran churches around the world today? What does it mean to be Lutheran in the contemporary global world, and how should we understand Lutheran identity from a minority perspective in the South? Are there in different social and cultural contexts different understandings of what it means to be a Lutheran? In what way do different social contexts imply various conceptions of the main tasks of Lutheran churches? How may multiple identities be both a challenge and a resource for Lutherans globally?

In Chapter Two Vítor Westhelle argues that when the majority of Lutherans in the world will be situated in the South, new theological questions are being formulated that conventional answers can no longer address. Luther's theology can be a resource to deal with some of these new challenges originating from new contexts, but a prerequisite is a theological approach that is aware of those issues that are important in the Global South. Westhelle introduces some areas in which Luther's theology might have some relevance in the contexts of Africa, Asia, and Latin America.

One such area is freedom and liberation. According to Westhelle, what Luther said about freedom is rather close to the liberation motif that has characterized theologies shaped in the third world to a large extent. Another area is Luther's theology of the cross and his understanding of Christ's real presence, which can be made relevant for a theology in a planetary perspective. Luther's conception of the three institutional spheres, namely the church, the economy, and politics, can also be interpreted in such a way that they are relevant, not only in modern and secularized Western societies, but also in other societies where Lutheranism is growing today. Here the church can be regarded to be a third sphere that keeps the economy and politics in relation, but still distinctly apart.

The next chapter, which is written by Göran Gunner, describes what are perceived to be substantial problems or important issues at stake within a sample of Lutheran churches around the world. What are regarded to be burning issues by Lutheran churches in different cultural contexts and different kinds of societies? It is quite obvious that there are a variety of opinions concerning what are the most important issues, depending on membership number and social context. Minority churches in Africa, Asia, and Latin America seem to face other challenges than majority churches in traditional European contexts.

One burning issue in many Lutheran churches is the situation of women in society and in the church. Some churches in Africa are growing rapidly and regard it important to increase growth, while some churches in the European context try to find ways to reverse the decrease in membership. Churches in the Global South are struggling to develop a Lutheran identity that is not dependent of Western culture. Several minority churches are dealing with issues concerning their relationship to Muslim majorities, and issues regarding the relationship between church and state are important in various contexts. The most common burning issue raised is related to the role of the church in the surrounding society, but minority churches have different perspectives on this issue than Lutheran churches in Northern Europe.

A different perspective on the role of Lutheran churches in the Global South is given by Ville Päivänsalo in Chapter Four. He explores some ways in which Christian identity has been expressed in the health work documents of the Lutheran churches and faith-based organizations in Tanzania and India. Even if some Lutheran accounts of health and development differ from each other significantly, Päivänsalo argues that a good part of the variation that shapes this work across cultures can be taken as theological richness rather than a problem. A wide array of Lutheran health work documents tell about a complementary unity, which means that even if perspectives vary and many agencies are minimalistic in terms of explicit faith, the statements do not tend to contradict each other.

Päivänsalo shows that both the Tanzanian and the Indian churches tell about the basis of faith of their health work rather extensively, even if the explored documents depict the pragmatic work in a largely non-confessional manner. He identifies both some important theological perspectives on the right to health, and some practical perspectives on Lutheran health work. One of his conclusions is that health work will be an important task for Lutheran churches in the Global South also in the future. Even if, for example, leprosy has almost been beaten and the global struggle against the HIV/AIDS pandemic has shown some signs of success, the health rights of the globally poor are still usually poorly fulfilled. Exploring the core aspects of the Lutheran health work so far can serve further ventures towards comprehensive visions of Lutheran responses to health-related human needs tomorrow.

Michael R. Trice discusses in Chapter Five what a productive Lutheran theology would look like in the contemporary post-Christian world. This is a world where more people believe in God than have a religion that expresses their belief, and where they are disassociated from organized religious life. Trice argues that there are three general characteristics of this post-Christian world. One is that the authority of the Church is a problem, since the Church is regarded to be a choice among an aggregation of choices in a world of pluralism. A second marker is a disconnection between "the story of God and us" and a world that may not find this story relevant. A third marker of a post-Christian world is a struggle for the coherence of an enclosed identity.

From this perspective Michael R. Trice discusses what a portal for Lutheran identity would need to be in a post-Christian world. His proposal is that Lutheran communities should address five questions aligned to the markers of authority, story, and identity. They need to consider how they understand the identity of the individual and the identity of the community of the believers. They need to reflect on the story of being human on this planet today, and they should also try to find out what is the radical question for the world tomorrow. A fourth question concerns our resources for responding to God's hope for the world, and the fifth question is what we should be doing as the highest aspiration of our vocational response to a loving God.

LUTHERAN TRADITION AND GENDER

The second theme of this book concerns Lutheran tradition and gender. The issues of gender and Reformation have been a subject of interest both to historical scholars and systematic theologians. Did the Reformation in any way contribute to the emancipation and liberation of women in church and society? Or did Lutheran theology mainly affirm traditional and patriarchal gender roles? These questions are not only of interest within historical research. Various versions of feminism have also an interest in analyzing the Reformation and its theologies in relation to gender.

Within feminist theology a crucial issue is if there are any liberating aspects of Lutheran theology in relation to gender and politics today. Are there any perspectives in Lutheran theology that can contribute to the liberation of women and a critique of patriarchal power structures? Or does feminist theology today presuppose a thorough critique of main positions within Lutheran theology? Within feminist studies there are different conceptions on these issues, and some of them are reflected in the contributions to this volume. However, the contributors seem to agree that even if there are ambivalences in the theology of Martin Luther, there are at least some liberating aspects in Lutheran theology.

In Chapter Six, Kirsi Stjerna argues that the emancipatory power of Lutheran theology rests on the core idea of justification by faith through grace. The diversity in the interpretation of this idea can be seen as a cause of celebration rather than a concern. From this perspective Stjerna argues that inclusivity, spirituality, and equality are core values within Lutheran theology. Inclusivity means the participation of women in Lutheran theological reflection. Spiritual theology involves the component of experience and entails a mystical dimension, which can nurture expectations of equality and inclusivity. The principle of equality can be regarded to be an implication of the Lutheran doctrine of justification by faith.

After reflecting on these three core values, Stjerna discusses what we can learn from the Reformation women and their theological concerns. Her thesis is that these women can exemplify the bearings of inclusivity, spirituality, and equality in the Reformation theological tradition. Of particular interest are two female theologians of the Reformation century, namely Argula von Grumbach and Katharina Schültz Zell. These women operated as situational biblically authorized lay theologians, and they applied protestant theology most notably in their defense of the vulnerable and the suffering. Thereby they speak to the transforming and emancipating power of faith and religious experience.

Else Marie Wiberg Pedersen argues in Chapter Seven that there are liberating aspects in Lutheran theology for a post-gender politics. By such a post-gender politics her aim is to go beyond any specific gender theories and rather employ an approach to which *homo*, the human being, is the main category. Her thesis is that it is possible to highlight features in Luther's theology that led to political and social improvements for the common people irrespective of sex, ethnicity, and social background. Luther's ambivalence towards women is possible to combine with his clear cut good theology of justice and grace in which *homo* is the central constitutive category.

According to Wiberg Pedersen, one liberating aspect for human beings in Lutheran theology is his theology of the cross. His idea of the priesthood of all believes emphasizes the equality of all human beings, women and men of faith. The principle of every human being at once just and a sinner (*simul iustus et peccator*) is also a liberating aspect pertaining to human life. Luther emphasized the importance of giving all children education in common schools, which had liberating and emancipating implications. In his commentary on *Magnificat* he interpreted Mary in such a way that she illustrates liberating aspects that point toward a humanization of the worldly regime.

In the next chapter Mary Elise Lowe gives a critical evaluation of queer Christologies that seem to lay aside the physical, time-bound, suffering, and resurrected body of Jesus Christ. Contemporary queer theologians argue that traditional claims that Jesus was male, had a masculine essence, was heterosexual and celibate have been theologically destructive for LGBTQI Christians. These theologians offer compelling queer portraits of Jesus, and many employ Judith Butler's textualist, materialized theory of the body. Inspired by Butler they develop a queer Christology that resists hetero-masculinist interpretations of Jesus.

Mary Elise Lowe challenges the dis-embodiment found in some of these queer proposals and argues for a fully-embodied queer Christology that weaves in commitments from Martin Luther's theology, especially his radical view of the incarnation, his assertion that the finite can bear the infinite, his view of the human person as *totus homo*, and his theology of the cross. Biologist Anne Fausto-Sterling's investigations of human sexual variation and philosopher Mark Johnson's theory of embodied cognition are also woven into this Christological proposal in order to ground claims about Jesus' body in emerging scientific research about human sexuality and cognition. Lowe's ambition is that such a fully-embodied Christology might offer queer theologians a way to re-embrace the body of Jesus Christ so that the incarnation can serve as the warp, weft, and direction to queer theological reflection.

Finally, Mary J. Streufert gives a critical analysis of theological anthropologies that claim a hierarchically binaristic gendered order of creation and create foreclosed human lives. Several Christian traditions advocate theological anthropologies that are rooted in gender essentialism and gender-based hierarchy. What it means to be human, these Christians argue, is to be hierarchically binaristic because God created humanity this way. Streufert gives an analysis of three such anthropologies operative within the

United States: the Roman Catholic Church, the Lutheran Church—Missouri Synod, and the Promise Keepers.

In her critique of these three positions, Mary J. Streufert argues that justification by grace through faith offers at least four benefits to theological anthropology. First, because the doctrine of justification is thoroughly theocentric and Christocentric, it unsets idolatry. Second, the doctrine of justification declares freedom from bondage. Third, justification alters our sinful status and relations with each other through God's alien righteousness. Fourth, it clarifies human vocation. Moreover, a feminist reading of justification strengthens current arguments on Law and Gospel that challenge its juridical distinctions into God's acts a wrath as the first move and love as the second.

LUTHERAN THEOLOGY AND POLITICS

The third theme of this volume is Lutheran theology and politics. Lutheran churches have often been uncritical of those in power and often closely allied with the state. Within family, economy, and the political order Lutheran ethic has developed a patriarchal principle, according to which the subordinate have to obey those in power. The state has been regarded as an order of creation and the political authorities have been looked upon as fathers of their countries who care for their children and expect obedience from them. Today, it seems to be necessary to revise this traditional social doctrine in Lutheran tradition. In what way can this be done?

A post-secular society poses new, challenging questions about the relationships between church, theology, and politics. In the Global South Lutheran minority churches need to participate in efforts to promote economic justice and political democracy. How can Lutheran theology respond to these challenges? Can churches rooted in the Reformation be a part of the return of religion in the public sphere? Is it possible to develop a Lutheran political theology that does not support existing political power? Can Lutheran churches contribute to social critique and liberation from different kinds of domination and oppression?

In Chapter Ten Tage Kurtén discusses the radical change which modern societies undergo when the secularism, which is taken for granted in modernity, is questioned. These changes open up for a post-secular way of understanding society and politics. The return of religion means that it is important to develop a political theology also within Lutheran tradition. However, according to Kurtén the traditional ways of understanding Lutheran social ethics must be abandoned. The traditional interpretation of the two kingdoms presupposes the idea of a common political and ethical language that unites all members of a society. When this presupposition is questioned, Lutheran theology must understand the task of Christian social ethics in a new way.

Tage Kurtén argues that Lutheran theology can learn a lot from Jeffrey W. Robbins, Raimond Gaita, and Stanley Hauerwas in its efforts to develop a political theology in a post-secular situation. Philosophers and theologians inspired by Ludwig Wittgenstein can give important insights in the meaning of a contextual understanding of language. The most important thing to be learnt from them is that a Christian cannot take for granted that her fellow humans would actually share her personal moral views. This should challenge everyone to be humble and to give room for "the other" to represent a way of life different from one's one.

Leif Svensson gives in the next chapter an analysis of Ernst Troeltsch's critical interpretation of Luther's ethics and the direction it has taken in contemporary "communitarian" critique of Luther. Many contemporary theologians follow Troeltsch in understanding an emphasis on the individual, obedience to secular authority, and an ethical dualism as characteristic features of Luther's ethics. This is also the case with the "communitarian" critique of Luther's ethics, which is developed by among others Jean Bethke Ehlstein, Alasdair MacIntyre, and John Howard Yoder.

Svensson shows that these "communitarians" concentrate their objections against Luther's ethics on what they identify as his strong individualism and neglect of community and tradition. The problematic individualism becomes very apparent when Luther's doctrine of the two kingdoms is interpreted in terms of a double morality. Even if this critique is influential, Svensson argues that a possible response to the critique might be to interpret Luther's ethics in a way that is proposed by David Yeago. His research provides a correction to the widespread picture of Luther's ethics as almost exclusively oriented to the individual and the inner dimensions of faith. Yeago calls attention to what Luther writes about the practices of the church, public discipline of Christians, and the role of God's law in Christian life. According to Svensson, an important research task is to further explore the insights of Yeago into the outer and bodily aspects of Luther's ethics.

In Chapter Twelve Victor Thasiah gives a vision of what a Lutheran political theology can look like by describing the theology and the work of John Rutsindintwarane, a Rwandan Lutheran community organizer. Rutsindintwarane embodies a political theology both responsive to a problematic history of relations between church and state and expressive of alternative possibilities in the context of civil society. His theology and his model for community organizing are described against the background of an analysis of the dominant, historical patterns of interactions between church and state in Rwanda and lessons germane to this relationship suggested for Christians post-genocide.

Thasiah argues that Christians can learn to maintain a critical distance to the state from the theological intelligibility of Rudsindintwarane's practices. Crucial to maintaining this critical distance is the development of political capacities for holding public officials accountable. However, this distance is not without certain positions of proximity. The vocation of the church includes critically cooperation with the same officials to address areas—social, economic, and ecological—of mutual concerns, especially those affecting one's community.

Why are churches not more forthrightly speaking out and acting to transform today's realities of domination? How might churches become places where subversions of reality can be nurtured and alternative public visions held forth? These are two questions discussed in a chapter by Karen L. Bloomquist. She proposes that *ecclesia* be considered an "event" of seeing, remembering, and connecting, of putting together what is fragmentary, pointing to what is true, enabling us to see and act, including in organizing actions with others. This implies the long-term challenge of nurturing and organizing communities of resistance against the dominant scripts and the systematic injustices they entail today.

Bloomquist argues that the challenge is to begin to see more deeply with a new vision rather than capture illusions that block our vision of what really is happening in our lives and world. This becomes possible as we remember a God who became radically incarnate and vulnerable in this world. This God frees and empowers us to engage with these realities today, remembering what has been forgotten in the past and remembering those who are forgotten around us and throughout the world today. We connect in ways that heighten the contradictions between the ideologies and the actual realities, we connect with those who are other from us, and we connect in collaborative actions with others for the sake of the world.

The final chapter in this volume is written by Elisabeth Gerle. She argues that Martin Luther drew on the Eros tradition and the Mystical tradition, but in new ways. He made an interpretation of Eros and passion that was more reflexive and mutual. The union was highlighted rather than desire for the bittersweet, non-attainable. His emphasis was further less individualistic than the modern readings of Luther claim and more directed towards the community. The desire and the love language of the *Song of Songs* became reflexive and mutual, expected to be played out in ordinary life, within the family, in economy, and in politics.

According to Gerle, the erotic imagery for Luther is a resource for ethics and politics. Luther used the *Song of Songs* to argue in favor of political authority and the love between the princes and the people. Such an idealization of political authority and of the princes is dangerous and easily led to complacency in relation to dominant structures of power. Today we need to question an overemphasis on technological rationality and of politics as pure technique for rational deliberation. This means that we may need more passion in politics. However, we need a passion that is realizing issues of power and tries to prevent productive differences to be an excuse for injustice.

PART ONE

Lutheran Identity in a Global World

2

Planet Luther

Challenges and Promises for a Lutheran Global Identity

VÍTOR WESTHELLE

A new time is dawning on us.

Dawn! That time before sunrise, the twilight, when a change is waiting in the wings; when darkness is about to disappear and the sun getting ready to peek out; when night makes way for the day. The dawn, as we know, announces a new day. What does the new day behold? What are its challenges? What does it promise? It is a new day making its appearance like a new born baby without a name. It is up to us to give it a name—beautiful or . . .

Indeed a new time is dawning on us. The world around us, its aura and terrain, especially in the religious arena, are changing. And with change, invariably, come challenges as well as promises. As far as the Reformation, in general, and Lutheranism, in particular, are concerned the demographics impose contextual challenges and will increasingly do so to Lutheran theology as we have hitherto known it. Most of the traditional confessional families have migrated to the south of the planet. Catholics, Episcopalians, Methodists, Presbyterians already have the majority of its membership outside of their original historical cradle. Lutherans are lagging behind, but already more than 40 percent of Lutherans are south (or in the Far East) of the north Atlantic axis, and growing to soon become in these new environments the majority of world Lutheranism. Luther is becoming planetary. But what seems more important is that this soon to become a majority in the new contexts are there, in these non-traditional settings, as *minorities* surrounded not only by other Christian denominations and independent or non-denominational churches, but by other religions as well. New questions are being formulated for a theological response that conventional answers can no longer address. Answers to questions copiously present in the West, as the challenge of work righteousness, secularization and so forth, no longer fit the bill. In this chapter I will deal with these issues in two parts. The first is of a polemical nature, the second has a more constructive character.

THE POLEMIC

Luther Research and Lutheran Demographics—the Correlation

A cursory review of publications in Luther research will show that there is no correlation to this change in the demographics of Lutheranism by a long chalk. The authors are with few exceptions from Germany, Scandinavia, and some from the USA. (An exception may be the Lutheran World Federation publication of annals of international conferences.) And if experience is what makes a theologian, as in Luther's Table Talk aphorism,[1] then context matters, for a context demarcates the scope of experiences one has; context challenges and changes texts. As the saying goes, "to each tribe its scribe." In "How Christians Should Regard Moses" (1525) Luther, reacting to some enthusiast preachers, offers the following comment regarding the reading of the Bible and the task of preaching:

> One must deal cleanly with the Scriptures. From the very beginning the word has come to us in various ways. It is not enough simply to look and see whether this is God's word, whether God has spoken it; rather we must look and see to whom it has been spoken, whether it fits us. That makes all the difference between night and day. (. . .) The word in Scripture is of two kinds: the first does not pertain or apply to me, the other kind does. (. . .) The false prophets pitch in and say, 'Dear people, this is the word of God.' This is true, we cannot deny it. But we are not the people.[2]

The same is true where theology is concerned. We need to know the people and the word that speaks to them, the word that pertains to its situation. Obviously this creates a problem for those of us whose job description entails the charge to do systematic theology. And certainly we should apply Luther's advice of how to read the Bible to Luther's own text and say, "yeah, this is Dr. Luther, but you are not the people to whom he is speaking."

---

1. Luther, *Table Talk*, LW 54, 7.
2. Luther, "How Christians Should Regard Moses," LW 35, 170.

Certainly that has been done in abundance in Luther research, which has the merit of reading Luther as not infallible. Such is the case in regard to Luther's words against the Jews, the Anabaptists, the Turks and so forth that Lutheran researches even within Lutheranism have long decried. Some of these criticisms have been done not only by theologians, but also officially by the LWF or by particular Lutheran churches. There is also a gray area of what is often considered Luther's idiosyncrasies, as it is often the case with his *scatological* (i.e. filthy, excremental, obscene) language, his obsession with the devil, etc. Then there is a third area that is not often touched, like his criticism of usury (particularly in the later works[3]), or the "third mode" of Christ's presence as formulated in the *Confession Concerning Christ's Supper* of 1528 (and quoted at length in articles VII and VIII of the Formula of Concord).[4]

God's Promissio and Luther's Promise

The question then is whether there are promises in Luther's or Lutheran theology that offer resources to face these changes and new challenges originating from new contexts. The word "promise" must be here underlined for it etches itself in God's own *promissio*. It is the word that calls forth a new reality and addresses its creation with a dispatch, an illocutionary speech act (the pragmatic force of an utterance) that calls for a response becoming thus a perlocutionary effect (the effect produced in the one being addressed) that the promise produces in us.[5] To address the response to Luther's locution, particularly when it comes in languages and pre-understandings far beyond Luther's, his contemporaries, and even present day Luther research, as represented (e.g., in the International Congress for Luther Research) requires new approaches that may not be conventional in most of Luther research. What is being responded to Luther's own promise for us as he translated God's *promissio*, or, in other words, what is the address that evokes a response? Or in other words, what is the illocutionary act that produces a perlocutionary effect. And the answer may lie not only at the deeper levels of Luther research, but also at the surface when we consider the impact of his persona, its emblematic significance.

---

3. To my knowledge, while almost everything of Luther has been translated into English, his long "Admonition to Pastors to Preach Against Usury" (*An die Pfarrherrn wider den Wucher zu predigen*, WA 51, 331–424) has never been translated. An exception has been the work of Ricardo Rieth, see, e.g, Rieth, "Luther on Greed."

4. Luther, *Confession Concerning Christ's Supper*, LW 37, 216ff.

5. Austin, *How to do Things with Words*.

In an article published in 1988, entitled *"Teufelsdreck,"* Heiko Oberman issues the following criticism of the tendency in Luther research to zero in the nodal point of the reformatory breakthrough going deeper and deeper into a debate that has created factions in European Luther research:

> The history of Luther research in this century is the history of concentration by contraction, moving in ever smaller concentric circles from the large grasp of European Reformation history around the turn of the [twentieth] century to an increasing preoccupation with the German Reformation, then with Luther's thought, and finally with the Reformation breakthrough and the young Luther.[6]

This concentration by contraction is the attempt of locating the illocutionary speech-act that set in motion the reformatory movement and elicited the response that goes by that name. But in the case of the Reformation, as in many other historical events throughout history the response exceeds what is prompted by the communicative act and saturates it with new meanings. Oberman indeed has a point in criticizing the contraction of Reformation studies, but not because it moves "in ever smaller concentric circles," but simply because it digs too deep. The problem in this shrinkage of the research lies in what is obtained in ever deeper levels of meaning and specialized research, missing the fact that Luther became an emblematic figure to catalyze multifaceted dormant expectations and discontent with the church of Rome and its commerce of indulgences. Robert Scribner may have overdone his case, but he has a point when he argued that the Reformation "attained wider significance because it quickly outran Luther's ideas, and achieved a near revolutionary impetus of its own."[7] To use a contemporary analogy the "near revolutionary impetus" became a sort of an "Occupy Rome" movement.

This dissociation between Luther's ideas, his prolific theological writings, and the emblematic figure he became is rather important and often missed as a topic in itself to be considered in Luther's research and the Reformer's significance as a catalyst of hopes of freedom in many places to this day. And this is the case even when complex and controversial issues in Luther's and Lutheran theology are paid no heed to.

---

6. Oberman,"*Teufelsdreck*: Eschatology and Scatology in the 'Old' Luther," 436.
7. Scribner, *The German Reformation*, 24.

Luther, a Figura

An interpretative method developed in literary theory by Erich Auerbach in an influential essay entitled *"Figura"*[8] will help to explain this often overlooked aspect of the importance of the Reformer. *Figurae*, figures, describe emblematic characters or localized events, which unlike concepts and doctrines that are rooted, belong to a context and are concretely located; they have a genealogy, a place, a time to which they belong. Yet they migrate! According to Auerbach, "a figural interpretation establishes a connection between two events or persons, the first of which signifies not only itself but also the second, while the second encompasses and fulfills the first."[9] The figural approach shows not only continuities but how a tradition is owned by incorporating historical circumstances and characters from other times and places. Such procedure appeals to *figurae* in order to establish legitimacy, even when the content and meaning is not the same of the one of the original *typos* (the Greek equivalent of the Latin *figura*).[10] Much of Auerbach's research on the figural phenomenon was actually developed by considering how Old Testament *figurae* appear in the New Testament, regaining a significance that, in one hand, makes a claim of legitimacy, and, on the other hand, invests it with a new meaning as to bring the old one into completion.

Luther became such a *figura*, not only *of* David or Paul, but also *for* many that came after him. This is not meant against Luther scholarship, but as something to be understood before other "deeper" aspects may be scrutinized and discerned. Can we understand that again? What was Luther if not a *figura* in the years that followed 1517, before the pamphlets of 1520 were widely recognized, not to mention before The "Bondage of the Will" of 1525, before the "Confession" of 1528, before his massive writings of the 1530s? The Reformer stood for something that was defined only by bare caricatured lines. But that is what helped decisively to launch a movement called the Reformation, way before any of the substantial issues defining differences between factions the Reformation took place, from the early

---

8. Auerbach, "Figura," 11–78. The essay was first published in 1944 while Auerbach was in exile in Istanbul, and was then followed and applied in his influential *Mimesis: The Representation of Reality in Western Literature*, originally published in 1946.

9. Auerbach, "Figura," 53. Auerbach (a persecuted German Jew under Nazism) wrote this essay in the context of the German Christians' anti-Semitic attempt to dissociate the New Testament from the Old Testament. But figures of the Old Testament are ominous in the New Testament.

10. Ibid., 28, 36–38. *Typos, morphe*, or *schema* (1 Cor 7:31) are the Greek words often translated as *figura* as the dominant language of early Christianity was changing from Greek to Latin, starting with Tertullian, one of the earliest Latin Fathers.

1520s on. To read 1517 from the standpoint of 1525 (with the Anabaptist disputes), or 1529 (with Zwingli), or 1530 (with Melanchthon in Augsburg and Luther in Coburg), or from 2013, will never get one into some decisive features of the Reformation, because they are figural, and decisively so.

One needs to look at the figure and how it is transfigured. Following are some brief examples that might offer us some food for thought insofar as the figural approach is concerned. Why were the people, condemned as heretics in the West Indies, as they were known in the early 1500 until 1555 (coincidentally or not the year of the Augsburg Peace Settlement), referred to as Lutherans in the *autos-de-fé*, when hardly anything of Luther's theology as such was known in those latitudes?[11] Why did Friedrich Engels appeal to Luther's figure to explain the groundbreaking impact of Adam Smith's political economy? For more recent "transfigurations" of Luther, here are a few: Why did Michael King Jr. change his birth certificate in 1957 to officially adopt the name of Martin Luther King Jr.? Why did Eduardo Hoornaert, a Belgian-Brazilian Roman Catholic historian say that Luther was the "theologian that taught the church to think with the people and from the people"?[12] Why did Leonardo Boff call Luther the "precursor of liberation theology"? Why did the Italian Roman Catholic philosopher Gianni Vattimo say in a recent interview that "we need a new Luther"?[13]

The examples can be multiplied, but the answer seems to be a simple one. The Reformer's impact and the Reformation movement as a whole was not read erstwhile starting from the dense texts of a Luther, a Zwingli, a Calvin, a Bucer, etc. Instead, and this is the crux, Luther stood and stands as a *figura* in and through which characters and events manifested themselves in concrete historical circumstances in which the figure of Luther intervenes to magnify the dimensions of characters and events relatively independent from the peculiar content of his theology, and simultaneously ground it contextually in new locations.[14]

---

11. Until 1555, the *autos-de-fé* included this line in the sentencing of heretics: "They left this kingdom to become Lutherans." Bastian, *Protestantismo y Sociedad en México*, 23; Westhelle, *After Heresy: Colonial Practices and Post-Colonial Theologies*, 18–19.

12. Hoornaert, "Matim Lutero: Um Teòlogo que Pensa a Partir do Povo," 9–17.

13. The Italian philosopher Gianni Vattimo said this in Buenos Aires when inaugurating a new chair in Ethics and Cultural Studies at TEATRO PRESIDENTE ALVEAR in April 2006.

14. Not only is the figure of the person, but the legendary event of nailing 95 theses to the door of the Castle Church in Wittenberg also the occasion for figural representation. At the Lutheran School of Theology at Chicago, the place I have been teaching for the last two decades, there is a very militant group of students that defend the cause of LGBT people that is called "Thesis 96."

Yet the figural approach is not phrenology, the analysis of the shape of the skull to determine the content of the mind—ridiculed by Hegel, but still held with respect by Goethe. The reason why the figure becomes so relevant is because there is some density underneath the surface that propelled the *figura* to appear. There is something more than Luther's silhouette profusely drawn in the legendary drawings and paintings of the nailing of the "95 Theses," or his seclusion in the Wartburg Castle. These portrayals and representations of Luther are not something like Andy Warhol's "Campbell's Soup Cans" painting, and his future was something more than "being worldwide famous for 15 minutes," as the painter's celebrated catchphrase goes. There was indeed something deeper that prompted the figure to emerge, which is as important as the figure itself is; *figurae* are not figments.

THE CONSTRUAL

This is not to suggest that the surface analysis of the figural approach is the only thing that is left of Luther that is significant for Luther's planetary phenomenon as much as my intention to call attention to the figural importance and relevance. I, therefore, introduce some areas in which Luther's in-depth theological contribution might still, or again, have some relevance, even, and most importantly, in contexts outside of the ones directly and historically linked to the Reformation heritage.

Freedom

If there is one motif that has characterized the insurgence of theologies shaped in the so-called Global South, since the second half of the twentieth century, it is the one of postcolonial freedom and liberation.[15] Luther's often cited opening theses in the treatise *The Freedom of a Christian* is commonly regarded as a paradox. A Christian person is free from all and simultaneously indebted to all. The supposed paradox is an illusion of modern Western imagination nurtured by highly mobile class societies in which freedom and duty or obligation are always relative categories, insofar as one prevails, the other is diminished. To understand the significance of Luther theses in his treatise it is important to remember that it emerged in the context of a medieval society's rigidity as to one's social location in estamental societies. Freedom was understood as that which one had toward those underneath, while duty was due to those above. Read with this key in mind, freedom means the liberation from those above in the social scale in the higher estaments. Duty, in turn, is due to those below. There is no paradox. There is

---

15. See Westhelle, *After Heresy: Colonial Practices and Post-Colonial Theologies*.

only subversion of the order of things. Freedom means obligation toward the downtrodden, and simultaneously liberation from those who oppress from above.

One has to remember that the Western understanding of freedom has been indelibly influenced by the Scottish Enlightenment and then, particularly, by John Stuart Mill (whose father, James Mill, was a significant figure of the Scottish Enlightenment). This is overwhelmingly a negative concept, or, to phrase it simply, it is "freedom from." To read this retrospectively into Luther is an anachronism. The second thesis of his treatise, that one is dutiful to all means not that he is leaving the topic of freedom, but that he is understanding freedom also in a positive sense, as a "freedom for," to bring about freedom. In other words, it is the basic theme of liberation theologies: to set the captives free. What Luther said about freedom is rather close to the liberation motif that has grown in the Third World and has defined its theology to a large extend, a third world that is now globalized

Cross and Christ's Presence

Crux sola est nostra theologia. The celebrated phrase of the early Luther (1518) has been explored and expanded to countless books on Luther's theology of the Cross. But if this Cross of Christ is identical to the cross we carry (as Regin Prenter argued persuasively[16]), what has being lifted up is not only its individual importance to our own condition. It has social and also ecological significance as well. God is there identified with suffering of the human and of the earth, and indeed with death itself. "There is one Cross. And it is plural."[17] This cannot be dissociated from Luther's understanding of the modes of Christ's real presence as we have it in his *Confession Concerning Christ's Supper* (1528). As the argument goes, the first mode of presence refers to the historical Jesus which was not a matter of contention by any party at the time of the Reformation (would only become such after Reimarus and Lessing more than two centuries later). The second mode of presence was the one that prompted Luther's "Confession." It was about Christ's real presence (instead of "representation" functioning as a symbolic rememoration) in the bread and the cup, the point of dispute with the likes of Karlstadt, Zwingli and Oecolampadius. But the third mode is the one that comes as a truly theological unexpected move, but logically coherent with the argument hitherto developed. If Christ is truly God according to his humanity, and if he is one with God, and God is everywhere (as in Luther's

16. Prenter, *Luther's Theology of the Cross.*

17. I am indebted to Neal Anthony former student and currently Senior Pastor at United Lutheran Church, Ponca, NE for this expression.

interpretation of the creedal placing of Christ at the "right hand" of God as being everywhere), then Christ is everywhere present. So this is Luther's conclusion written one year before his dispute with Zwingli in Marburg: "since he is a man (. . .) and apart from this man there is no God, it must follow that (. . .) everything is full of Christ through and through, even according to his humanity."[18] "Even according to his humanity" is the crucial point here. There is no presence without materiality, without something that has mass and body.

This "third mode of presence" follows logically from what precedes. It did not need to be there for he had taken care of the argument of his antagonists with the "second mode" over more than 200 pages. But it is this "third more of presence" that makes possible for a theology in a planetary perspective. Christ is everywhere, not spiritually as would be easy to assume, but according to his humanity, according to matter, to embodied humanity, that, finally for Luther, is what matters. There, where the world's crucible is, God is in the flesh, in the rock, in the tree, wherever pain and death are at stake and the resurrection is a promise, a new creation. And this makes it imperative the usage of the word "planet," for unlike "global" that refers to a self-contained totality, "planet" refers to a little piece of a stellar system, called the Sun, which in turn is a tiny piece of what is called a constellation, which is small part of the dimensionless universe. Theodor Adorno might have learned something from his Lutheran mentor in Frankfurt, Paul Tillich, when he said that only a materialist can believe in the resurrection of the body.[19] Of course, he went beyond Tillich, who with his rounded-up system would never go so far, and be so faithful to this bold affirmation of someone who did not even confess the Christian faith (for he was a secular Jew). Or in the words of the Reformer himself: "No, comrade, wherever you place God for me, you must also place the humanity for me."[20]

Ecclesiology

In the Genesis lectures of 1535 and 1536 Luther offers a vision of the church that also entails promises. He discusses it in the context of the institution of the "orders." The first of them is the *ecclesia* which is instituted with the establishment of the Shabbat. Since it precedes the *oeconomia* and the *politia*, Luther's image of the church is one, as he says, "without walls and without any pomp."[21] Some of Luther's speculations in his creative interpretation of

---

18. Luther, *Confession Concerning Christ's Supper*, LW 37, 218.
19. Adorno, *Negative Dialectics*, 401.
20. Luther, *Confession Concerning Christ's Supper*, LW 37, 219.
21. Luther, *Lectures on Genesis 1–5*, LW 1, 103.

the text are beyond anything that a contemporary critical reading of the text would allow.[22] And yet his imaginative reading underscores a theological vision of the church highly relevant for an ecclesiology today. The church established in Paradise is an apophatic church. It is the tree of the knowledge of good and evil, which Luther equates with the tree of life (*arborvitae*). This was "Adam's church altar and pulpit."[23] But what is interesting in Luther's reading is an implicit ecumenical vision when Luther says that "it does not appear preposterous that ... there stood several trees of the species arborvitae."[24] So these trees "would have been the church at which Adam, together with his descendants, would have gathered on the Sabbath day."[25] This vision of a multiplicity of trees for the worship of the descendants of Adam suggests first that there is not a single center to identify the true church. But even more, it implies also that the descendants of Adam are from all religions on the planet. Or to phrase it aphoristically: to each religious creed, its tree.

Running the risk of becoming too allegorical, the metaphor of the tree is for several reasons quite fitting for the church or the religious factor as such. Consider the following characteristics. Trees are free standing organisms grounded on the earth. Among the living organisms they live the longest and grow the tallest always in search for light. They adapt to scarcity of space and through photosynthesis they transform carbon dioxide into oxygen, which after all is that which we require to be alive. Hence we have the importance of trees for the ecosystem. Not by chance has deforestation been emblematic to exemplify our sinful condition. Of course, this idyllic vision of such apophatic church disappears with the fall, which in Luther's speculation happens on that first Shabbat. But it still remains in Luther's mind as an ideal of which the church, now with walls, policies and pomp, dimly mirror itself. Yet "the origin is the goal," in the celebrated expression of Karl Kraus. The difference that the fall represents is that now the church has to borrow from the spheres of the *oeconomia* and *politia* its specific functions to build and organize itself, and with them come along also the shortcomings that the fall impinged upon these institutions. And trees keep falling.

---

22. I am not considering here the thesis of Peter Meinhold about glosses in the text added by a second generation of editors influenced by the emerging Lutheran orthodoxy. The concern here is about the imagery used and not with the dogmatic formulae that sometimes is of dubious origin as the discussion of the loss of the *imago* that sounds as if coming from Flacius Illyricus. Ibid., LW 1, 60.

23. Ibid., LW 1, 95.

24. Ibid.

25. Ibid., LW 1, 105.

Between Economy and Politics

The cultural anthropologist Roberto DaMatta offers a terminology that is useful in reading Luther's view of the church as this place gripped between the other two institutional spheres. The terms "economy" and "politics" in their modern Western connotations really do not convey what Luther, following a long medieval tradition, called *oeconomia* and *politia*. The modern Western concepts of "economy" and "politics" have different connotations. Since the industrial revolution the concept of economy dissociates what in antiquity and medieval times was still housed in the domestic sphere, namely, production for the sustenance of life and its sexual reproduction. And since the American and French revolutions, politics gained emancipation from a set order of flux of authority represented by monarchies in which the ruler is only bound to the rules he himself establishes.[26] Hence the coinage of the modern expression: "political economy" is a notion unconceivable in earlier times. But outside of the modern West there still remains a distinction of these domains even as modernization is a planetary phenomenon. This is why I believe the distinction DaMatta makes, in discussing Brazilian society, between "house" and "street," is important to understand *oeconomia* and *politia*. The house is seen as a realm that controls the domains in which much of sexual reproduction takes place, and significant amount of production of goods is allocated there. The street, on the other hand, serves as a metaphor for the space in which public affairs take place and human inter-subjective matters are administered.[27]

This terminology seems to address rather well the way to understand Luther's distinction between *oeconomia* and *politia*, but also to address worldwide contexts in which the space of intimacy, sexuality, and often also of production for the sustenance of life, are protected from the public sphere, even architecturally so. The domestic space in those latitudes is often the space that in the modern West takes the form of health insurance and retirement pension. But such is not the case in many other contexts where "health insurance" and "pension" is still a matter of the household. This helps to explain, for example, the dissention taken by some African churches of the Anglican and the Lutheran communions over the way the West takes its own position on question of human sexuality and homo-affectivity. Even if morality plays a role in opposing the "liberal" Western position, it is not the primary cause of the strife; it is a question of how to keep the house in order, the *oiko-nomos*, and make it sustainable for generations to come. And this is done also by keeping one protected from what happens in the "street," in the

---

26. Morse, *New World Soundings: Culture and Ideology in the Americas*.
27. DaMatta, *A Casa e a Rua: Espaço, Cidadania, Mulher e Morte no Brasil*.

public domain, often inimical, in some contexts, to the domain of intimacy, the domestic.

The Third Space

The way in which the economy became so much intertwined with politics is what accounts for a particular phenomenon characteristic of the West, called secularism. Secularism can be defined, to use the terminology I have suggested, as the street invading the house, or the other way around, the house invading the street. What disappears then is this "third space" that Luther called *ecclesia*, the church that keeps the economy and politics in relation, but still distinctly apart. Arguably no one understood this better than Walter Benjamin in his discussion of Parisian galleries, arcades, or *passages*. These are the architectural expression of the mingling of house and street, of economy and politics. In describing these recently created arcades, Benjamin offers the following comment:

> Already the inscriptions and signs on the entranceways (one can just as well say "exits," since with these peculiar hybrid forms of house and street every gate is simultaneously entrance and exit), already the inscription which multiply along the walls within (. . .) have about them something enigmatic.[28]

The recent instantiations of those early modern galleries are today's shopping centers and malls. Not by chance they have become the *ersatz* of the church for secularized societies.

Luther's distinction of the orders or "spheres of promises" (Elisabeth Gerle and Hans Jonas) is no longer descriptive of modern and secularized Western societies, but it is a diagnostic tool to understand the Western peculiarity and, most importantly, other societies where Lutheranism is growing and in which even as modernization took place secularism has not taken hold; the "house" and the "street" remain as discreet dimensions, and religion, to use a more generic word for *ecclesia*, is a space in-between, something like what that Victor Turner called "betwixt and between"[29] and Homi Bhabha defined as a third space. It is an "interruptive, interrogative, and enunciative" space which blurs the limitations of traditional boundaries.[30] It is a hybrid space, which is not a result of two essences that combined to form a third. It is like a suspension and disruption, not a synthesis; something that is neither in nor out but both at the same time.

---

28. Benjamin, *Arcades Project*, 871.
29. Turner, *The Forest of Symbols: Aspects of Ndembu Ritual*, 93–99.
30. Bhabha, *The Location of Culture*.

These three then, *oeconomia*, *politia*, and *ecclesia* remain as foundational institutional realities that Aristotle, in the *Metaphysics* VI, described as the basic and discrete human faculties (*dianoia*): *poiesis* as the practice that creates objective realities defines the order of the *oeconomia*; *praxis* as the inter-subjective communicative action with no material result corresponds to *politia*; and *theoria*, the passive enduring of being an observant, defines the *ecclesia* or religious observance in general.

If the three spheres have been corrupted by the fall (the first to be corrupted, according to Luther, was the church for the origin of sin took place in the first Shabbat[31]) they remain as divinely instituted as spheres of promise in which sanctification or holiness takes place. Luther stresses that with great emphasis when he distinguishes between being holy (*heilig*) and being blessed or saved (*selig*). "For to be holy and to be saved [or blessed] are two entirely different things. We are saved through Christ alone; but we become holy both through this faith and through these divine foundations and orders."[32] Now, if we connect this to Luther's third mode of presence, blessedness or salvation can be everywhere for Christ may, according to his humanity, be there. It is not confined to a region or a particular religion, but embraces the entire planet. Sanctification, being holy, however, is the labor of love in the instituted spheres that everyone is called to serve in.

THE TREE—A PLANETARY METAPHOR IN LIEU OF A CONCLUSION

The importance of seeing blessedness or salvation embracing the entire planet: this is the reason why for Luther the tree or trees in paradise were the fit metaphor for the church. And the metaphor is even more fitting as the tree, as it grows in the front yard, or in a park, stands between the house and the street. The church's ultimate goal is observant receptivity, which is proper to translate literally *theoria*. But after the fall the church needs to borrow from the *oeconomia* its buildings and all the objective realities that make it up, and from the *politia* the rules of inter-subjective actions that establish the liturgy as well as other inter-personal functions such as counseling, parish counsel and committee meetings. As an instituted reality it is dependent on the *oeconomia* and *politia*. This is why the church has this hybrid character and can be said to exist only as an event; it happens. It is not of our doing. It is only apt to end with some lines of a poem, a *poiema* by Joyce Kilmer entitled "Trees":

---

31. Luther, *Lecture on Genesis 1–5*, LW 1, 70.
32. Luther, *Confession Concerning Christ's Supper*, LW 37, 365.

> I think that I shall never see
> A poem lovely as a tree.
> (...)
> A tree that looks at God all day,
> And lifts her leafy arms to pray
> (...)
> Poems are made by fools like me,
> But only God can make a tree.[33]

BIBLIOGRAPHY

Adorno, Theodor W. *Negative Dialectics*. New York: Continuum, 1997.
Auerbach, Erich. "Figura." In *Scenes from the Drama of European Literature*, 11–78. Minneapolis, MN: University of Minnesota Press, 1984.
———. *Mimesis: The Representation of Reality in Western Literature*. Princeton: Princeton University Press, 1953.
Austin, J. L. *How to do Things with Words*. Oxford: Clarendon, 1962.
Bastian, Jean Pierre. *Protestantismo y Sociedad en México*. México: Casa Unida, 1983.
Benjamin, Walter. *Arcades Project*. Cambridge, MA: Belknap, 1999.
Bhabha, Homi K. *The Location of Culture*. London, Routledge, 1994.
DaMatta, Roberto. *A Casa e a Rua: Espaço, Cidadania, Mulher e Morte no Brasil*. Rio de Janeiro: Rocco, 1984.
Hoornaert, Eduardo. "Matim Lutero: Um Teòlogo que Pensa a Partir do Povo." In *Reflexões em Torno de Lutero*, edited by Martin N. Dreher, 9–17. São Leopoldo: Sinodal, 1984.
Kilmer, Joyce. *Trees and Other Poems*. New York: Doubleday Doran, 1914.
Luther, Martin. *An die Pfarrherrn wider den Wucher zu predigen* (1540). WA 51. Weimar: Hermann Böhlaus Nachfolger, 1914.
———. *Confession Concerning Christ's Supper* (1528). LW 37. Philadelphia: Fortress, 1961.
———. "How Christians Should Regard Moses" (1525). LW 35. Philadelphia: Fortress, 1960.
———. *Lectures on Genesis 1–5* (1535–1538). LW 1. St. Louis: Concordia, 1958.
———. *Table Talk* (1531–1546). LW 54. Philadelphia: Fortress, 1967.
Morse, Richard. *New World Soundings: Culture and Ideology in the Americas*. Baltimore: John Hopkins University Press, 1989.
Oberman, Heiko. "*Teufelsdreck*: Eschatology and Scatology in the 'Old' Luther." *Sixteenth Century Journal* 19.3 (1988) 435–50.
Prenter, Regin. *Luther's Theology of the Cross*. Philadelphia: Fortress, 1971.
Rieth, Ricardo. "Luther on Greed." In *Harvesting Martin Luther's Reflections on Theology, Ethics, and the Church*, edited by Timothy J. Wengert. Grand Rapids: Eerdmans, 2004.
Scribner, R. W. *The German Reformation*. Atlantic Highlands, NJ: Humanities, 1986.

---

33. Kilmer, *Trees and Other Poems*, 18.

Turner, Victor. *The Forest of Symbols: Aspects of Ndembu Ritual.* Ithaca, NY: Cornell University, 1967.
Westhelle, Vítor. *After Heresy: Colonial Practices and Post-Colonial Theologies.* Eugene, OR: Cascade, 2010.

3

Burning Issues

GÖRAN GUNNER

The question of "burning issues" is part of a research project discussing how Lutheran tradition is constructed and understood in a sample of Lutheran churches around the world today. In this part of the project I concentrate on present-day burning issues, collecting examples and exploring what are perceived to be substantial problems or important issues at stake for different churches today. The churches included in the study have been chosen within the Lutheran World Federation (LWF).

To ask about the burning issues for a Lutheran church at a national level is a challenge in itself. The question is open to interpretation by the respondent and the answers are not easy to compare between countries. What comes to mind first? Internal challenges for a church or external challenges? Internal challenges raised by issues coming from outside the church or issues raised from the internal life of the church? External issues being raised when society or the state pose questions to the church or international challenges the church body needs to take into account such as peace issues, environmental challenges or questions on human rights and democracy?

To get appropriate answers I asked high-ranking people in Lutheran churches the question, either directly to a president of the church or an archbishop/bishop or the people they considered best placed to answer the question. In a number of countries I also asked researchers with knowledge of the church to answer the same question. I am fully aware that if I had had the opportunity to put the same question to lay people and Sunday churchgoers, the answers might have been quite different. So the answers here represent a perspective very much from the top of the church, from people who tend to be elected to the position of representing the church.

If you look at the number of existing Lutheran churches, it is clearly not possible to deal with all of them. To arrive at a representative sample, some general parameters were taken into consideration, such as examples of churches in Africa, the Americas, Asia and Europe. I wanted to reach at least one of the major churches in each part of the world from the point of view of the number of members, as well as a minor church body. I also wanted, if possible, to include at least one majority church—if there was one—and one minority church.

CLARIFYING DISTINCTIONS FOR CATEGORIZING LUTHERAN CHURCHES

Before exploring the "burning issues" in the chosen churches I will set out some clarifying distinctions to enable some kind of comparison to be made between the different settings for the churches involved.

The first distinction is the number of Lutheran followers in a country that will situate each church on a scale from several million followers to a couple of thousand, the result being "big" and "small" churches. Historically the big churches have been in Northern Europe, a view of Lutherans that persists in the minds of many people to this day. Certainly there are big churches in Northern Europe, in Germany and the Nordic countries. But, today some of the biggest Lutheran churches are to be found in Africa (Tanzania and Ethiopia) as well as in Asia (Indonesia). It is worth mentioning that in most countries only one Lutheran church body exists, whereas in some countries there are many churches belonging to the Lutheran family, such as in Indonesia, India, and Germany.

The membership number can also be considered in relation to the population in a country at large, for instance where it results in a situation where the grouping is the religious majority or minority in relation to the main bulk of the population as well as in relation to other Christian denominations and people of other faiths. There is a majority of Lutherans in Sweden, Norway, Denmark, Finland and Iceland but the same also goes for Namibia, even if the majority is not that big. At the same time, some of the churches geographically close to the origin of Lutheranism are not big at all. So, we use the distinction *minority—majority*.

One traditional and rather simplistic way of dividing the Lutheran church family has been between *traditional contexts* and *new contexts*. The traditional contexts often have the attribute "Lutheran" attached, as in "traditionally Lutheran contexts," while the new contexts seldom have "Lutheran" attached. The traditional contexts are those European countries that are closely connected geographically to the historical Martin Luther and where the Lutheran faith was adopted centuries ago. The new contexts have been established by immigration when *immigrants* brought the Lutheran church with them, such as, for example, coming from Europe to Brazil, Argentina, South Africa and the USA. But there are also immigrants who came from places such as India and China to Malaysia. Quite a lot of the Lutheran churches were established as a result of missionary activity, and today they are independent Lutheran churches in different settings. There are also some churches established by natives when they returned home after becoming Lutherans abroad in, for example, Malawi. To differentiate between these circumstances, I use the distinctions *traditional context, immigrant context, missionary context* and *returnee context*.

Of course, there will also be a variety of theological positions and stand-points depending on history, context, and present-day burning issues. Hopefully, this chapter, will pin-point some of the variety. In view of the complexity of the situation, let us introduce just one of the countries involved in this study. Indonesia has twelve churches belonging to the Lutheran World Federation family. Taken together they account for more than 5.8 million members—some would say seven million—outnumbering all other countries except Germany and Sweden. Only one church would use the concept "Lutheran" in its name and all would prefer to use "Protestant" or "Reformed," but they all have a Lutheran identity through the LWF, even if they also stress their Calvinist heritage. One way of putting it is "we are still in the process of becoming Lutherans." This produces a unique situation—so many churches and the total number of members—in a country with the largest Muslim population in the world.

Thus, the numbers below include churches related to the LWF in different regions. The numbers in brackets are the number of churches taken into account in this study.[1] The first number inside the bracket indicates new context with missionary background and minority situation, the second new context with immigrant background in minority situation, the third traditional context in majority situation and finally, traditional context in minority situation.

---

1. Statistics from the LWF. See *Member Directory*.

	<5,000,000	5,000,000-1,000,000	1,000,000-100,000	100,000>15,000
Africa	2	2 (1,0,0,0)	11 (2,0,0,0)	16 (1,1,0,0)
America	-	1 (0,1,0,0)	2 (0,1,0,0)	16 (1,1,0,0)
Asia	-	1 (1,0,0,0)	10 (3,0,0,0)	41 (3,2,0,0)
Oceania	-	-	-	1
Europe	1 (0,0,1,0)	8 (0,0,2,0)	12 (0,0,1,1)	19 (0,0,02)

In this study the minority churches in a missionary context with more than 1 million members are the Protestant Christian Batak Church and the Malagasy Lutheran Church. The majority churches in traditional context with more than one million members are the Church of Norway, the Church of Sweden, and the Evangelical Lutheran Church in Denmark. Also with more than one million members but in an immigrant minority context is the Evangelical Lutheran Church in America.

Lutheran churches with between 100,000 and one million members in a missionary as well as a minority context are the Evangelical Lutheran Church in Southern Africa, the Christian Protestant Church in Indonesia, the Indonesian Christian Church, the Simalungun Protestant Christian Church, and the Evangelical Lutheran Church in Malawi. The Evangelical Lutheran Church of Iceland represents a traditional majority context, the Evangelical Church of the Augsburg Confession in Austria a traditional but minority context and the Evangelical Church of the Lutheran Confession in Brazil an immigrant minority context.

Finally, churches with less than 100,000 members and living as minorities in a missionary context are the Lutheran Costa Rican Church, the Evangelical Lutheran Church in Jordan and the Holy Land, the Protestant Church in Sabah, and the Lutheran Church in Malaysia and Singapore. Minority churches in an immigrant context are the United Evangelical Lutheran Church, Argentina and Uruguay, the Evangelical Lutheran Church in Southern Africa (N-T), the Basel Christian Church of Malaysia, and the Evangelical Lutheran Church in Malaysia. Two minority churches in traditional context are included in the study: the Evangelical Church of the Augsburg Confession in Slovenia and the Evangelical Lutheran Free Church of Norway.

In the following I will deal with burning issues thematically and I am aware that one "burning issue" may fit under more than one theme.

FEMALE AND MALE

Let me now turn to gender issues and the situation for women in the church. This issue highlights not only a content aspect but also demonstrates a methodological difficulty in the study. The response may differ substantially depending on who has been chosen as the informant.

I will use a couple of examples, the first being Madagascar. All respondents—male and female—would agree that the position and situation of women is not related to biblical issues but to the Malagasy culture, traditionally very restrictive to women outside the household. A female theologian expresses it as: "Due to male leadership in the church, women's issues are disregarded. It is always men who decide, both in church and in society, so the concerns of women are not very important. Men do not want to lose power."[2] A male theologian agrees that the male view on women is dictated by culture and needs to be challenged. In contrast, one of the male leaders of the church, when asked if this is a burning issue for the church, claims it is not a big problem at all. Rather, it is a problem created by pressure from the West forcing the question on to the agenda.[3] In Brazil, when asked about burning issues, male leaders stressed leadership and land issues while female leaders directly related to women issues. They talk about how important it is for women to come together to share their lives and issues about suffering, violence, submission, silence and how to overcome violence in their families.[4] Another example can be Norway with a different context but with questions concerning the need of inclusive language in the church: "Though the need for making women visible is recognized, and the acceptance of women ministers is widespread, the limit is set at feminine God-talk."[5]

These examples clearly show that the answers depend largely on who is responding to the question about burning issues. When the church at a structural national level is asked to respond to the question on burning issues, the people who answer turn out to be overwhelmingly male. While they will talk about the situation concerning women as well as gender if they are asked a direct question, they will not raise it as a burning issue. But if a woman is the person answering, issues relating to gender and to the situation of women in society and in the church become a "burning issue." In this case the border-line do not relate to big or small churches, to traditional or

---

2. Interview, Fianarantsoa, Madagascar, 02/06/2010.
3. Interview, Antanarivo, Madagascar, 05/06/2010.
4. Interview, São Leopoldo, Brazil, 09/06/2009.
5. Thomassen, "Construction of Gender, Liturgies, and Dichotomies from a Norwegian Perspective," 204.

new contexts, to minority or majority situations but to the role of women in a male context. The same all over the world but with local design.

EXPANDING OR DECREASING CHURCHES?

Some of the churches in this study are based on historic missionary activity but today independent local churches and very different, depending on their Asian or African context. The Indonesian and Malaysian churches exist in a Muslim majority context and the same goes for the Lutheran church in Jordan and the Holy Land. The churches in a Muslim majority setting face particular challenges in terms of doing mission work since the constitution in places like Indonesia and Malaysia prohibits sharing the message with Muslims. Nonetheless, even if the Muslim majority context basically restricts the possibility for the church to grow through evangelistic activities, several churches say mission and evangelism are a top priority. "We are still converts and have a burning desire to tell others. There are ways of spreading the good news."[6] Another way of expressing the situation is: "The only way is to pray, to be friendly with them."[7] So they mainly depend on growth through a stable birth rate but may also recruit members from other denominations and in some cases from groups with traditional religiosity. But there is also a threat from emigration, especially for the church in Jordan and the Holy Land.

The situation in some of the African churches is very different. The church in Madagascar is growing rapidly with new members coming frequently through evangelization and new local congregations becoming established on a regular basis, especially attracting people from country areas. One of the "burning issues" is how to increase growth. We know that other African churches—not included in this study—have also seen a similar increase in membership through active evangelization, such as the Evangelical Lutheran Church in Tanzania, which has nearly six million members and the Ethiopian Evangelical Church Mekane Yesus, which has over five million members. The Evangelical Lutheran Church in Malawi was established in 1982, not by missionary work but by lay people coming back to Malawi after becoming Lutherans abroad. Active evangelization has helped the church to grow.

One church in the traditional context expresses concerns in similar terms to the African churches. The Evangelical Lutheran Free Church of Norway can be looked upon as a tiny minority church in relation to the majority Church of Norway. Still, the Free Church places mission in the

6. Interview, Kuala Lumpur, Malaysia, 02/12/2010.
7. Interview, Kuta Kinabalu, Malaysia, 05/12/2010.

forefront as a "burning issue" and wants to reach out with the gospel to new secular Norwegians in the towns and cities. Even the Church Synod has assembled with the sole objective of "praying for people to meet Jesus Christ and be saved."[8]

In South and Central America the Lutherans are a minority in relation to the Roman Catholic majority. The Evangelical Church of the Lutheran Confession in Brazil places evangelism in the centre: "We should evangelize the Lutherans who are already baptized and we should evangelize the people of the country who are not members of any church or by tradition are members of the biggest church—the Catholic Church."[9] The Lutheran Costa Rican Church is a growing church. The church is still rather small but has grown steadily since its founding. This has been done by means of it being a church that identifies with the social struggle in the country, a church "for the poor," such as women, landless farmers, immigrants and LGBT people.[10]

Churches in the traditional context seem to be in a different situation. In both Austria and Slovenia the majority faith is Roman Catholicism and the Lutherans are a minority. A church leader from the Evangelical Church of the Augsburg Confession in Austria pin-pointed the burning issue as being people leaving the church. This is due to the decreasing birth rate, especially in small church communities, mixed marriages between Lutherans and Roman Catholics, and 1,500 persons leaving the church on a yearly basis, in most cases as a "consequence of increasing secularization." In some areas there are no longer enough followers to maintain the critical mass needed to implement the mission of the church or to keep up with services in villages every Sunday.[11] The concern of the Evangelical Church of the Augsburg Confession in Slovenia is almost identical based on it being a small minority church. The membership is shrinking because the birth rate is decreasing in society as a whole and as a consequence there are no longer any children in the church. The critical mass of people is lacking in some of the local areas, and that affects the church.[12]

Even if it is not stressed as "the" burning issue, the material in the study shows that the number of members is decreasing in the traditional Scandinavian Lutheran churches as well. In Sweden, the Church of Sweden had 7.3 million members in the year 2000 whereas ten years later it was 6.5 million. The Evangelical Lutheran Church in Denmark lost about 63,000

8. Interview by mail, Oslo, Norway, 18/01/2013.
9. Interview, São Leopoldo, Brazil, 09/06/2009.
10. Interview, San José, Costa Rica, 18/06/2009.
11. Interview with respondent from Austria, Brussels, Belgium, 05/11/2011.
12. Interview with respondent from Slovenia, Novi Sad, Serbia, 04/05/2012.

members during the same period and the Church of Norway lost about 33,000. All of these are majority churches that still count about 80 percent of the Danish population, 77 percent of the Norwegian population, and 67 percent of the Swedish population as members.[13]

Of course, as a consequence, both majority churches and minority churches in the traditional context claim the challenge to be how to stop this trend and reverse the decrease in membership and church attendance.

So in this issue it is possible to see the difference related to context—traditionally, immigrant, or missionary with growing churches in Africa and Asia while shrinking in Europe. This is in accordance with other findings and Douglas Jacobsen writes: "When scholars today say that Christianity is moving south, it is this phenomenal Christian growth in Africa (and in Latin America) that they have in mind."[14] And the Lutheran tradition is part of this development with what is here named the missionary contexts growing.

THE WESTERN HERITAGE

The Evangelical Church of the Lutheran Confession in Brazil is a "big" church in South American terms. It emerged from German immigration to Brazil when immigrants brought the Lutheran church with them to a new setting. The church remained an ethnic church for many decades and people still consider: "The Lutheran church is a German church." This has changed in the last 60 years, but with it being a rural church one of the burning issues is turning the German identity into a Lutheran identity and bringing the Lutheran identity into the big cities. Confessional unity in the context of religious pluralism creates new challenges in new situations.[15] It is possible to see the same kind of heritage in the United Evangelical Lutheran Church in Argentina as well, even if there has been a period of missionaries from the US in the 60s and the 70s. Even if the people today have lost the German language in country areas, the identity is still embedded in German/Lutheran immigrant rural surroundings and a big challenge for the church now is moving with the people into the cities.[16] The Evangelical Lutheran Church in Southern Africa (N-T) is in a similar position. A German-speaking Lutheran church was transformed into a South African church, the majority of

---

13. Eriksson and Gunner, "Exploring a Heritage," 32, 8, 26.
14. Jacobsen, *The World's Christians*, 164.
15. Interview, São Leopoldo, Brazil, 09/06/2009.
16. Interview, Buenos Aires, Argentine, 11/06/2009.

the members still being German-speaking. The burning issue is how "to get the context more into the church, for it to be more South African."[17]

One burning issue for several of the Lutheran churches in Malaysia is how the traditional Lutheran heritage brought by missionary work—with its architecture and gothic Western buildings as well as Western-style vestments—can be developed to be Malaysian. Of course, in this huge country with all its islands, it may imply different identities to talk about the Malay and "the church still being relevant as a Malaysian church."[18] At the same time, it is a struggle since in this society to be Malay tends to mean to be Muslim and the church needs to fight to be included in the Malaysian culture and heritage. The church needs a powerful message for people outside the church—not abandoning culture—to avoid being dismissed as "the white man's religion." For the Chinese groups, it is about being contemporary Chinese in a Malaysian society maintaining as much as possible of the cultural heritage, such as festivals on the Chinese calendar, without retaining their religious significance. At the same time a "new" influence is coming via the charismatic movement. It is attractive to people and feels compatible with the indigenous tradition, which may create tension with the "old" Lutheran tradition of worship. There are two ways of expressing the concern: "The church is now more open to the charismatic as long as we keep the basic faith" and "it's an issue we are struggling with."[19]

In the Indonesian churches, the situation is somehow different. The churches in this study are to a high degree contextualized in the culture as Batak churches, evident in church architecture, decoration, and music. However, new charismatic movements trying to renew the church are considered to reject these customs and introduce new values. "The charismatic people will lose their culture, tradition and identity." This is also threatening contextualization through music in the church. So here it is a burning issue to accept that "people long for the spiritual experience" yet at the same time want to be able to keep the Batak tradition.[20]

In Madagascar, the rapid growth of the church is very much the result of the revival movement, the Awakening, originating in the early twentieth century. An issue for the church is how to keep the Awakening inside the church and host a development opening up for both the Lutheran tradition and an emphasis on prayer, laying on of hands, and exorcism and expressed

17. Interview, Johannesburg, South Africa, 28/5/2010.

18. Interviews, Kuala Lumpur, Malaysia, 02/12/2010.

19. Interviews, Kuala Lumpur, Malaysia, 02/12/2010 and Kuta Kinabalu, Malaysia, 05/12/2010.

20. Interviews, Pematang Siantar, Indonesia, 27/11/2010 and Tarutung, Indonesia, 29/11/2010.

as "just a change of activities between regular Lutheran and the Awakening." It is also about relating to the traditional Malagasy religion:

> In reality, however, there is no clear boundary between Christianity and traditional religion because, on the one hand, many Christians still remain attached to their traditional beliefs, and on the other hand, an increasing number of traditionalists are influenced by Christianity.[21]

This opens a rather new burning issue: what to do when the Bible is used outside the church in order to legitimize Malagasy traditional religion and attracting many followers, including Christians.

We are here dealing with minority churches in new contexts and still very different contexts depending on the background. The churches originating from immigration are still struggling with the image that to be Lutheran is to keep the original western culture and language also in the new setting. The churches founded by missionary activities are struggling with how to be loyal their own cultural heritage in relation to Western Lutheran tradition.

FINANCIAL IMPLICATIONS

When asking about burning issues at a conference, researchers associated with seminaries connected to the Evangelical Lutheran Church in America stressed financial issues or just said "money." One of the leaders of the church explained that, in terms of the changes emerging in society, the need was to be looking into cash flow, where money is located, how money is used, and how to release monetary assets for best use.[22] It was a high-priority issue for the Evangelical Lutheran Church of Iceland as well as for the state and society in general after the Icelandic financial crisis.[23] The traditional big churches in the West take financial issues into consideration in the context of the economic crisis.

All the African, East Asian, and South and Central American churches express concern about the financial situation and how they are going to be able to maintain church buildings and fund running expenses and salaries in the future.

However, this is not only a burning issue as regards each church individually; it affects relationships between the churches as well. There is a

---

21. Razafindrakoto, "The Bible Outside the Realm of the Church." Paper presented 01/06/2010.
22. Interview, San Fransisco, USA, 20/11/2011.
23. Interview, Reykjavik, Iceland, 07/05/2009.

fear that churches with resources might reduce the assistance they provide to churches in need. A leader in the small Lutheran Costa Rican Church claims that the church is completely dependent on financial support from abroad. If that support were to be reduced, the church would no longer be able to work to the same degree with the issues they consider to be of the utmost importance, such as indigenous peoples, immigrants, women, children, young people, sexual diversity and HIV.[24]

But there are also concerns that the West is using financial support to put pressure on churches. One church leader expressed the concern that the West and the LWF are trying to impose issues on the church when the local church requests financial support. It is experienced as pressure from the West, and that the "dollar dictates" the agenda. One example given is that in order to receive a scholarship for theological training the church had to accept a 40 percent quotient of female theological students, and another is that the question of homosexuality is a question "forced" to be a subject of study.[25]

At the LWF conference "Identity, Survival, Witness" it was said that LWF documents refer to the "three blocks" with big power and financial resources—Germany, Scandinavia and the US. In contrast, the new contexts "lacked power, felt inadequate to provide intellectual leadership that could challenge Western academics and, worse, constituted a tiny minority."[26] So this is basically a division between an influential Western hemisphere (Northern Europe and the US) with financial resources and the rest of the world. In some cases this is addressed as a burning issue in this study. There is no doubt that one of the "burning issues" for Lutheran churches, regardless of whether they are big or small church bodies and where they are situated on the globe, is that of finance. Obviously, this follows in the wake of the economic crisis across the world.

INTERNAL CHURCH MATTERS

One issue that comes up in African and Asian settings relates to the lack of pastors/priests. The Protestant Church in Sabah, on the part of the island of Borneo that belongs to Malaysia, lists the lack of pastors as a burning issue. As an example, it is difficult for only one pastor to provide spiritual support for 42 villages and 6,000 people. The church does have young people ready to train for the ministry but lacks the financial means to support them

---

24. Interview, San José, Costa Rica, 18/06/2009.
25. Interview, Antanarivo, Madagascar, 05/06/2010.
26. Westhelle, "Transfiguring Lutheranism," 11–12.

during their studies.[27] The small Evangelical Lutheran Church in Malaysia also raised the shortage of pastors as an issue— "the young have no interest in serving the church"—and the fact that salaries are very low.[28] The same goes for another of the small churches, namely the Lutheran Costa Rican Church.[29] The problem may revolve around leadership issues on a wider basis and on the need for training for local leaders.[30] "We should prepare for good leadership to be involved with youth, women and poor people,"[31] or even to teach "the church members to do good deeds."[32]

Internal issues can also be specific, such as with the United Evangelical Lutheran Church—Argentina and Uruguay. Since the time of American mission this small denomination, with its small parishes, has been running schools. A burning issue is that the schools will always need attention and the church is "stuck between a general political discourse that is not favorable and the public schools being in a terrible situation."[33]

When asked about burning issues without any specific clarification, it is up to the respondent to decide if the question is to be seen as related to internal church matters or to the surrounding society, or a combination of the two. In some instances it is internal church matters that first spring to mind.

CHALLENGES FROM THE SURROUNDING SOCIETY

In Malaysia the churches have seen a resurgence of Islam as well as rising radicalism owing to the fact that certain political parties are using religion as an instrument for Islamization. They have witnessed incidents that include churches being attacked and burned down in religious tensions. In this situation there is a need for "harmony in our country" —an "inter-religious dialogue to live in harmony."[34]

Christianity in Indonesia is in the minority. The most burning issue for the church is inter-religious tolerance—there is a struggle for harmony among people from different faiths. In some parts of the country the situation is worsening locally but not across the nation as such. "We interact day by day in the same place in the same state but it is becoming more

27. Interview, Kuta Kinabalu, Malaysia, 05/12/2010.
28. Interview, Kuala Lumpur, Malaysia, 02/12/2010.
29. Interview, San José, Costa Rica, 18/06/2009.
30. Interview, Kuta Kinabalu, Malaysia, 05/12/2010.
31. Interview, São Leopoldo, Brazil, 08/06/2009.
32. Interviews, Pematang Siantar, Indonesia, 27/11/2010.
33. Interview, Buenos Aires, Argentine, 11/06/2009.
34. Interviews, Kuala Lumpur, Malaysia, 02/12/2010 and Kuta Kinabalu, Malaysia, 05/12/2010.

and more difficult to live together" and "The encounter can be anything from close and friendly to sharp and cruel."[35] There are examples that the churches locally have been closed because of disagreement with Muslim majorities. A number of churches have been burned down or closed. There are also problems when building a church since the people in the surrounding area will object. This is not being done by "ordinary Muslims" but by "extremists" (words like radical movements, fanatics and radicalization are also used) and the government cannot do much about it since they cannot go against any Muslims. One way it is phrased is: "Most Muslim people are good people and only a small number are extremists" or "From time to time we face serious problems."[36] The issue is how to enable the church to live in harmony with its neighbors. So, the church organizes dialogue and encourages its members to develop dialogue with its neighbors.

A major burning issue for small minority Lutheran churches living within a Catholic majority in the European setting is exemplified by Slovenia. Even if the Lutherans and the Catholics are historical churches, there are complications with mixed marriages between Catholics and Lutherans. The problem is that Lutherans cannot take communion in the Roman Catholic Church and, because of that, the Catholics agree to mixed marriages but insist that any children should be brought up as Catholics. Today up to 50 percent of marriages are mixed and the result is that the Evangelical Church loses the children.

In the US, one of the burning issues is to position the Evangelical Lutheran Church in America as an alternative face of Christianity in America. There is a perception of Christianity in the US today that has been created by the Christian Right and organizations like the Moral Majority. In this situation the church wants to show an alternative Christianity in order to serve its neighbors. An example of the type of action the Church takes is to be "open to people living in same-sex marriages," something that is viewed as a continuation of being open and inclusive, grounded in the message of Christ.

In both Indonesia and Malaysia an issue that is often raised is the fragmented face of Christianity. Both the diversity of Lutheran and Reformed churches and the large variety of denominations, combined with weakness at the level of national Christian bodies, are considered to be a problem. At a time when you fear pressure from the outside, including even physical assaults on both individuals and churches, you need a strong voice in

---

35. Interviews, Pematang Siantar, Indonesia, 27/11/2010 and Tarutung, Indonesia, 29/11/2010.

36. Ibid.

relation to society and the state. In Brazil the Evangelical Church of the Lutheran Confession in Brazil stresses the importance of dialogue with evangelical, charismatic movements, as well as with representatives of liberation theology.

The Evangelical Lutheran Church in Jordan and the Holy Land is situated at the centre of the historic places connected with the life of Jesus and Biblical history, and is a focus for Christian pilgrimage. Membership-wise, it is one of the very small churches and the local congregations are geographically spread across different countries. The burning issues are connected to the political situation and the question of Palestine/Israel. As the church is an integral part of Palestinian society, issues like peace and reconciliation, the end of occupation, the wall and worsening living conditions are on the agenda. However, owing to developments in Egypt and Syria, concerns also extend to the Middle Eastern situation as a whole. The call from this small Lutheran church emanates from fear for the future that people will place more hope in violence and weapons than in a peaceful resolution of the conflicts of the Middle East with non-violent methods.[37]

In the Lutheran setting, the relationship between church and state has for a long time been associated with the Nordic folk churches being state churches. The Church of Sweden has gone through a process of disestablishment (2000) while the issue is still on the agenda in the other churches. It is an issue being discussed in society and at state level as well as inside the church. In Denmark the burning issue can be described as follows:

> Part of this conflict is also over how the relationship between church and state, and how free the church is to mind its own affairs. Being a national folk church in between a state church model and a free church model is an ongoing tension because there will always be people who wants more or less state in the governing of the church.[38]

In Iceland, around two-thirds of respondents in public surveys favor a separation between the church and the state but there is disagreement on the issue among the pastors in the church. Some want to keep the relationship between church and state as it is now, while others want disengagement.[39] In Norway the discussion in the church has focused on how to retain a folk church when there are changes and a gradual loosening of the bonds between church and state.[40]

37. Interview, Bethlehem, Palestine, 21/09/2011.
38. Lodberg, "Burning Issues in the Evangelical Lutheran Church in Denmark," 78.
39. Interview, Reykjavik, Iceland, 07/05/2009.
40. Jensen, "The Formation and Identity of the Church as a Present Challenge in Norway," 64.

In Malaysia the churches have seen the state become an Islamic state, with Islam as the religion of the state, in the space of a generation. The government wants to prohibit the Malayan-speaking Christians from using the word Allah. For the churches it is a burning issue not to give in. They know "Allah" is just the beginning and the government wants a total of 150 words in Malay to be prohibited. "You will not even be able to use the word Gospel since it is in the Quran." Or put another way: "The Malay Bibles will be contaminated because of the word Allah." There is also tension concerning the indigenous people—who are not Malay—when the government tries to draw them into the Muslim faith, including providing local Christians in villages with a lot of benefits if they change their religion. The perspective of local Christians is that the government is creating problems for them.[41]

The relationship between the state and religion is also a burning issue in Indonesia. The state is giving in to a request that the country with the biggest Muslim population in the world should be dominated by a Muslim atmosphere by means of legislation and the constitution. There is a fear of what the churches call a "Shari'aisation" of the country, and it is felt that it has already started, creating a situation with religion (Islam) and the state being one and the same. Religious tolerance exists according to the law but is interpreted in a way that is discriminatory against Christians. Examples are that Muslims are not allowed to convert to Christianity (though Christians may, of course, convert to Islam) and there is no possibility for interreligious marriage unless there is conversion to Islam. Religion is shown on people's ID cards, making it difficult for Christians to get work in government and industry, and to gain entry into state universities; in some schools Christians have to wear Muslim dress. The government has issued new laws resulting in "churches being closed by the government and no permits being issued to build." "We can feel it—it is getting worse."[42]

The Evangelical Lutheran Church in Denmark, a national folk church, lists the refugee situation as one of its main burning issues. The issue is not new—it has been there since the 1940s. It is not just a challenge to the church but may cause friction and even a split between those arguing for the church as a place where refugees can seek asylum and those arguing for strict laws to be followed so as to control the influx of refugees. Another burning issue is the protection of the environment symbolized by church bells ringing for the environment during the UN Summit on Climate Change in Copenhagen, which met with considerable opposition from politicians. The church

---

41. Interview, Kuala Lumpur, Malaysia, 02/12/2010.

42. Interviews, Pematang Siantar, Indonesia, 27/11/2010 and Tarutung, Indonesia, 29/11/2010.

is finding its place "in society and it serves as a battleground for different theological and political opinions about the future of the church and Danish society."[43] An example from Sweden is a discussion in the church where authoritative decisions are taken concerning bioethics and new reproductive technologies.[44]

The question of homosexuality and same-sex marriages has become an important issue in recent years. Today same-sex marriages may be performed in several European countries including Sweden, Norway, Denmark and Iceland, and also in Brazil, Argentina, Canada and South Africa, as well as in several states in the United States. When a state or society looks upon same-sex marriages as a natural development, the church needs to relate to the issue and can be in the forefront against discrimination. In terms of the family of Lutheran churches inside the LWF, the Evangelical Lutheran Church in America and the Church of Sweden have decided to marry same-sex couples. These decisions have been followed by discussions on how a theological justification can be found for the endorsement of same-sex relationships.[45] In the other Lutheran majority churches in Northern Europe same-sex marriages are a burning issue, as for example in Iceland with a debate in the church about the same-sex marriage legislation.[46]

The decisions taken have created tension between Lutheran churches. In the interviews a few voices raised concerns about the Swedish point of view. Does the respondent mention the issue just because I come from Sweden and they need to disagree with the decisions taken by the Church of Sweden when a Swede turns up? Is it just to say, "we disagree" while at the same time firmly denying that homosexuality and same-sex marriages are issues existing in their own setting? The question has been raised by a few church leaders, such as in Madagascar and Malawi, not as "the" burning issue but at the end of the interview and in one case after a Western missionary raised the issue as part of the conversation.

In Brazil the church put forward questions connected to land reforms and reforestation as well as expressing concerns for the situation of indigenous people.[47] In Costa Rica the church aims at being "a people's church" and to include people in poor neighborhoods, on Indian reservations, in small country villages, indigenous people, immigrants, those suffering from HIV/AIDS, and people who are oppressed owing to their sexual orienta-

---

43. Lodberg, "Burning Issues in the Evangelical Lutheran Church in Denmark," 78.
44. Bråkenhielm, "Ethics and Ecclesiology," 82–83.
45. Ibid., 81.
46. See Bóasdóttir, "Same-Sex Marriage," 107–8.
47. Interview, São Leopoldo, Brazil, 08/06/2009.

tion. They express these burning issues in terms of human rights, natural resources and ecology.[48]

Today the churches in South Africa want to take on the struggle of the people and pinpoints as a burning issue the fact that the gap between rich and poor is becoming ever wider. They want to focus on issues such as unemployment, developing and empowering rural communities, land distribution, electricity, the massive migration to cities, HIV/AIDS, paying tax, and laws and regulations oppressing the people. "The churches have to help the people to find a way to survive and to keep those responsible accountable."[49] Whatever they declare to be the main burning issue, churches in the non-Western world list similar issues as being hugely problematical, such as HIV/AIDS in Malawi[50] and Indonesia and poverty in Indonesia[51]. Another more general way of expressing the desire to be a part of society is the "need for the church to be part of nation building and the common good of society."[52]

The most common burning issue raised is related to the church's surrounding society but differs a lot between churches. The traditional majority Lutheran churches have aspirations to play an important role in society in relation to different ethical (and political) issues and to provide a forum for different opinions on both theological and ethical matters in relation to their present and future development. Sometimes this involves responding to crucial questions raised in society or by the governing bodies in the state and that includes the relationship between the state and the church.

The minority churches in traditional context express concerns and discrimination over against the majority church (Catholic) and the difficulties in ecumenical dialogue for a small church. The minority churches in new context with Muslim majority populations express jointly the burning issue as challenges from Islamic movements also creating severe problems in the relation to the state and co-existence on local level. This is not just a fear but a reality with churches burnt down and severe discrimination. Another minority church expressing grave problems is the Lutheran church in the Holy Land partly living under occupation and facing the unsolved on-going conflict. There is also a clear indication that the minority churches—with immigrant or with missionary background do have physical survival for people in the country as the burning issue. The minority Lutheran churches

---

48. Interview, San José, Costa Rica, 18/06/2009.
49. Interview, Johannesburg, South Africa, 26/05/2010 and 28/05/2010.
50. Interview, Lilongwe, Malawi, 09/06/2010.
51. Interviews, Tarutung, Indonesia, 29/11/2010.
52. Interview, Kuala Lumpur, Malaysia, 02/12/2010.

focus on justice and against discrimination in their own context or, put another way, "How to live your faith in this unjust country."

CONCLUSION

"Burning issues" for Lutheran churches seem to depend on the local context. One striking difference is that churches in traditional Lutheran settings—majority or minority situations—are facing a decreasing membership rate while churches in the Global South and not the least in Africa are growing churches but both situations create burning issues for the churches.

The context clearly determines what is on the agenda. Asian Lutheran churches situated in Muslim majority contexts are dealing with issues relating to discrimination and violence from the majority society and thus the relation between church and state. Churches in traditional Lutheran context, as in Scandinavia, deal with the ethical issues challenging the society as well as with the relations between state and a majority church. The churches in Africa and Latin America seem in a higher degree to deal with social issues and injustices in society.

BIBLIOGRAPHY

Bóasdóttir, Sólveig Anna. "Same-Sex Marriage. A Burning Issue in the Evangelical Lutheran Church of Iceland." In *Exploring a Heritage: Evangelical Lutheran Churches in the North*, edited by Anne-Louise Eriksson et al., 97–114. Eugene, OR: Pickwick, 2012.

Bråkenhielm, Carl Reinhold. "Ethics and Ecclesiology: Burning Issues for Church of Sweden—and Beyond." In *Exploring a Heritage: Evangelical Lutheran Churches in the North*, edited by Anne-Louise Eriksson et al., 79–96. Eugene, OR: Pickwick, 2012.

Eriksson, Anne-Louise and Göran Gunner. "Exploring a Heritage: An Introduction." In *Exploring a Heritage: Evangelical Lutheran Churches in the North*, edited by Anne-Louise Eriksson et al., 1–44. Eugene, OR: Pickwick, 2012.

Jacobsen, Douglas. *The World's Christians: Who they are, Where they are, and How they got there.* Wiley-Blackwell, 2011.

Jensen, Roger. "The Formation and Identity of the Church as a Present Challenge in Norway." In *Exploring a Heritage: Evangelical Lutheran Churches in the North*, edited by Anne-Louise Eriksson et al., 49–66. Eugene, OR: Pickwick, 2012.

Lodberg, Peter. "Burning Issues in the Evangelical Lutheran Church in Denmark." In *Exploring a Heritage: Evangelical Lutheran Churches in the North*, edited by Anne-Louise Eriksson et al., 67–78. Eugene, OR: Pickwick, 2012.

Member Directory. The Lutheran World Federation. Online: http://test2.lutheranworld.org/lwf/index.php/who-we-are/people/member-directory (accessed 10/10/2013).

Razafindrakoto, Georges A. "The Bible Outside the Realm of the Church." Paper presented at a seminar, Lutheran Graduate School of Theology, Madagascar, 1 June 2010.

Thomassen, Merete. "Construction of Gender, Liturgies, and Dichotomies from a Norwegian Perspective." In *Exploring a Heritage: Evangelical Lutheran Churches in the North*, edited by Anne-Louise Eriksson et al., 191–206. Eugene, OR: Pickwick, 2012.

Westhelle, Vítor. "Transfiguring Lutheranism: Being Lutheran in New Contexts." In *Identity, Survival, Witness: Reconfiguring Theological Agendas,* edited by Karen L. Bloomquist, 11–23. Geneva: The Lutheran World Federation, 2008.

4

Lutheran Perspectives on the Right to Health in a Global World

VILLE PÄIVÄNSALO

Lutheran health work has had a high profile in many countries in the Global South, but how should the inheritance of the past medical mission be reframed in our global age? In this chapter, I explore some ways in which the Christian identity has been expressed in the health work documents of the Lutheran churches and faith-based organizations (FBOs) in Tanzania and India as well as in some corresponding documents at a global level.

Lutheran accounts of health and development differ from one another significantly in terms of their visions and missions, for a start. However, for a smooth cross-cultural cooperation to succeed, both local and global level understandings of the foundational guidelines that apply to the work have to be either similar or complementary to one another. In biblical terms, the quest for a complementary approach stems, for example, from Romans 12:6–8 as quoted in the *Lutheran World Service: India 2002* report:

> If our gift is serving, let us serve; if it is teaching, let us teach; if it is encouraging let us encourage; if it is contributing to the needs

of others, let us give generously; if it is leadership, let us govern diligently; if it is showing mercy, let us do it cheerfully.[1]

Nowadays Lutheran health services are provided or sold to all people in need regardless of their race, religion, or gender. Beyond this guideline, a good part of the variation that shapes this work across cultures can be taken as theological richness rather than as a problem. For the most part I would defend such a complementary approach, though I am well aware that many issues of both theology and praxis continue to be truly challenging.

ENDURING NEED FOR CHRISTIAN HEALTH WORK

The human right to health, as originally stated in the *Constitution of the World Health Organization* (1946)[2] and subsequently in a host of human rights documents, has gradually become fully integrated into mainstream democratic theories of justice as well. At least since Amartya Sen's *Development as Freedom*[3] and the Millennium Development Project, health rights have belonged to the core of social justice debates all over the world. However, there is still a lot of work to be done.

Today, India endeavors to reach health-related development goals through a number of central policy reforms, including the National Rural Health Mission, but overall its investments in public health remain drastically inadequate in the face of the health needs of its poor.[4] Development has been fragile in Tanzania as well. There, however, the government has re-emphasized the importance of collaboration with the voluntary sector.[5] In this case that largely amounts to the FBO sector. In both countries, the economic, political, and environmental developments are unstable enough to postpone realistic welfare state scenarios far into future. Voluntary organizations will thus be needed to supplement the public health systems for a long time—these will include Lutheran health agencies.

In many regions in these countries it has become difficult to maintain the cornerstones of Christian health work, namely Christian hospitals. Even so, this situation also means there are opportunities. The close link between health rights and the rights to nutrition and water, as well as the alleviation

---

1. Lutheran World Service India, *Lutheran World Service: India 2002*, 2.
2. World Health Organization, *The Constitution of the World Health Organization* (1946).
3. Sen, *Development as Freedom*.
4. Taneja, *Health Policies and Programmes in India*; Drèze and Sen, *An Uncertain Glory: India and Its Contradictions*, 143–81.
5. Lynge, *Tanzania: The Darling of the Donor Community*; The United Republic of Tanzania, *Health Sector Strategic Plan III*.

of poverty and the promotion of holistic health, is widely recognized nowadays. For instance, in 2002, in *Prophetic Diakonia: "For the Healing of the World,"* Karen Bloomquist et al. reported a shift in the Lutheran World Federation (LWF) discussions beyond "the classical, charity-oriented work of diakonia."[6]

One thing that such "moving beyond" could mean is re-emphasizing responses to world hunger—as Graig L. Nessan has done with extensive biblical quotes about caring for the hungry, the sick, and the poor alike.[7] Yet, in addition to prophetic diakonia and responses to hunger, the lasting inheritance of more direct Lutheran responses to both physical and more holistic health needs is also noteworthy.

REMEMBERING THE INHERITANCE

In Sub-Saharan Africa, inspired by people such as the towering figure of David Livingstone (1813–1873), medical mission became an integral part of the mission movement towards the twentieth century. Carl-Erik Sahlberg mentions Johann Jacob Greiner (1842–1905) as the first Lutheran missionary in East Africa. Arriving in Dar es Salaam from Ethiopia in 1887, he then moved to Zanzibar the following year and discovered a connection with other Germans who had just started medical work there.[8] Around 1905, German Lutherans opened a dispensary in the Machime district (close to Kilimanjaro) and a hospital in Lutindi. Lutheran healing ministry in the emerging Tanzania—independent since 1961—was closely connected to ecclesiastical work. While the healing power of Jesus, both for the body and the soul, was seen in the hands of doctors and nurses, the work was medically-oriented and there tended to be tension between it and traditional African concepts of healing.[9]

In Tanzania by 1961 missionaries were running half of the hospitals. Today, under the auspices of the Christian Social Service Commission (CSSC), there are almost 90 operating hospitals, which amounts to approximately 40 percent of hospitals on the Tanzanian mainland, and about 100 operating health centers. Most of the hospitals belong to the Catholic Church, followed by the Evangelical Lutheran Church in Tanzania (ELCT) with its 23 hospitals, which are partly funded by the government. The network of Christian health centers comprises about 20 percent of health

---

6. Bloomquist, Granke, and Rasolondraibe, *Prophetic Diakonia: "For the Healing of the World."*

7. Nessan, *Give Us This Day: A Lutheran Proposal for Ending World Hunger.*

8. Sahlberg, *From Krapf to Rugambwa: A Church History of Tanzania*, 60.

9. Ibid., 100.

centers on the Tanzanian mainland—and there are also Christian and Muslim dispensaries all over the country.[10]

In India, Christian mission often followed the motto *to teach, preach, and heal*, with unsuccessful attempts of medical mission already in the 1730s (Danish-Halle Mission).[11] Regular medical mission in the country was started by fully-qualified medical doctor and missionary John Scrudder (The American Board of Commissioners for Foreign Missions) arriving in Madras in 1836. His granddaughter Dr. Ida Scudder (1870–1960) also become one of the pioneers of Christian health work by establishing a one-room clinic in Vellore in 1900, paving the way for the widely admired Christian Medical College (CMC) and Hospital, Vellore.[12]

Another major figure of the relatively early medical mission in Southern India was Dr. Anna Sarah Kugler (1856–1930), the founder of the Guntur Mission Hospital for women and children in 1897. When she applied to the Board of Foreign Lutheran Mission of the General Synod of the Evangelical Lutheran Church in the USA in 1882 and subsequently served as a missionary of the Women's Home and Foreign Missionary Society of the General Synod in Guntur, she had a strong vision to bring people to the Christian faith by relieving their physical suffering. Her approach was that medical work functioned, in addition to plain service in terms of modern medicine, as *praeparatio evangelium*.[13] Kugler's approach also included a profound concern for women's rights. In 1887, she called forth a "civilization which recognizes women as an equal and not an inferior."[14]

Today, the Christian Medical Association of India (CMAI, originally founded in 1905), an umbrella organization for Protestant health work, coordinates the work of around 330 functioning member hospitals and health centers. About 30 of these belong to Lutheran churches in India.[15] The great inheritance of the Protestant medical mission has been difficult to maintain in the changing health and health care circumstances of India, a country that still bears more than a fifth of the world's burden of disease. Nowadays, the health work coordinated by the Catholic Health Association of India (CHAI) is much broader than its Protestant counterpart: the number of

---

10. Boulanger and Criel, *The Difficult Relationship between Faith-Based Health Care Organizations and the Public Sector in Sub-Saharan Africa*, 81–82; The Evangelical Lutheran Church of Tanzania, *ELCT Health*.

11. Röllinghoff, *Zeittaffel der evangelischen "Ärztlichen Mission" in Deutschland*, 4.

12. Jeyakumar, *History of Christianity in India: Selected Themes*, 37–40.

13. Vethanayagamony, "'A Deliver on a White Horse:' The Pioneering Journey of Dr. Anna Sarah Kugler," 93–94.

14. As quoted in ibid., 95–96.

15. Christian Medical Association of India. *Church Health Boards*.

CHAI member institutions extends to around 3,400 including "484 large hospitals."[16]

COMPLEMENTARY DIVERSITY IN VISION AND MISSION

Let us now turn to the vision statements of the Health Charter of the Evangelical Lutheran Church in Tanzania (ELCT) and the Indian Lutheran Health Ministry (ILHM). The ELCT has focused its vision on society at large: "A society with healthy individuals and communities whereby physical, emotional, mental and spiritual needs are met and balanced resulting in peaceful and joyful life."[17] The vision of the ILHM is more about its own health work, namely, "[t]o partake in God's purpose of healing in its fullness."[18] It is worth noting that whereas the Tanzanian version highlights the perspective of the needs of the "individuals and communities," the Indian version talks about participating in the ministry (or responsibilities). However, although these two visions are quite different as such, they can, by and large, be regarded as complementary rather than incompatible.

The lengthy mission statement of the ELCT begins with a perspective on witness: "To witness and glorify God through provision of holistic affordable and accessible quality care supported by community and other stakeholders."[19] This is followed by a list of eight goals that the church will pursue. The first of them is that care is to be provided "to all people irrespective to creed, status or social inclination."[20] The rest of the goals could largely be from any public sector health agenda, but the identity in faith is also indicated, particularly in the notions of "biblical teachings on caring for the body (the temple of God)," keeping "life sacred," and exercising "good stewardship."[21] In the context of the ELCT's overall mission, the charter thus depicts the church's health sector provision "[a]s the healing arm of the church [which] aims to demonstrate Christ's love in offering healing and compassion for those people in need."[22]

Akin to the ELCT, the ILHM uses the language of witness in the description of the mission of its member churches in the field of health: "Mission of the UELCI [United Evangelical Lutheran Churches in India] member

16. Catholic Health Association of India, "Home."

17. The Evangelical Lutheran Church in Tanzania, *The Health Charter*, 4.

18. The United Evangelical Lutheran Churches in India, *Caring for Life: Indian Lutheran Health Ministry*, 2.

19. The Evangelical Lutheran Church in Tanzania, *The Health Charter*, 4.

20. Ibid., 4.

21. Ibid., 4–5.

22. Ibid., 3.

churches is to witness Christ through healing and health services."[23] The actual mission statement of the ILHM is brief and more about the role of this umbrella organization: "To enable the member church's healing ministries to gather strength in togetherness and expand its reach to communities."[24] However, it is "witness" in particular that stands out as a unifying theological notion in the expressed health work missions of both the ELCT and the UELCI.

In both Tanzania and India, a particular area of health work has been to respond to HIV/AIDS. This pandemic has implied further emphasis on theologies of human dignity and the body. Preventive health education and community health (with ecclesiology) have also ranked among the key issues in the field.

The UELCI program on HIV and AIDS points out, to begin with, that "all people are created as images of God" who may have life "in all its fullness."[25] ELCT Health, particularly through its program The Local Community Competence Building & HIV and AIDS Prevention in Tanzania & Zambia (LCCB), has integrated preventive education with a strong community aspect into its work. Indeed, the "LCCB recognises that the most effective responses to HIV and AIDS are community driven."[26]

SUBNATIONAL PERSPECTIVES: TANZANIA

Individual Lutheran hospitals both in Tanzania and in India can have their own vision and mission statements, often expressed with values and guiding biblical references. The Itete Lutheran Hospital, South-Tanzania, opened its *Annual Report 1997* with a quote from Numbers 21:8–9, which tells about a bronze, life-giving serpent in the wilderness in the times of Moses. This is interpreted to inspire the idea of getting well through turning "to the services provided in the name of JESUS Christ our saviour" (emphasis in the source).[27] After this foreword, the rest of the report unfolds in the same way as that of any secular hospital.

The Nkoaranga Lutheran Hospital, in the Arusha area of Tanzania, begins its *Annual Report for the Year 2011* with a quote from Luke 10:9: "Heal

---

23. The United Evangelical Lutheran Churches in India, *Caring for Life: Indian Lutheran Health Ministry*, 2.

24. Ibid., 2.

25. The United Evangelical Lutheran Churches in India, *Services: HIV and Aids Programme*.

26. The Evangelical Lutheran Church in Tanzania, *ELCT Health*, HIV/AIDS.

27. Itete Lutheran Hospital, *Annual Report 1997*, 1.

the sick who are there and tell them, the Kingdom of God is near you."[28] The stated mission of the hospital is "to provide quality health care to our people so as to alleviate disease burden within our community ultimately glorifying GOD" (emphasis in the source).[29] The Bumbuli Lutheran Hospital in the North-Eastern Diocese uses somewhat different terms, when formulating its vision, in its *Annual Report 2011*: "A leading hospital in Tanzania offering excellent health services with the love and compassion of Christ."[30]

Straightforward references to God, Christ, and witness in the forewords or introductions to health work might seem peculiar to Western observers. However, Stephen Munga, bishop of the North-Eastern Diocese, has emphasized that assisting people and providing social services is indeed mandatory to the church and depicted such diakonia as a quintessential aspect of *holistic evangelism*. He regards holistic evangelism as spreading the good news both in word and practice, but distinguishes it clearly from proselytism, which is about attempting to convert people to faith.[31]

Frederic Svensäter has pointed out further, based on his interviews on healing mainly in the Iringa diocese, that it is quite natural in Tanzania to see faith in God and Christ as connected to liberation from all kinds of problems including illnesses. To be a healer or "medicine man" (in many Bantu languages *mganga*) is traditionally very much appreciated among Tanzanians, and Christ fits smoothly into the role of a "supreme healer."[32] Such a belief appears to be on a continuum with a belief in the love of God that "does not want anything higher than to deliver people from all kinds of burdens, whether in sickness, spiritual oppression or material shortage."[33]

Whereas God's love and the compassion of Christ may appear as rather unproblematic starting points of faith both in terms of Lutheran theology and inclusive dialogical cooperation across cultures, the concepts of holistic evangelism and Jesus' healing power might sometimes complicate cooperation and, in some cases, the process of healing as well. Yet it should be borne in mind that Bishop Munga's account of holistic evangelism excludes proselytism. In this respect it is roughly compatible with non-confessional health work, or at least it encourages a dialogical attitude in a context where approaches that are assumed to be non-confessional are often regarded as

28. Nkoaranga Lutheran Hospital, *Annual Report for the Year 2011*, 2.

29. Ibid., 4.

30. Bumbuli Lutheran Hospital, *Annual Report 2011*, 5.

31. Munga, "The Church in Partnership with the World: Quest for an Ecclesiological Method," 56–61.

32. Svensäter, "Concepts and Practices of Healing within the Lutheran Church in Tanzania: With a Special Focus on Iringa Diocese," 125, 135.

33. Ibid., 125.

somehow biased at the very least. At the practical care level, ELCT Health strives for at least as high medical standards as any non-confessional quality health agency does, thus implying that any understanding of Jesus' healing power should be compatible with high-level medical practices.

SUBNATIONAL PERSPECTIVES: INDIA

The Bethesda Hospital, a Lutheran hospital that stems from the heritage of Anna Kugler in Ambur, South India, states its mission as follows: "Comprehensive care of the body and the soul of any person regardless of caste, creed, color, and religion in the true spirit of Christ."[34] This "House of Mercy" also highlights Exodus 15:26 on the front page of its brochure: "I am the Lord who heals you." In addition, Matthew 25:40 is quoted on doing something "unto one of the least of" Jesus' brothers as doing something unto Jesus.[35] Such references underline the biblical basis of Lutheran health work in the service of people irrespective of their religion or, for example, caste.

The Ruth Sigmon Memorial Lutheran Hospital (RSMLH) in Guntur "aims to deliver health care to all people through concern and love through the healing power of Christ."[36] This mission statement is explained further with a reference to the idea that truth will set people free, for example, in this context especially the truth of Christ's sacrifice on the cross and the healing power of Christ. In turn, the concept of freedom is clarified as freedom "[t]o live right and to enjoy God's World."[37]

In these hospital-level formulations, both loving God and the work and healing power of Christ are openly referred to, resembling some of the corresponding statements in Tanzania. On the other hand, as in Tanzania, the practical objectives could be from the agenda of any non-confessional health organization. Areas of special focus can be perceived, though. For instance, the first of the ten practical objectives of the RSMLH is "to establish a clinic with optimum facilities for providing health care with emphasis on women and children."[38] A similar emphasis is to be noted here as in Kugler's work over a century ago: a special concern for women's health.

The Gossner Evangelical Lutheran Church has promoted activities in the areas of education, health, agriculture, interprofessional service, financial self-reliance, and spiritual ministry.[39] Even if the public health services

---

34. Bethesda Hospital, *House of Mercy*, 7.
35. Ibid., 12.
36. Ruth Sigmon Memorial Lutheran Hospital, *Healing Through Christ*.
37. Ibid.
38. Ibid.
39. Singh, "Globalization and Human Resource Development," 168.

of the country actually improve, this type of a broad development agenda can be extremely useful.

In its pioneering stage, as Rev. A.C. Oommen has put it, Christian health work in India was largely about responding "to urgent, desperate calls for health in the face of sickness and death, when nothing else was available."[40] However, such circumstances are still to be found in several parts of India today, and steady public health development cannot be taken for granted. Dr. K.M. Shyamprasad, Chancellor of Martin Luther Christian University in Shillong, took a stance on this front in 2012. Shyamprasad especially urged the Indian government to improve its regulation of public health.[41]

However, even properly functioning public health services do not necessarily imply that church-related health and social work should wither away or be merged entirely into the system that has a secular outlook. The significance of the spiritual dimension in the faith-based facilities might become important in the markets, for this is what these institutions can provide in particular; but whether for theological or pragmatic reasons, the faith dimension has tended to be expressed in rather minimally explicit terms in health and development programs coordinated by the Lutheran World Service (LWS), basically a global-level humanitarian and development agency.

LUTHERAN WORLD SERVICE

Health work has been an important aspect of the broader humanitarian and development initiatives of the LWS, or the Department of World Service (DWS) of the LWF. In its *Global Strategy for 2007–2012*, the DWS formulates its rather secular vision as follows: "People of the world living in just societies in peace and dignity, united in diversity, and empowered to achieve their universal rights, to meet basic needs and quality of life."[42] The mission of this organization, however, tells about a faith-based identity: "Inspired by God's love for humanity, World Service responds to and challenges the causes and effects of human suffering and poverty."[43] In addition, the *Global Strategy for 2007–2012* reports on a "mandate" from the LWF member churches, which

---

40. Oommen, "New Challenges in the Healing Ministry of the Church of India," 101.

41. Shyamprasad, "Waiting for a Law."

42. The Department of World Service, *Global Strategy 2007-2012: Uphold the rights of the poor and oppressed*, 5.

43. Ibid.

is to "Bear Witness in Church and Society to God's Healing, Reconciliation and Justice."[44]

The new strategy of the DWS enshrines its vision and mission almost unchanged. The updated vision only includes a reference to the "full potential" of the people of the world in addition to their universal rights and introduces itself as "[r]ooted in Christian values of love, reconciliation and justice."[45] The language of witness is not used here in terms of speaking of Jesus as the supreme healer. The work of the DWS is mandated by its member churches and its "uniqueness is to be locally rooted and globally connected."[46] In the foreword of this strategy, however, the director of the DWS, Rev. Eberhard Hitzler, highlights the motto of the department: "Uphold the rights of the poor and oppressed" (cf. Ps 82:3).[47] The motto provides a biblical insight to the rights-based approach characteristic of the work of this agency. In another text, Hitzler uses the term "theology of the cross" when he distinguishes the diakonia of the DWS from the "gospel of prosperity" type of approaches that he denotes as being common in today's Africa.[48]

The Lutheran World Service India Trust (LWSIT) functions as an independent national agency. Interestingly, its vision includes the notions of *secular* society and communal harmony: "People of India living in just, secular and peaceful societies, in communal harmony and with dignity, united in diversity and empowered to achieve their universal rights to basic needs and quality of life."[49] The mission of the LWSIT is virtually the same as that of the DWS. In the organization's *Annual Report 2011* Dr. Vijayakumar James, executive director of the LWSIT, emphasizes the calling of the LWSIT "to empower the last, the least, and the lost."[50]

Despite the overall secular outlook of such documents, it is nonetheless clear enough that the work of the LWSIT has its deep foundations in faith. The message from the executive secretary of the UELCI and also the President of the LWSIT Board of Trustees, Rev. Dr. Augustine Jeyakumar, in *The Indian Lutheran News* helps to clarify this approach in a broader

---

44. Ibid.

45. The Department of World Service, *World Service Global Strategy 2013-2018*, 5–6.

46. Ibid., 5.

47. Hitzler, "Foreword," 4.

48. Hitzler, "The 1972 EECMY Letter: Could It Be Written Today and What Would Be a Possible Response?," 220.

49. Lutheran World Federation India Trust, "Lutheran World Service India: Since—1974", Home.

50. James, "Foreword," 5.

perspective. While Jeyakumar points out that all religions "emphasize fraternity, love, peace, and equality" amidst all kinds of difficult conditions day by day, "the churches and Christians are called to trust in the transforming power of the Gospel and to share that faith among others."[51] Such an approach implies that the content of the ethical perspective that is promoted is assumed to be widely shared across different religions and world views, but the Christian faith dimension is also firmly embedded in the work in its entirety.

In Tanzania, from 1964 to 2006 the DWS worked through the Tanganyika Christian Refugee Service (TCRS), which has since then continued as an autonomous organization and associate program linked to the LWF/DWS. The vision statement of the TCRS is: "Empowered communities living in a just, democratic society, united in diversity and enjoying quality of life and God given dignity."[52] Its mission statement is non-confessional in character. Nevertheless, these TRSC formulations do not include the concept of the secular state as the LWSIT's has done.

As far back as several decades ago, in their annual reports from the year 1979, both the Lutheran World Service India (LWSI) and TCRS profiled themselves as non-confessional in character in virtually all respects other than their names. In the health sector in particular, by its fifteenth anniversary, the TCRS reports having built seven health centers and 19 dispensaries.[53] The LWSI, in turn, was then five years old and already very active in the community health work involving immunization, nutrition supplements, health education, and home visits, for instance.[54] It is difficult to measure the value of such a pragmatic witness for the church.

Whether or not to include explicit insights of faith in health and development work was actually a debated question already in the 1960s and 1970s. After a short summary, I will return to some insights on this issue in the Makumira Consultation held in 1967, insights that could still be valuable today for future Lutheran health work and forms of service across continents.

PARTIALLY OVERLAPPING PERSPECTIVES

When it comes to the explicit dimension of faith, both the Tanzanian and Indian churches cover the faith basis of their health work quite extensively,

51. Jeyakumar, "Message from the Executive Secretary," 1.
52. Tanganyika Christian Refugee Service, Home.
53. Tanganyika Christian Refugee Service, *Annual Report 1979*, 3.
54. Lutheran World Service (India), *Annual Report 1979: Preparing the Ground . . .*, appendix.

although the documents I explored depict the pragmatic work in a largely non-confessional manner. The globally connected DWS and its key partner organizations are characteristically less explicit about faith in their foundational statements as well. Taken together, however, the above-mentioned Lutheran documents reveal a fairly vivid array of theological standpoints in their visions, mission, and corresponding guidelines.

Some of the Lutheran perspectives on the right to health and the promotion of health-related development are more theological and others more practical. Beginning with the primarily *theological perspectives*, at least the following ten can be identified:

1. Glorifying God—witnessing God's love
2. *Praeparatio evangelium*—holistic evangelism
3. Christ as the supreme healer—the healing power of Christ
4. Partaking in God's purpose of healing—freedom to practice God's love
5. Human dignity—keeping life sacred—the temple of the Holy Spirit
6. Caring for, and empowering, the suffering least—theology of the cross
7. Ecclesiology of the body—the healing arm of the church
8. Enjoying God's world—enjoying quality of life
9. Prophetic diakonia—restoring the world with the rights of the least
10. Rootedness in Christian values—inspiration by God's love

Although many of these theological perspectives are largely compatible with corresponding non-confessional accounts of love, healing, dignity, quality of life, rights, and service, they can also function as starting points for intriguing forms of explicit theology. In particular, there are clear Bible references in their support (usually plenty of them) and some of these references have also been quoted or paraphrased in the documents studied in this chapter.

Another set of perspectives, *practical perspectives* (sometimes overlapping with the theological ones) concerns what is primarily the practical nature and scope of Lutheran health work:

11. Maintaining basic health facilities—curative treatments for bodily health
12. Promoting holistic health—well-being with a spiritual dimension
13. Focusing on women, children and other vulnerable groups

14. Preventive health education—preventive HIV and AIDS work (in communities)
15. Advancing multidimensional human development—preconditions for well-being
16. Requesting the implementation of social and health justice and human rights
17. Enabling responsible living—transformation of individuals and communities

Maintaining basic health facilities is still at the core of Lutheran health work, but depending on the needs that emerge, the trend among many Lutheran agencies seems to be towards other types of faith-related health and development work. The above-mentioned 17 perspectives, as represented on a single list, could be of some use for further ventures that promote a multidimensional and dialogical approach while avoiding unnecessary parochialism.

Tensions among the perspectives in question could necessitate rationing among the different options. For example, it might be worthwhile to avoid the *preparatio evangelium* approach (2) if—cf. Bishop Munga above—in practice it entailed proselytism with a failure to demonstrate God's love. At the same time, I would highlight the ecclesiology of the body (7) because it could serve as an umbrella concept in the search for complementary approaches among most of the other theological and practical perspectives.

Although all of the enlisted 17 perspectives may be rather abstract as such, I have repeatedly pointed out their connectedness to real-life service among the poor and the ill. This type of conceptual approach means that future-oriented scenarios may often also be informed by what can be learned from down-to-earth historical inheritance.

SOME MAKUMIRA INSIGHTS REVIVED?

The Evangelical Lutheran Church in Tanzania served as the key organizer of the Consultation on Health and Healing in Makumira in 1967, which was chaired by Dr. John Wilkinson from the East African Presbyterian Church.[55] Bishop Stefano R. Moshi, Mkuu (Head) of the ELCT, emphasizes in that context that the Church does *not* do medical work with a view to winning more converts. This would "not show God's love and compassion for man in

---

55. This consultation was a follow-up of so called Tübingen consultation, in 1964, initiated by the Commission on World Mission of the LWF two years earlier. World Council of Churches, *The Healing Church: The Tübingen Consultation 1964*.

his suffering."[56] In turn, Rev. Cuthbert K. Omari, from the University College of Dar es Salaam, underlined a holistic and responsible understanding of the human person. Originally created as body, mind, and spirit, any sick person needs healing in all of these respects, and not only for themselves. Here on earth, says Omari, Christians are to seek health "in order to live for the service of God" and thereby also for the service of their neighbors as God's co-workers.[57]

In the early 1970s, the rapidly growing Ethiopian Evangelical Church Mekane Yesus (EECMY) was influential in promoting the concept of holistic healing in Eastern Africa. For instance, in a consultation the LWF held in Nairobi, Kenya, in 1974, the representatives of the EECMY emphasized "the restoration of man to liberty and wholeness."[58] However, in 2009, when commenting on the EECMY's original search for holistic healing, the Director of the DWS Eberhard Hitzler suggests that now the situation is completely different. Nowadays the gospel as word is being preached vigorously in East Africa, but marginalization, oppression, and violence—not to mention the lack of many basic conditions of life including health facilities—are widely prevalent.[59] Hence he asks for more attention to be paid to the holistic gospel today, but from a very different angle than that of the EECMY in the 1970s.

Back in the Makumira Consultation of 1967, Dr. Aart van Soest from Tübingen focused on the practical planning of church-related medical work: he urged the recognition of "[a]n existing and unmet need."[60] For example, no hospitals should be maintained as monuments of prestigious service, but the needs of one's neighbor should guide the selection of the means to be adopted. Equally, no Christian medical schools need to be established if there is sufficient medical education already available—although in India, van Soest points out, there indeed was that need and Christian organizations responded to it well.[61]

As regards the topic of this chapter, I would add here that insofar as the right to health is about the real needs of others, the need-based and the rights-based approaches are bound to overlap to a large extent. Similarly, if

---

56. Moshi, "Foreword," 1–2.

57. Omri, "Health and Healing in the Creation," 31.

58. The Ethiopian Evangelical Church Mekane Yesus, "Serving the Whole Man: A Responsible Church Ministry and a Flexible International Aid Relationship," 14.

59. Hitzler, "The 1972 EECMY Letter," 220.

60. van Soest, "The Strategy of the Healing Ministry of the Church," 87.

61. Ibid., 90.

the right to health is not primarily a right to adequate responses on the basis of real health needs, I do not know what it is.

TOWARDS COMPREHENSIVE VISIONS OF HEALTH WORK

Health and healing are not marginal issues either in the Bible or in the life of human beings in general, and health work has often been among the top priorities in Christian mission. A wide array of Lutheran health work documents demonstrate a comparatively strong complementary unity: perspectives and contexts vary and many agencies are quite minimalistic in terms of writing about faith explicitly, but the statements do not tend to contradict one another.

There are also deep tensions between the approaches. One of the most important theological perspectives in confronting them is the ecclesiology of the body—included in (7) above. In the body of Christ, different members have different talents and tasks. However, even at the level of theological analysis we have reason to be reminded: there is no perfectly healthy communion or church, or the body of Christ, here on earth. Hence, this perspective does not provide grounds for expecting perfectly functioning divisions of labor in the field of health work—not even an approximation of that—although it can help us mitigate the tensions.

The practical challenges ahead are considerable as well. Virtually any major crisis is bound to entail devastating health consequences for a great number of people. For example, leprosy has almost been eradicated and the global struggle against the HIV/AIDS pandemic has shown some signs of success, but the health rights of the poor across the world are usually inadequately fulfilled even today—and insecurity about tomorrow is as prevalent as ever. The world cannot afford to neglect the potential to be harnessed in agencies, communities, and individuals (partly) motivated by some of the ten faith-related perspectives listed above.

Lutheran churches do not characteristically have a surplus of financial or human resources these days, but times are not easy for the Catholics, either, and yet their health work is notably viable in many contexts. Equally, charismatic healing theologies are rising rapidly. Exploring the core aspects of Lutheran health work to date can serve further ventures towards comprehensive and sustainable visions of Lutheran responses to the profound health-related human needs of tomorrow.

BIBLIOGRAHY

Bethesda Hospital. *House of Mercy*. Ambur: Bethesda Hospital, 2008.
Bloomquist, Karen, Robert Granke, and Péri Rasolondraibe. *Prophetic Diakonia: "For the Healing of the World."* Report, Johannesburg, South Africa, November 2002. Geneva: The Lutheran World Federation, 2002.
Boulanger, Delphine, and Bart Criel. *The Difficult Relationship between Faith-Based Health Care Organizations and the Public Sector in Sub-Saharan Africa*. Antwerp: ITGPress, 2012.
Bumbuli Lutheran Hospital. *Annual Report 2011*. Bumbuli: Evangelical Lutheran Church in Tanzania, North Eastern Diocese, 2012.
Catholic Health Association of India (CHAI). "Home." India: CHAI, 2013. Online: http://chai-india.org/?p=1499 (accessed 30/06/2013).
Christian Medical Association of India (CMAI). *Church Health Boards*. New Delhi: CMAI, 2013.
Drèze, Jean, and Amartya Sen. *An Uncertain Glory: India and Its Contradictions*. London: Penguin, 2013.
Hitzler, Eberhard. "The 1972 EECMY Letter: Could It Be Written Today and What Would Be a Possible Response?" In *Serving the Whole Person: The Practice of Diakonia Within the Lutheran Communion*, edited by Kjell Nordstokke and Frederick Schlagenhaft, 217–22. Minneapolis: Lutheran University Press, 2009.
———. "Foreword." In *World Service Global Strategy 2013–2018*. Geneva: The Lutheran World Federation. Online: http://www.lutheranworld.org/sites/default/files/DWS-StrategicPlan-2013-low_0.pdf (accessed 28/10/2013).
Itete Lutheran Hospital. *Annual Report 1997*. Tukuyu: Medical and Deaconic Department, Konde Diocese, ELCT, 1998.
James, Vijayakumar. "Foreword." In Lutheran World Federation India Trust, *Annual Report 2011*. LWSIT, 2012, 4–5. Online: http://www.lutheranworld.org/sites/default/files/India-Annual-Report-2011.pdf (accessed 29/10/2013).
Jeyakumar, Augustine. "Message from the Executive Secretary." *The Indian Lutheran News: The E-Newsletter of the United Evangelical Lutheran Churches in India* 6 (Issue 4, 2011) 1.
Jeyakumar, D. Arthur. *History of Christianity in India: Selected Themes*. Delhi: Indian Society for Promoting Christian Knowledge, 2002.
Lutheran World Federation. *Lutheran World Service: India 2002*. Kolkata: Lutheran World Service India, 2003.
Lynge, Kristina. *Tanzania: The Darling of the Donor Community: A Critical Review of the Failure of Past Development Aid Efforts*. Saarbrücken: LAP Pambert, 2008.
Lutheran World Service (India). *Annual Report 1979: Preparing the Ground* . . . Calcutta: LWSI, 1979.
———. *Lutheran World Service: India 2002*. Kolkata: LWSI, 2003.
Lutheran World Federation India Trust (LWSIT). "Lutheran World Service India: Since—1974." Kolkata: LWSIT. Online: http://www.lwsi.org (accessed 29/10/2013).
Moshi, Stefano R. "Foreword." In *Health and Healing: The Makumira Consultation, February 1967*, 1–2. Arusha: The Medical Board of the Evangelical Lutheran Church of Tanzania, 1967.
Munga, Stephen. "The Church in Partnership with the World: Quest for an Ecclesiological Method." *Africa Theological Journal* 32.2 (2009) 39–63.

Nessan, Graig L. *Give Us This Day: A Lutheran Proposal for Ending World Hunger*. Minneapolis: Augsburg Fortress, 2003.

Nkoaranga Lutheran Hospital. *Annual Report for the Year 2011*. Usa River: Meru Diocese, ELCT, 2012.

Omri, Cuthbert K. "Health and Healing in the Creation." In *Health and Healing: The Makumira Consultation, February 1967*, 28-33. Arusha: The Medical Board of the Evangelical Lutheran Church of Tanzania, 1967.

Oommen, A.C. "New Challenges in the Healing Ministry of the Church of India." In *The Healing Ministry in the Church in India: A Compilation of The Dr. Jakob Candy Orations*, edited by Vijay Aruldas, 93-104. New Delhi: Christian Medical Association of India, 2001.

Röllinghoff, Werner. *Zeittaffel der evangelischen "Ärztlichen Mission" in Deutschland*. Tübingen: Deutsches Institut für Ärztliche Mission, 1984.

Ruth Sigmon Memorial Lutheran Hospital. *Healing Through Christ*. Guntur: RSMLH, 2013. Online: http://ruthsigmonmemorial.webs.com/ourmission.htm (accessed 27/10/2013).

Sahlberg, Carl-Erik. *From Krapf to Rugambwa: A Church History of Tanzania*. Nairobi, Kenya: Evangel Publishing House, 1986.

Sen, Amartya. *Development as Freedom*. Oxford: Oxford University Press, 1999.

Shyamprasad, K.M. "Waiting for a Law." In *Inclusive Media for a Change*. Delhi: Im4Change, 2012. Online: http://www.im4change.org/latest-news-updates/waiting-for-a-law-dr-km-shyamprasad-16032.html (accessed 28/10/2013).

Singh, C. K. Paul. "Globalization and Human Resource Development." In *Just Asia: The Challenge of a Globalized Economy*, edited by Viggo Mortensen, 167-68. Geneva: Department of Theology and Studies, the Lutheran World Federation, 1998.

Svensäter, Frederic. "Concepts and Practices of Healing within the Lutheran Church in Tanzania: With a Special Focus on Iringa Diocese." In *Church Life and Christian Initiatives in Tanzania: A Report from a Field Study 2001*, edited by Klas Lundström, 117-40. Uppsala: Swedish Institute of Missionary Research, 2002.

Taneja, D.K. *Health Policies and Programmes in India*. 11th Edition. Delhi: Indian Public Health Association, 2013.

Tanganyika Christian Refugee Service. *Annual Report 1979*. Dar es Salaam: TCRS / The Lutheran World Federation, 1979.

———. *Tanganyika Christian Refugee Service*. Dar es Salaam: TCRS. Online: http://www.tcrs.or.tz (accessed 29/10/2013).

The Department of World Service (DWS). *Global Strategy 2007-2012: Uphold the Rights of the Poor and Oppressed*. Geneva: The Lutheran World Federation. Online: http://193.73.242.125/What_We_Do/DWS/DWS-Documents/DWS-Stratplan.pdf (accessed 28/10/2013).

———. *World Service Global Strategy 2013-2018*. Geneva: The Lutheran World Federation. Online: http://www.lutheranworld.org/sites/default/files/DWS-StrategicPlan-2013-low_0.pdf (accessed 28/10/2013).

The Evangelical Lutheran Church in Tanzania. *ELCT Health*. Arusha: ELCT, 2013. Online: http://health.elct.org (accessed 29/10/2013).

———. *The Health Charter*. Arusha: ELCT, 2010.

The Ethiopian Evangelical Church Mekane Yesus. "Serving the Whole Man: A Responsible Church Ministry and a Flexible International Aid Relationship." In *Proclamation and Human Development: Documentation from a Lutheran World*

Federation Consultation, Nairobi, Kenya, October 21-25, 1974. The Lutheran World Federation, 1975, 11-17.

The United Evangelical Lutheran Churches in India. *Caring for Life: Indian Lutheran Health Ministry*. Chennai: UELCI, 2010.

———. *Services: Hiv and Aids Programme*, 2013. Online: http://www.indiamart.com/united-evangelical/services.html#hiv-and-aids-programme (accessed 29/10/2013).

The United Republic of Tanzania. *Health Sector Strategic Plan III: July 2009-June 2015: "Partnership for Developing the MDGs."* Ministry of Health and Social Welfare, 2008. Online: http://ihi.eprints.org/970/1/HealthSectorStrategicPlan.pdf (accessed 08/02/2013).

van Soest, Aart. "The Strategy of the Healing Ministry of the Church." In *Health and Healing: The Makumira Consultation, February 1967*, 85-91. Arusha: The Medical Board of the Evangelical Lutheran Church of Tanzania, 1967.

Vethanayagamony, Peter. "'A Deliver on a White Horse:' The Pioneering Journey of Dr. Anna Sarah Kugler." *Gurukul Journal of Theological Studies* 22.2 (June 2011) 93-109.

World Council of Churches. *The Healing Church: The Tübingen Consultation 1964*. Geneva: WCC, 1965.

World Health Organization. *The Constitution of the World Health Organization*. WHO, 1964. Online: http://www.who.int/governance/eb/who_constitution_en.pdf (accessed 27/12/2012).

5

"There's an App for That!"

A Post-Christian Lutheran Response

MICHAEL R. TRICE

Last summer I visited the National Palatine Museum in Rome, where a special exhibit was on display that focused on over 1,500 years of the Christian story evident in written correspondence. In the exhibit's dimly lit, air-conditioned hallways, I turned a corner and blinked hard at two documents seated side-by-side, against dark velvet. On the left was the colorful opening salvo of the Second Vatican Council. On the right in stark relief rested the papal bull ordering the excommunication of Martin Luther. The inches between these documents compressed centuries of Christian hardship and theological fortitude. Although I left to view other works, these texts drew me back twice to silently gaze downward. And then, in a breath the contours of Christian identity for our time slowly rose up from the thin space between these texts.

Martin Luther nailed on the parish doors his early sixteenth century pastoral response to alleviate the terrified conscience before God; Paul Tillich's mid-twentieth century engrossing sermon on Isaiah and the shaking of the foundations was an analogous response of radical grace to a ruptured post-holocaust world. Like the documents at the National Palatine Museum, Luther and Tillich emit clarion calls for serious ecclesiological change, refined theological fortitude, and even renewal, in Christian identity. Today, those of us throughout the Lutheran world would do well to acclimate ourselves to our new historical situation. Take a deep breath and cast aside presumptions of privilege. Today we are citizens *within*—and not merely rapping at the gates *of*—a post-Christian world.[1] That day is here.

THE POST-CHRISTIAN WORLD—THREE MARKERS

What is a post-Christian world? This is a world where more people believe in God than have a religion that expresses their belief. They are disassociated from organized religious life. It is a global context that is itself an aggregate of numerous geographical and cultural contexts with their own particular theological narratives for Christian identity and truth. The proliferation of particular contexts is not a cause of, but rather signals the end of, an age of Western Christian ideological supremacy that was itself the last ember of Constantinian Imperial Christianity. In this world, institutions are not necessarily looked to as centers of moral authority, exemplified in how today's religious leaders are envied when they mutually *represent* and *resist* their own institutions. From this decentered religious platform, Pope Francis is able to speak from a fuselage about God's love for homosexuals without disavowing Catholic Church teaching on the matter. It is his honest charisma that draws Christians and those who are not Christians, who value an authentic response rather than a complex rhetorical concealment.

The world is listening to Christianity, but it is listening differently. In the heart of the local post-Christian world of the U.S. Pacific Northwest, as a theologian I am a post-systematic constructive Lutheran theologian. This designation means that we have surpassed systems, where they are necessary but *never* sufficient for constructing the fullest, relevant theological retort today. In my context, theological truth must be relevant in order to amplify the narrative of hope-amidst-the-inexplicable that isn't a mere jingle on paradox and providence. By way of example and in terms of the inexplicable, my theological students, who consider themselves the radical loyalists to organized Christian life, require that I enumerate a theology of evil and restorative hope, and in the same course carve curricular space for a praxis-based method of the "religious first-responder" that helps them prepare as leaders for tragic events in local communities, like guns in elementary schoolrooms. In this context whenever I excise the threads of privilege and presumption, theological discourse bursts into life. Our post-Christian world is both a dilemma and an opportunity. In both cases, wishing it away

---

1. Much has been written about the post-Christian world. To understand more of these trends, I encourage a reading of the edited volume Bender and Klassen, *After Pluralism: Reimagining Religious Engagement*; and the recent book, Granberg-Michaelson, *From Times Square to Timbuktu: The Post-Christian West Meets the Non-Western Church*. Both of these texts take seriously rhetoric of post-Christian encounter by framing it within a helpful and straightforward interpretation of pluralism.

is a massive disservice to ourselves and to the world that is the seat of our call.

For heuristic reasons, let's imagine together three general characteristics or markers of this post-Christian world, which assist us in explicating the above points in more manageable form. These markers being: 1) the *authority* of the Church, 2) the *Story* of God and Us, and 3) the search for human *identity*.

THE *AUTHORITY* OF THE CHURCH

First, Christian ecclesial authority (even prior to Constantine's christening of it) assumed an interior authoritative structure that likens to Russian Matryoshka dolls, i.e., beginning with the primacy and unity of the Church as the outer shell. Every embodiment of the Church was conceived of as deeply nested within this outer skin, and related to the whole body. These included liturgical expression in community, theological discernment, moral social connection, and individual ethical responsibility.

Consider the marker of Christian identity today: The image of an ecclesial Matryoshka is turned inside-out, reflected in (1) global disagreements on matters of human sexuality that herald Christian separatism, rather than acknowledging the *apriori* unity we share in Christ; (2) a global weakening of social bonds and corporate memory that are a generative power in liturgical expression, where empty churches are not well equipped to refit communal memory to a new immigrant population in the neighborhood; (3) the introduction of the moral marketplace through the revolutionary arrival of social organizing and networking typified in Clay Shirky's enormously popular work: *Here Comes Everybody*[2]; and, (4) secular alternatives from Teach for America to Greenpeace that inspire the emerging generation with values (however admirable) that are not derived from the teaching of the Church and which draw no necessary redeeming virtue from it. All in all, contemporary society can well determine moral and ethical action and bypass the Christian narrative as having any relevance in the marketplace of ideas and action. The Church is not irrelevant, but it is relegated to a choice among an aggregation of choices in a world of pluralities and possibilities, like marbles in a fishbowl. Feeling decentered?

Here is a problem for pluralism: The Church does not see itself as a choice among other choices. And, in fact, the Church is not a consumer product, like a choice of coffee, or wine, or bread on store shelves. Instead, the Church even and especially in local expressions, is making cosmological claims about the relationship between God and humanity in a complex

2. Shirky, *Here Comes Everybody: The Power of Organizing without Organizations.*

universe. The Christian narrative in all of its particularity in the world is still making claims that, far beyond an assent of the will, ask for a modicum of belonging. When we join a group we become members, but when we truly belong to a narrative we are disciples. In life cosmological claims are not so much believed as they are encountered, and this is a problem for pluralism in the world that finds it difficult to coherently belong like a disciple in cosmological terms. This is also a problem for the Church whenever it focuses on membership over discipleship and mistakes four walls for a Story.

THE *STORY* OF GOD AND US

The second marker of a post-Christian world begins with the narrative to which we belong. For Christians, this is titled: the "Story of God and Us"; it covers creation-loss-redemption and return to God, enacted through community liturgy, theological moral memory, collective action, and the individual ethical response.[3] A popular complaint throughout church and society is that we have misaligned our story to the urgent needs of the world today, in effect pursuing internal and tribal arguments while paying less attention to our call for the healing of the world "out there." Think about the protracted scandals and decade-long fights on sexual orientation and practice. In the twilight of these sex wars, Lutherans are exhausted by a family fight, which nearly brought the house down upon us. Having served for eight years (2004–2011) in the Office of the Presiding Bishop in the Evangelical Lutheran Church in America (ELCA), I witnessed our bishops, clergy, and laypeople traverse what was one of the most punishing times of their vocational lives. Sex matters, and the world suffered through our own Lutheran self-demolition. Everything has a cost.

The misalignment in the Story of God and Us has nothing to do with sex, of course. It has to do with a disconnection between the Story and a world that may not find the Story relevant. We need be aware that the single most influential measurement of religious relevance is whether a cosmological Story responds to suffering in a believable way. In this world, there is a disconnection between the Story we tell about God's love for the world and the inundation of struggle humans face on the planet. We call this the theological problem of theodicy: "Why does a loving God allow us to suffer (. . .) so much?" This question is our theological canary in the coalmine, revealing what has gone awry in the middle term between the Story of God *and* Us. The mediating distance between God *and* Us includes pogroms,

---

3. I find Kristen Kvam's understanding of story and the relationship between God and humanity very constructive in Kvam, "God's heart Revealed: Luther on the Character of God and the Vocation of Humanity," 57–67.

and the holocaust, *and* genocide, *and* domestic violence, *and* the slaughter of the innocents, *and* a groaning ecology, *and* the innumerable tales of daily suffering that assault the psychological scales of moral permissibility. Too much of a bad thing can become an intractable weight on hope, which like a nonrenewable resource, can one day refuse to rise in a human life. The Christian narrative must have an existentially stellar response to human suffering that is generative of hope. Does God care, and if so, how does the Church tell that story in a way that is relevant today?

This misalignment and the relevant response is not a new predicament. For instance, Friedrich Nietzsche warned that our Christian prescriptive grammar for ontological sin was insufficient as a serious accounting to the wrenching experience of human cruelty in the world today. By way of our forebear, Luther's project was *precisely* set to resolve this incommensurability in his own time, where he struggled for the soul of the Christian Story. His goal was to re-identify the language of redemption in the Church for the sake of his congregants. He was an uncompromising student of rhetoric and translation, wittingly choosing explosive language to expose the struggle; *The Babylonian Captivity of the Church* roiled his adversaries. His theological reimagining of grace rooted in the Pauline epistles and the gospel accounts was a breakthrough that eased the consciences of people he knew personally from the very terror of death and damnation. For Luther as for us the misalignment of Story, and this reality of disconnection, is nothing new. In a post-Christian world, we must belong to a narrative where a response of hope takes suffering seriously. And, finally, hope is more than a matter of relevance. In our cosmological Story hope also aims at being *true*. If we mistake hope as merely a matter of relevance then we render that truth irrelevant from the start.

THE SEARCH FOR *IDENTITY*

The third marker of a Post-Christian world is a struggle for the coherence of an enclosed identity. Twentieth century philosophy and psychology disarmed us of the delusion of a centralized ego, opting instead for human identity as an aggregate of powerful, desirous forces.[4] We live in a world where systems (of knowledge and authority) are less valuable than the integration of incomplete information—life as a perpetual wiki, where a wiki is a grab of nonintegrated information. We live in an age that values individual experience, where we are equally weary of enclosed systems that

---

4. So much has been written about this issue. I commend a classic thinker, Edmund Schlink, in his treatment of the whole Self in Luther's anthropology. See Schlink, *Theology of the Lutheran Confessions*, 37–66.

describe truth in objective terms. In our world today, the human story is not principally valued in terms of the integration and coherence of truth, but rather our popular story is the human psyche in a consummate Wiki or Google search for meaning. We say yes to networked community but no to a functional teleology for how it all fits together. A noted public hunger for dystopian book and film, and tellingly, the meteoric rise of the apocalyptic cult of the walking dead in popular culture, are outgrowths of our new hyper-displacement where one is everywhere and nowhere at once, the vanishing "I."

To illustrate this point about human identity, think of the ubiquitous I-Phone. By name, an I-Phone is a misnomer; its primary designation already disfigured by the word we use to describe it. The point is not *I-here*, but rather *You-everywhere*. Here is what I mean: Not in truth a phone, an I-Phone is a lightweight object that fits in your hand like a prayer book. It is a medium, allowing access to everything. The I-Phone user chooses which part of everything to access through portals, which are small, uniform (yet uncoordinated) squares that fit on the I-Phone screen called Apps (applications). From rising to sleeping, Apps are the portals of observance, of spontaneous genuflection, for framing any part of everything, be this the weather, social networking, economic analysis, or dog grooming. The I-Phone is the surprise, disruptive technology that mirrors the human experience of identity in the world today. Standing, walking, or driving, our heads and hands are bowed to access parts of everything without existing fully anywhere. Zombies.

WHAT ABOUT A LUTHERAN APP?

Given the three markers I'm suggesting as a quick heuristic to the post-Christian world, what would an App or portal for Lutheran identity need to be in this current age, where today human authority, story, and identity are shaped by forces *external* to the core history and tradition of Christian veracity? We begin by asking ourselves whether there are some questions that a Google search cannot answer. If it is true that the aggregate accumulation of information does not suffice for coherent spiritual depth, then the Christian-Lutheran story will have a singularly meaningful contribution to make in the post-Christian world. Put positively, do we have a *sensus fidelium*, or sense of the faith that we profess in the world? This exercise toward a Lutheran App is precisely about that positive work of theological discernment.

So, what would a Lutheran App look like that addresses the three prevailing markers of a post-Christian world: *Authority, story,* and *identity*? I suggest to particular Lutheran communities seeking renewal that there are five questions aligned to these aforementioned markers. These five questions represent a single inquiry toward embodying a Lutheran App today. I am not presenting an exhaustive treatment for Lutheranism, which would undermine my entire approach below. I'm instead constructing five questions as constitutive of a single inquiry, and then commending this inquiry to Lutheran communities who desire to share a common story together tomorrow. Throughout, I am providing suggestions for approaching an answer to each of these questions within the inquiry.

SEARCH FOR IDENTITY AND THE STORY OF BEING HUMAN

The first question is a simple one: *Who are we?* This question is aligned to the third marker, or the Search for Identity. In terms of the individual, and taken from the above account, can we today reimagine the geographies of the Self at home as an aggregate identity? In terms of the community of believers, where the Body of Christ is no longer nested like Matryoshka dolls, can we consider our identity as a Church that begins with the particular individual and ends with a community's deeper unity in Christ? Unlike a Google algorithm that provides a parade of aggregated responses, for our purposes, the Christian algorithm is located in the *particular* yet unified stories and experiences that begin and end in the human walk with God. However we frame our identity, from the road to Emmaus to any number of urban byways that define human life today, who we are *must* make a distinction between calculable optimism and resurrection hope, *must* make sense of what a Rabbi in Newtown, Connecticut called "sacred darkness" at the refuse of public trauma and death, and *must* be clear about a vision of humanity's prevailing purpose in the cosmos and beyond. A Lutheran constructivist theology responsive to our current historical situation must be able to provide depth to the public quest for spirituality where human beings today adhere to an aggregate of religious and personal identifiers.

The axis of Lutheran identity is experienced at the hyphen between our sinfulness and God's redeeming hand. *Simul-et (both-and)* is the beating heart of that identity. *Saint-sinner*: As *both* saint *and* sinner, we are freed up for our neighbor in the world. *Gift-response*: Both God's gift of grace *and* our response to this grace in faith is the mediating power of our Story in the world. From the individual to the community, we are stitched together as a priesthood of believers where we respond to the gift of grace in our own lives, in our families, and within our local communities. In this way, Lutheran identity never begins at the macrocosm. Instead, our identity is the constitutive narrative of God's grace and our response, grounded in individual lives that comprise the community of believers. Luther consistently opted for the word *Gemeinde* (community/congregation) over *Kirche* (Church) in his work, with an emphasis on the believing community celebrating their baptisms and receiving the Eucharist, over the adiaphoraic hazards of institutional life. We are seventy-five million narratives stitched into a single story of grace, and this is what we call Church. In terms of our identity, internal particularity is central to our communitarian narrative coherence.

The second question is as follows: *What is the story of being human on this planet today?* This question is aligned to the second marker of the Story of God and Us. This is a first-order cosmological question that is deeply theological for us. Our response must not get lost in the trappings of theological jargon. Bishop Paulos Mar Gregorios, who served in the Orthodox Syrian Church of the East, and Methodist Liberation theologian Dr. Elsa Tamez, provide two of the finest examples for answering this question albeit in unique ways. They both take the story of our planet as a first-order theological problem. Both call Christians to answer this question from beyond what Gregorios called "Christomonism" in our approach to God, and what Tamez identifies as "monocentrism" in our perspective of humanity.[5] Taken together, these theologians call us to refrain from providing answers that omit the fullest expression of both God's unity and our humanity. The challenge here is not to undervalue the complex features of everything we know and believe about both. In terms of approach, this suggests that Lutherans should answer this question not by what we think we know, but by first fully discovering what we do not.

Our theological horizons are expansive enough to make an accounting of human sin and redemption of humanity through the death and resurrection of Christ. And yet, do we know how human beings in the world today experience cruelty and suffering while also being able to exhibit kindness (*kindredness*) that is the embodiment of Christ incarnate in the world? In every attempt to locate this question, we must take seriously not global typologies, but rather the multiplicity of cultural, religious, ethnic, political, gender-related, and technological aspects of our shared humanity on the planet at this moment. We can emphasize how the act of incarnational love requires a response that rises first from the experience of our particular

---

5. Mar Gregorios, "Human Unity for the Glory of God," 209–12; see also, Tamez, "Breaking Down Walls in our Globalized Society: A Relevant Ecumenism," 15–30.

stories, our interpretations of humanity, our vocations on the planet, and our direct eschatological sense of God's mission for the world at this time.

History like tradition is dynamic, depending on how you experience these. Experience contextualizes history and tradition for us today and is therefore a primary source of authority for us. Dr. Ivone Gebara is a Latin American Catholic Liberation Theologian who assists us as Lutherans in speaking from experience not as an add-on, but rather as a central authority to all that we are.[6] Post-Christian theology void of experience is as potentially conceptually rich as German Idealist philosophy, but unfortunately no one reads these luminaries anymore. Our cosmological response as the story of being human on the planet today requires that we value experiences first, drawn from our multiple cultural narratives, including the songs, art, and other artifacts of our identities. This questing after our humanity is always diminished when it isn't grounded in the experientially plural.

The answer to the story of being human on this planet today must likewise draw from multiple fields and disciplines, including psychology, sociology, trauma studies, neurology, quantum physics, and emerging local expressions (from literature to music) that also have a cathartic impact on a globalizing audience. Our theological responses to this question must make use of the insights of secular humanists and Ultra-Orthodox Jews, in order to decipher the shared threads for interpreting our humanity today. What are our fears and joys, our capacities for hoping and for enduring trauma, our ambitions and disappointments, our privileges and disparities? Where do we feel we are going and what do we believe will be our future? There is no universal response to this question, but only perhaps. We do experience the world and indeed the universe in a distinct manner from any other era. We have the horrors of the graves of war alongside the wonder of hundreds of new planets that we are discovering in a mysterious universe. We should be able to speak about the human experience in the twenty-first century in a way that illustrates the imprint of our identities today.

Our Lutheran response to the previously unthinkable tragic event, or to the joys of a world being drawn nearer (and also farther) from itself via emerging technologies, must be aligned to the soil of our experience. Otherwise, theology—however pastoral—will sound like a platitude. Do we, as Lutherans, have a vibrant sense of the sinner made saint today? And do we refer to this in ways that the world understands? Once we respond to these and other inquires for being human in the world we will be equipped to answer what we believe are the fundamental questions the human race has about its present and its future.

---

6. Gebara, *Longing for Running Water: Ecofeminism and Liberation.*

THE RADICAL QUESTION

Our third question is: *What is the radical question for the world tomorrow?* This question is aligned to the first marker, or the *Authority of the Church*. The radical question for tomorrow is located in the emerging challenges to the world itself; and will be more aligned not to, say, environmental degradation, but to a theological quest to understand the complexity of our humanity in the midst of the challenge of environmental degradation itself. Luther's radical question for the sixteenth century was: How is the human being justified before God? His project focused on a response that never lost sight of the question and the human being ensconced within it. The human being was in fact the question itself. Much philosophical and theological work was made in the twentieth century on the human as Question, and we can draw from that without eclipsing the earth. What we must not do is allow narrow social justice ideologies, or broad missional pronouncements, unhinged from the grounding story of being human on the planet today, to cloud the identification of this question.

In a world where broad or narrow ideological and physical walls are more commonplace, even an articulate vision and mission statement for organized religious life may sound reasonable to Lutherans in the in-crowd, and at the same time be misaligned to the human question taking place *underneath* issues of ecology, or urban violence, or generations of poverty and displacement. Asking after the world and all that lives in it is a very different project from providing a statement of mission of confessional allegiance, which may function more as a wall than a call. It is an odd feature of institutional life that mission statements can balkanize us from the world, hemming us in when our intention is to act out. With the urgencies of our time, we should locate the question and implement our response, and simultaneously care less for mission statements from the start.

The *response* to the radical question is first located in the Story of God and Us; at core, the response is theological too. Otherwise, well-meaning organized religious life will address social injustices in the world that require our dedication and sweat equity; but if we cannot identify the "why" inside of the "what" then particular social justice platforms will misalign the whole internal story and fail to be a coherent response to the world. That is to say, the particular social justice platform results may be a success, but the failure will take place at the root of hope, which is the source of nutrition for any specific social justice effort.

Finally, the response to the question of the religious other requires us as Lutherans to engage the new pluralism, by locating and deciphering the radical question together amidst numerous ecumenical and additional religious expressions of faith.[7] Pluralism does not require (nor could it, really) uniformity in response; locating the question alongside religious others, however, is an essential part of our Lutheran renewal to be further refined.[8]

RESOURCES AND ASPIRATIONS

The fourth question is not: What is our strategy? Organized religious life, particularly in the Northern hemisphere, is quick to produce strategic, outcome based and scalable options that utilize novel jargon to get granular in responding to the question we have circumscribed. However, between the question and our plan is God's hope. What does God *want*? As Christians we must assume that every response we offer is to demonstrate God's hope, so our fourth question is this: *Given God's hope for the world, what is our core set of resources for responding to that hope?* The history of theological discourse, the traditions of the Church with all of its expressions, and the gospel narratives, are some of our key resources. For Lutherans, closer to our core are the vocational rousing of the Spirit, the gospel-based virtues of faith active in love, and the Christian set free for the world through a loving God. At our core is the grace-endowed Christ event itself, and behind that veil is the mystery of God who chooses life over judgment.

At the level of *resources*, notice that I have mentioned neither a strategic plan nor financial exigency. The resources to which I am referring are our *core* gifts that we have been given to steward on behalf of God's hope for the world. One of these is the Lutheran understanding—even charism—of grace, which is a particular spiritual gift of the Christian voice to the world.

A Lutheran App in the post-Christian world needs to ask the *aspirational* question, which is our fifth question. This is a tricky enterprise. Aspirational questions in religious life are typically determined by committee and, in final form, appeal more to the less inspirational least common

---

7. For engaging co-religious interlocutors in aligning story or text, I recommend looking to Rabbi Peter Ochs and Fr. Frank Clooney, S.J. for methodological approaches that range from "scriptural reasoning" to "comparative theology," as a way of thinking anew about engaging the religious "other." Begin with Ochs, "Scripture."

8. The classic for understanding religious pluralism in America is still highly recommended here. It is a text made possible with assistance from the Olaus Petri Foundation at Uppsala University: Hutchison, *Religious Pluralism in America: The Contentious History of a Founding Ideal*.

denominator than to the original higher aspiration itself. Grand ideas have a way of being whittled down. There is a way of avoiding this form of diminishment. Christians should not traffic in reasonable possibilities. Adherence to the gospel of Christ, loving your neighbor, welcoming the stranger, dying for your friend, loving your enemy, preaching the good news to the whole world, taking care of widows and orphans; none of these are for the faint of heart. These aspirations reside at the core of the faith we profess. Are we listening? If so, then in every opportunity to respond to God's hope for the world, our aspirations must be centered on the Story of God and Us, and focused on the singular, specific, undeniable, and deeply meaningful ways we should respond to God now.

As a community of believers, we do not have a magisterium. We do have a global community of pastoral theologians. This means that our local communities engage one another "without a net," so to speak; at our best we thrive in the hyphens of life, as mediators of internal discernment, especially when conflicts arise. Experience in ecumenical and interreligious circles teaches me that this internal self-mediation at the individual and communitarian aspects of our faith lives, sensitizes us to the narratives of others. For instance, in 2010 when Lutherans sought forgiveness from contemporary descendants of the Anabaptist community for our share of atrocities against that community, or in the succeeding years after 1982 as Lutherans around the world repudiated an aberrant anti-Judaic theology at our roots, these efforts revealed a capacity for mediation that led toward corrective efforts and restoration of relationships. This ability to be *both* who we are in our particular forms *and* open to refinement by others, arises from the same deep scripturally-based hermeneutic of gift-response at work in us that is first-and-foremost encountered in the individual made righteous before a loving God. We do well not to undervalue the formative power of this first hermeneutic moment for our entire ecclesiological life. If we have a Lutheran App in the world, then "grace-in-particular" is close to its proper name.

In order to avoid any residual diminishment, we might ask the fifth question this way: *What is our "Moon Shot"?* I don't mean to imply here a parade of socially responsible service projects, as a first-order response. I mean that our response to God's hope for the world requires us to ask, what a popular blogger today calls the gonzo airdrop into deep "What, really?" territory. That is, with these other four questions in tow—from identity to response—Lutherans must dig deep from our *sensus fidei* and, with all we have learned thus far, take on a major effort for our renewal in the world: Ask ourselves what the highest and deepest aim is of all we are, of everything we indeed must be in the world, and then go and do that thing. This is not a resurrection of semi-Pelagianism. It is rather an appeal to the kind of love activated through faith of George Forell, to Robert Schreiter's interpretation of the sinner freed from the narrative of the lie, to Deanna Thompson's courage to hope after serious lament, and to Luther's true freedom of a Christian in service to the neighbor. In this world, what is the one thing we should be doing as the highest aspiration of our vocational response to a loving God?[9] Everything we do thereafter will be aligned to that moon shot.

Every aspirational moonshot has three qualities in common: (1) It locates a significant challenge for the world that must be named; (2) it identifies a potential solution[s] to that challenge; and (3) it seeks a breakthrough that must take place as an irrevocable solution to that challenge. Consider Luther. His moon-shot was the radical question of the human being seeking justification. His challenge was the terrorized conscience. His solution was a reformation of the language of justification. And, his solution required of him (and indeed a whole movement) a new grammar and syntax for interpreting core theological truths. These truths washed across and renewed our understanding of justification, election, free will, the Christian civil life, the Christian relationship to the political order, Law and Gospel, the sacraments as edifiers of divine grace, and the role of the state in Christian affairs. The list goes on. Following decades of hard work, by the compilation of the *Book of Concord* in 1577, a new movement offered a response to the radical questions not only of his day, but to what Luther believed was necessary to the future of the Story of God and Us. Luther could introduce all of this amongst friends who furthered his project, in the experience of debilitating political stress and persistent physical ailment, and with the serious possibility of being assassinated. So, in the twenty-first century, what is our moonshot today as Lutherans?

All in all, the language of a moonshot is a simple heuristic device to describe the highest aspiration of calling where we don't let ourselves off the hook. As we mark the 500th anniversary of the start of the Reformation, do we today have as clear an understanding of our imprint on the world? If not, then we should look to these five questions as ways of taking seriously an inquiry that must be a central part of our project in a post-Christian world today. If the questions seem rudimentary, it is only because they are. There is nothing like 500 years to seriously evaluate where we are going as readily as we celebrate from whence we've come.

I will close with where I started. That day at the National Palatine Museum in Rome, as I stared at the papal bull of Luther's excommunication alongside the opening salvo of the Second Vatican Council, I found my gaze falling into the slight rift between these two documents. Time and again,

---

9. Schreiter, *Reconciliation: Mission and Ministry in a Changing Social Order*, 32.

my view slipped into that miniscule space between them. You can sense the gravity of so much historical distance compacted in a small margin of space. What did I see there, that rose up so lightly but intractably between those documents? "Gratitude." My father would say to me as I held his hand a few days before his death, his body becoming a shipwreck. "Gratitude?" I asked. "Yes, to feel God so close when we travel so far away. To know that being together makes the world bearable. To surprise even ourselves when we don't lose faith under great duress. The whole world groans and me in it, but I cannot suppress an overwhelming sense of gratitude."

BIBLIOGRAPHY

Bender, Courtney and Pamela E. Klassen, editors. *After Pluralism: Reimagining Religious Engagement*. New York: Columbia University Press, 2010.

Gebara, Ivone. *Longing for Running Water: Ecofeminism and Liberation*. Minneapolis: Fortress, 1999.

Granberg-Michaelson, Wesley. *From Times Square to Timbuktu: The Post-Christian West Meets the Non-Western Church*. Grand Rapids, MI, Eerdmans, 2013.

Hutchison, William R. *Religious Pluralism in America: The Contentious History of a Founding Ideal*. Ann Arbor: Sheridan, 2003.

Kvam, Kristen E. "God's Heart Revealed in Eden: Luther on the Character of God and the Vocation of Humanity." In *Transformative Lutheran Theologies: Feminist, Womanist and Mujerista Perspectives*, edited by Mary J. Streufert, 57–68. Minneapolis: Fortress, 2010.

Mar Gregorios, Paulos. "Human Unity for the Glory of God." In *The Ecumenical Review*, vol. 37, no. 2, (1985) 209–12.

Ochs, Peter. "Scripture." In *Fields of Faith: Theology and Religious Studies for the Twenty-first Century*, edited by David F. Ford, Ben Quash, and Janet Martin Soskice. Cambridge: Cambridge University Press, 2005.

Schlink, Edmond. *Theology of the Lutheran Confessions*. Minneapolis: Fortress, 1961.

Schreiter, Robert J. *Reconciliation: Mission and Ministry in a Changing Social Order*. New York: Orbis, 1992.

Shirky, Clay. *Here Comes Everybody: The Power of Organizing without Organizations*. London: Penguin, 2008.

Tamez, Elsa. "Breaking Down Walls in our Globalized Society: A Relevant Ecumenism." *Ecumenical Trends* 38.7 (July/August, 2009) 15–30.

PART TWO

Lutheran Tradition and Gender

6

For the Sake of the Future

Rekindling Lutheran Theology on Spirituality, Equality, and Inclusivity

KIRSI STJERNA

Critically and compassionately—these could be the Lutheran mantra words for re-exploration of the roots of Lutheran faith and for imagining the future promise of Lutheran theology as an agent of transformation. As Lutheran theology's emancipating power rests on the reformation's core theology of justification by faith through grace, its relevance today depends on its ability to nurture inclusivity, equality, and spirituality in the spirit of the original reformations. After reflecting briefly on the promises of these three core values in Lutheran vision, the Reformation women and their theological concerns are introduced: The Reformation women can exemplify the bearings of inclusivity, equality, and spirituality in the Reformation theological tradition.

LUTHERAN VISION IN PLURAL

Lutherans have a history of disagreeing among themselves. The debates (among Lutherans and with others) have fundamentally always something to do with the reformation principle of *sola scriptura*. The same texts of the canon (*norma normans*) can be interpreted with remarkable differences, which the Lutheran hermeneutics allows while also expects a reasonable connection with the interpretative tradition articulated in the confessions (*norma normata*). The nature of Lutheran biblical and confessional tradition is, thus, quite complex with its inherent options for diversity. With differences in biblical interpretation and either rigidity or over-flexibility with the Confessions, debates are ongoing—and only enhanced with the entrance of feminist scholarship and gender perspectives to challenge traditional positions on an assortment of issues.

Lutheran theology already benefits from feminist scholarship of the scriptures and the corrected vision from there towards inclusive proclamation of the Word. With the confessional texts, Lutherans have yet to systematically address their "exclusivist" limitations: written in the sixteenth century, by a small representative of exclusively Lutheran male voices, all at least in public heterosexual, and all involved with professional theology, academia or leadership functions, the texts can hardly be straightforwardly "applied" as normative today and without a re-assessment of the foundations with the help of feminist (and modern historical) scholarship and other critical approaches. Also essential is to embrace and learn from the global diversity within the Lutheran tradition. This is what inclusivity entails—owning to and celebrating diversity in its many meanings.

Lutheran tradition holds an element of diversity in both its teaching and practice. The inter-Lutheran controversies that led to the writing of the Formula of Concord did not run their cause in the sixteenth century. Even if standing firmly on the common doctrinal foundation of "justification by faith through grace alone," Lutherans globally speaking continue to disagree in several essential areas, as well as with a galore of issues that could be considered adiaphora.

For example, the sacrament of baptism: while in unanimity about the centrality of the practice of the sacrament in Lutheran churches, the purpose and effectiveness of the sacrament is celebrated by Lutherans with quite different emphases around the globe. Whereas some practice baptism primarily for its ecclesiological function in providing membership, identity and a calling as a Christian, others strive to consider its benefits in sight of the mystery of justification and its transformative effects as the spiritual wash. Whereas some focus on the personal meaning of baptism in one's faith life here and now, others stress baptism's necessity for salvation in general. The dubious words of the *Augsburg Confession's* article nine leave room for diversity in emphasis.[1] Similarly, the sacrament of Eucharist allows diversity

---

1. See *Augsburg Confession*, article IX on Baptism. See Stjerna, *No Greater Jewel: Thinking about Baptism with Luther*; Trigg, *Baptism in the Theology of Martin Luther*; Wood, *One Baptism: Ecumenical Dimensions of the Doctrine of Baptism*.

in its practice. For instance, whereas in some Lutheran communities infants are welcome, in others stricter parameters are in place for who can receive and who can assist in administering. The differences speak of the contextual factors in Lutherans' interpretation of their foundational documents, the bible and the Lutheran confessions. They also reflect differences in appropriating the core Lutheran doctrine of justification by faith.

Lutherans are not on the same page about the full meaning of justification by faith. This is demonstrated with the mixed responses to the findings of the Finnish "Mannermaa" school and also to the Joint Declaration of 1999. Some take pride in the Lutherans' traditional emphasis on the "forensic righteousness" and wish to underscore the differences between Lutheran versus Roman Catholic versus Eastern Orthodox understandings of justification; others start from the point of considering a shared vision between the traditions on the many dimensions of the doctrine and stress the importance of the "effective righteousness." The basic differences pertain to Christology and expectations regarding Christian life, and thus spirituality. On the one hand Lutherans can with the forensic justification perspective teach about the liberating power of justifying faith that grants person the status of forgiveness and a new relationship with God; on the other, Lutherans can with the effective justification perspective teach about the ontological reality change a personal encounter with God brings about and what Christ's presence in person's life entails in relation to others. Obviously, if only one perspective to justification is emphasized, the promise of this justification vision is diminished. It makes a difference in terms of spirituality—and also philosophically—whether Lutherans are satisfied with proclaiming Christ as a "favor" only or whether they embrace also the meaning of Christ as a "gift" "for me" and appropriate the doctrine of justification as mystically as it deserves.[2]

The point made here is this: There is significant diversity imbedded in the interpretation of the Lutheran core theology and the practice of central traditions. The diversity of Lutheran ways and practices around the world can be seen as a cause of celebration rather than a concern. There is evidence that, with its emphasis on "word alone"—and in Luther's model—Lutheran theology can nimbly speak with a distinct language in different contexts, with much flexibility in the practical matters, without losing its identity. There are issues, however, that are in a different category, where flexibility can allow for behaviors that stand against the basic values of the reformation theology about Christian freedom received in justification and that can

---

2. Examples of the polar opposites are the Forde school vs Mannermaa school. See Mannermaa, *Christ Present in Faith* (English translation of *In Ipsa Fide Christus Adest*, 1978); Forde, *Justification by Faith: A Matter of Death and Life*.

thus effectively cloud the positive power of Lutheran theology: the status of women is one of these issues (and related, matters relating to sexuality).

ON WOMEN, SEXISM AND INCLUSIVITY AS THEOLOGICAL CONCERNS

Not all Lutheran churches today ordain women or are even actively considering it. Conservative schismatic groups around the globe actively preach against women's equal status and ordination, this occurring also in churches already historically ordaining women (e.g. Finland and USA). Closely related, the rights of gay and lesbian persons are still heavily debated, with wide gaps between different Lutheran positions. In this matter that qualifies as an urgent human rights issue, the global Lutheran church could proclaim powerfully towards a positive change with a unified front. Lutherans' ambiguity regarding women's status in the church is related to its teaching of sex, gender, and sexuality; Lutheran theology's ambiguity in these matters is not about "good diversity" but contributes to the ongoing crimes of injustice and violence against women.

On a positive note, in academic theological discourse, the vitality of the ongoing participation of women is increasingly recognized in the Lutheran theological tradition built on historically predominantly male voices. The unraveling insights from research that acknowledges gender as an essential factor in all theology, across the disciplines, promises positive reforms for Lutheran hermeneutics and positions. Research originated by women and underscoring the importance of gender in regards to experiences of faith and in theological imagination can, however, still meet significant hermeneutical suspicion from those who consider "serious" theological discourse "free" from gender concerns. Traditional Lutheran theology can still be "bothered" by feminist Lutheran scholarship that from many disciplines is offering unsettling observations for Lutherans to consider, starting from the basics of their theology (e.g. language about God; notion of grace and salvation; sin; issues of theological anthropology). Resistance to the use of inclusive language in scholarship and liturgy reflects unresolved tensions in different Lutherans approaches to theology, and in basic understandings of God and humanness.

The recognition of the gender factor in all theology, including Lutheran theology, is a discovery that rattles the foundations. Neuralgic theological issues are brought under scrutiny in this "reformation of reformations" that can begin with the doctrine of justification, and with simple questions that will complicate the status quo: How well does Lutheran theology globally endorse inclusivity and equality for women? How has the doctrine of justification worked out in the lives and spiritualities of women? How can women's experiences enhance contemporary understanding of justification by faith? Related, the question of sin calls for readdressing in light of women's specific experiences: a constructive approach to sin can be found in the experiences of sexism with long roots in Lutheran biblical interpretation, theological tradition, and liturgy.

Naming sexism as a matrix of sins that prevent inclusivity, equality, and justice for women, and considering violence against women as a spiritual concern, brings the status of women effectively into the arena of theological discourse. Examining the foundations of Lutheran theology and adjusting its priorities in light of (also) women's experiences are essential for the credibility of Lutheran spiritual theology: How could Lutheran theology with credibility speak to women's and men's spiritual concerns unless the issues (and crimes) of injustice and inequality are receiving sufficient theological attention? In many ways, the inclusion of women (of today and past) and their experiences offers opportunities for a reality-check of the relevance of the Lutheran message.

LUTHERAN SPIRITUALITY IN VISION

The relevance of Lutheran theology is most imminently felt in the lives of men and women today in the area of spirituality. Namely, in spirituality, the core issues of Lutheran reforms and theology are translated into relevance for daily life. Enhanced teaching of spirituality per se, then, provides a natural access or "return" point for people with spiritual needs but who have wandered away from the church and fail to see the relevance of "being religious." The word spirituality has thus much promise for the Lutheran future that has rich historical resources to offer in this regard.

Not only volumes of Luther's and other reformers' works, but also the Lutheran confessional texts offer valuable resources for particularly Lutheran spirituality. Luther's Catechisms have already proven themselves as the "lay bible" for Lutherans through ages seeking for guidance for their faith and daily lives as Christians. Even the more politically oriented texts, such as the *Augsburg Confession*, are written on the basis of a particular spiritual vision about God and godly life, which allows for their spiritual use in new circumstances. Engaging the confessional texts in this spirit promises more possibilities for both inter-Lutheran and ecumenical unity—which in the larger scope of things would seem to factor in the credibility of the Christian Lutheran message in the world hungry for spiritual direction.[3]

The ambiguous word spirituality needs re-introduction in Lutheran language.[4] Most simply, it means "piety" or religious health and awareness. With spirituality, the attention is on "the quality or state of being concerned with religion or religious matters: the quality or state of being spiritual (...)" Lutherans can, with Bernard McGinn, assert that "Christian spirituality is the lived experience of Christian belief (...) in both its general and more specialized forms (...)."[5] In all, the term *spiritualitas* speaks to the reformation concern of authenticity and relevance of Christian faith in personal life.

The sixteenth century reforms were largely ignited in response to the obvious spiritual ills and hunger that led Martin Luther and others to develop new theological perspectives. Far from desiring to instigate chaos, Luther's priority was to effectively name God's grace in the midst of human life, as tangibly and personally as possible. Luther's primary concerns were spiritual: returning to the authenticity of faith, leading people to experience in faith the immediacy and real presence of God in all the complexities of human life, while underscoring the fundamental equality of sinners and saints as beggars of God's mercy already freely given.

Luther wrote several works that have served Lutheran spirituality through the ages. Some of the most powerful are his *The Freedom of a Christian, Catechisms, Personal Prayer Book*, and *A Simple Way to Pray*.[6] The Catechisms in particular spell out a particular theology for daily life

3. See Krey and Krey, *Luther's Spirituality*. See Hendrix, "Martin Luther's Reformation of Spirituality," 242–43.

4. Wiseman, *Spirituality and Mysticism*, 3–4 writes that the word "spirituality" refers to 1) a fundamental dimension of the human being; 2) a lived experience that actualizes that dimension; 3) an academic discipline that studies it. (Schneiders, quoted in Wiseman, 4), names spirituality as "the experience of consciously striving to integrate one's life in terms not of isolation and self-absorption but of self-transcendence toward the ultimate value one perceives." (Van Ness, quoted in Wiseman, 5), states that "the spiritual dimension of life is the embodied task of realizing one's truest self in the context of reality apprehended as a cosmic totality."

5. "Spirituality" in *Merriam-Webster*. Bernard McGinn: "Christian spirituality is the lived experience of Christian belief in both its general and more specialized (...) It is possible to distinguish spirituality from doctrine in that it concentrates not on faith itself, but on the reaction that faith arouses in religious consciousness and practice. It can likewise be distinguished from Christian ethics in that it treats not all human actions in their relation to God, but those acts in which the relation to God is immediate and explicit." McGinn, Meyendorff, and Leclercq, *Christian Spirituality: Origins to the Twelfth Century*, xv–xvi.

6. See Luther, *A Simple Way to Pray*, LW 43, 191–209; Luther, *Personal Prayer Book*, LW 43; WA 10.II, 375–406; Luther, *The Freedom of a Christian*, LW 31, 333–77; WA 7, 49–73 (Latin), WA 7, 20–38 (German); Luther, *Catechisms* in the *Book of Concord*.

and a practical model for a spiritual approach to Christian life. Similarly Luther's advice to his barber on how to pray puts in practice the doctrine of justification with an intentional method to enhance the reader's spiritual awareness. These texts continue to draw readers with their practical advice for "how to" and by addressing the experiential dimension of faith. And that is of interest to people, even those who consider themselves non-religious. There is a reason why spirituality and with that, mysticism, are on the rise.

Spiritual theology involves the component of experience and entails a mystical dimension. "Mystical" can be defined with Bernard McGinn simply as the dimension of Christian faith tradition and practices that concern "the transformative presence of God."[7] "[T]he mystics invite us to imagine and even to explore an inner transformation of the self based on a new understanding of the human relation to God." Mystical life is about a process, "an itinerary or journey to God."[8] In this regard, Luther's spiritual theology that unfolds the mystical dimension—and experience—in the life of the one justified by faith.

The Finnish Luther School with Tuomo Mannermaa has (unintentionally) led to rediscovering the mystical dimension of Luther's notion of justification in its "effectiveness" in particular.[9] Disagreements abiding on what ultimately constitutes mystical and on Luther's attitudes towards mystics—and about the forensic and effective dimensions of justification—the Finnish research has demonstrated how impossible it is to fully appreciate the depths of Luther's idea of justification by faith, without accepting the mystical foundation of it all. His treatment of the doctrine of justification in his *Two Kinds of Righteousness* and *Commentary on Galatians* are just two examples of the centrality of the mystical dimension of his spiritual theology that in mystical language articulates a vision for a transformed Christian life.[10]

---

7. See McGinn, *The Foundations of Mysticism*. Also, McGinn, *The Essential Writings of Christian Mysticisism*.

8. McGinn, *The Essential Writings of Christian Mysticism*, xiv. Also, see Wiseman, *Spirituality and Mysticism*; Soelle, *The Silent Cry: Mysticism and Resistance*.

9. See Mannermaa, *Christ Present in Faith*; Mannermaa, *Two Kinds of Love*. See Hoffmann, *Theology of the Heart*. See Stjerna and Schramm, *Spirituality: Towards A 21st Century Lutheran Understanding*.

10. See Luther, *Two Kinds of Righteousness*, LW 31, 297–306; WA 2, 144–52; Luther, *Commentary on Galatians*, LW 26/WA 40.I; LW 27/WA 40.II. "But this most excellent righteousness, the righteousness of faith, which God imputes to use through Christ without works (. . .) is a merely passive righteousness (. . .) we only receive and permit someone else to work in us, namely, God. (. . .) This is a righteousness hidden in mystery, which the world does not understand. (. . .) it must always be taught and continually exercised. There is no comfort of conscience as solid and certain as this passive

For Luther, faith entails a life-changing religious experience and a transformed reality. He reflected on his own transformation upon reading Paul's letter to the Romans (1545 Preface to the Latin edition of his works), "There I began to understand that (. . .) the righteousness of God is revealed by the gospel, namely, the passive righteousness with which merciful God justifies us by faith (. . .) Here I felt that I was altogether born again and had entered paradise itself though open gates."[11] With his own example, Luther underscored that faith matters on a personal level. Luther's theology of justification can be seen as his unfolding the meaning and the experience of the saving faith in the life of the justified. He pointed at Christ's "for you" gift as the foundational faith experience that transformed one into Christlikeness. He preached about the life-changing power of the experience of freedom of conscience from all that binds—freedom originating from the transformative experience of being forgiven in/with/because of Christ, and an experience that would bind Christians to serve others.[12]

Luther's contribution in spiritual theology has so far received insufficient attention. This is an opportunity for Lutheran theology today, in junction with adjusting the interpretation of the reformation's original concerns: Recent scholarship has begun to unfold the emancipatory power of the sixteenth century reformations first and foremost in the realm of spirituality. Scott Hendrix among others has suggested that the Reformation was about reformation of spirituality.[13] Even if Protestants—with the dismissal of many of the Catholic traditions—lost many important food channels, a familiar faith language and frameworks for thinking and living spiritually,[14] it was the "reformed" spiritual theology that fueled the Protestant theologians to radically criticize the church and its leadership, its power structures

---

righteousness. (. . .) it is a merely passive." LW 26, 3–11; WA 40.I, 40:5–52:6.

11. Luther, *Commentary on Romans*, LW 34, 336–38 (333–77); WA 54, 186:9–10 (185–86).

12. See Luther, *The Freedom of a Christian*, LW 31, 333–77; WA 7, 49–73 (Latin); WA 7, 20–38 (German).

13. Scott Hendrix writes, "Luther and the evangelical movement proposal to change the actual patterns of Christian living, and they urged that patterns upon the faithful as the genuine way of being spiritual, as authentic spirituality." Even if he disliked the word "Geistlichkeit" when referring to the religious activities of the religious professionals, the word can also refer to the genuine Christian life that Luther wished to reform. "If spirituality is taken in the sense of piety or living the Christian life, then I am convinced that Luther initiated a reformation of spirituality; or, to say it another way: the Reformation which Luther initiated was also intended to be Reformation of spirituality." Hendrix, "Martin Luther's Reformation of Spirituality," 242–43.

14. See Gregory, *The Unintended Reformation* and his blaming the Protestant reformations for secularization of the Western world and the ensuing spiritual freeze.

and all the injustice and illness they saw resulting from the Church losing its spiritual focus and center.[15]

The new theology with a radically inclusive vision of what is spiritual, suggested that everybody was equally holy and worthy—just as everyone was equally needy for grace. The Protestant spiritual theology conspicuously spiritualized or sanctified the secular realm (just as it benefitted from the secular authorities' securing and implementing the theologically-induced reforms on practical level). Their renewed spiritual theology nurtured expectations of equality and inclusivity, and led to events that shifted power structures in the church and in the society. The impact of the new theological vision was tangible in people's lives, for better or for worse. The areas and urgencies where Lutheran theology today can continue to make a tangible difference remain the same: (1) promoting spiritual wellness and authenticity of faith with all people, (2) ensuring equality of all beggars for God's grace in church and society, and (3) pursuing inclusivity of all sinners equally liberated to embrace and proclaim the Word, and thus transform the world. At the core of Lutheran theology's promise for transformation and emancipation stands the original principle of equality, both spiritual and political.

ON EQUALITY AS A LUTHERAN CORE VALUE, WITH A REALITY CHECK ON THE STATUS OF WOMEN

Lutheran doctrine of justification by faith makes matters of equality—and with that, justice and freedom—a priority among theological and spiritual concerns. If Lutheran theology does not proclaim and labor towards full equality in all the senses of the world, then what is the core mission of the tradition committed to the Christian gospel of grace and freedom? Considering equality as a theological and a spiritual priority, in turn, reveals the opposites as ugly manifestation of the original sin. Inequality, injustice, bondage/ forced servitude, harmful hierarchies are all manifestations of sin that needs resisting. All forms of gender-inequality, sexism, and the undercurrent of misogynism that feed violence against women (and children), once named as theological matters and as sins as such, become issues that Lutheran theology can reject as unacceptable and do all in its power to find remedies for. The urgency to fight these sins lies not only in the practical devastation they cause in human lives, but also because these transgressions

---

15. E.g. Scott Hendrix on Luther urging Christians to "affirm and participate in the world, its stewardship and its governance." Luther calls "all baptized Christians to a deeper connection with Christ, that is a deeper spirituality, in the world." Hendrix, "Martin Luther's Reformation of Spirituality," 258.

reflect detrimentally on Lutherans' understanding of God, humanness, issues pertaining to freedom or bondage of the will, and the many aspects of the salvation doctrine.

The status of women question brings the sins of sexism and violence against women to the forefront: Recognizing sexism as a sin and as a fuel for violence towards women is important. Recognizing sexism as a force that feeds off the distorted images of humanness, sex/gender and sexuality and justifies different forms of inequality and abuse of power is a theologically urgent task, with political ramifications. A common sense deems it diabolical that in modern "free" society women still need to be afraid to walk out at night alone, that every three minutes a woman is assaulted, raped, or killed—that it is allowed to happen without a full-blown strategy to suppress both violence against women and sexism that feeds it. Lutheran theology can address the roots of the problem, as well as facilitate appropriate action in the society.

Lutheran theology's distinction between the realms of *coram Deo* and *coram hominibus* is helpful in this regard: passive and helpless as humans may be in regards to redeeming themselves *coram Deo*, active Christian action is the word for life *coram hominibus* with a plenty of options for choices and deeds. Whereas in the former existence there is no human action but God's only, in the latter there is much room for human action, with God's fuel. Issues of violence and sexism and inequality belong in the latter realm to tackle with a theological ammunition. Not doing that compromises basic teaching of Christian freedom *coram hominibus*, and would imply that something might be terribly wrong with *coram Deo* matters as well.[16] Lutheran theologians can with their scholarship promote positive changes in the kingdom of God: In the model of Luther's theology of the cross, naming the reality in the face of human suffering and in light of the gospel precedes offering theological responses that can effect changes in tangible ways; history has demonstrated that.

With Luther's original reformation theology and the contribution of feminist and liberation theologies, Lutheran theology has good resources to promote theologically argued and politically enforced equality between the sexes, and of all people.[17] With Luther and intentionally including

---

16. "Violence" in *Merriam-Webster*. On violence related to gender, sex and race, see Rothenberg, *Race, Class, and Gender in the United States. An Integrated Study*, esp. 481–84. On countering distorted images of women, see Cooper-White, *The Cry of Tamar: Violence against Women and the Church's Response*, 64–66, 80–81.

17. E.g., Luther stresses the created and spiritual equality of the sexes, with much compassion and respect for Eve and the other OT women he considers heroes of faith; he also reads motherhood into the salvation history like no other theologians before

women's experiences in Lutheran theological hermeneutics, the negative culture can be countered with a healthier understanding of maleness and femaleness and sexuality—and of God. The original reformation theology of spirituality—centering on the message of Christian freedom resulting from the experience of gift-forgiveness-in-faith—can still powerfully foster emancipation and equality and, first of all, inclusivity.[18]

TESTING THE PRINCIPLE OF INCLUSIVITY: LEARNINGS WITH THE REFORMATION MOTHERS

Inclusivity is the noble Christian principle that made early Christian communities appealing. Inclusivity—in praxis and in scholarship—is crucial for the credibility of the Lutheran theological tradition today. The principle of inclusivity can be applied in all scholarship and it calls for focused study on the experiences and roles of women in Christian tradition. In the following, the Reformation women are brought into the conversation on the reformation theology's potential with its core values of equality, inclusivity and spirituality. Examining their contributions opens new avenues for contemporary Lutherans to connect with the tradition and towards re-creating an inclusive theological tradition where women's contributions are incorporated into the main story.

First a few words about the Reformation's impact in women's lives: Study of the sixteenth century women reveals the instrumental contribution of women in the spreading of the evangelical theology even if public ministry or writing theology were not considered a woman's realm; women were not expected to, or prepared to, write theological summae—kitchen and household was to be their world. (Luther's wife Katharina von Bora was a poster woman for this calling, as was Wibrandis Rosenblatt, who married four times: she had the ideal resume for a reformer's wife who was able to set up a parsonage in multiple times in new towns and both adopt and give birth to several children, in her case eleven.) With the sixteenth century Reformation, basic gender roles in the church or the society hardly changed. Women's domestic calling was heavy-handedly re-enforced by the Protestant preachers. Domestication of women in the to-the-core patriarchally arranged society was one of the ways that actually served the success of

---

him. See e.g., Stjerna "Grief, Glory and Grace: Insights on Eve and Tamar in Luther's Genesis Commentary,"19–35; and articles by Kris Kvam and Jane Strohl; Stjerna, "The Case of Women: New Perspectives, New Interests in Luther and Reformation Studies."

18. E.g., the matter of inclusive language, the significance of which goes beyond pronouns. See e.g. *Guidelines for Inclusive Language*. See also Johnson, *She Who Is: The Mystery of God in Feminist Theological Discourse*; Ruether, *Sexism and God Talk. Toward a Feminist Theology*.

the reformation: the new teachings laid roots through homes, the women's room of operation.

With the beginning steps towards basic public education for boys and girls, higher education and scholarly activity was considered "for men only." Few women were able to break the barriers in this until the secular laws opened universities for women. Women have, though, found ways to bypass the obstacles. The visionary writers of the Middle Ages are a brilliant example of such creativity. In the Reformation era, the examples are fewer but outstanding. (E.g. Olimpia Morata, an Italian court-educated scholar had language skills surpassing those of her male academic associates, she was called an "Amazon" for her academic aspirations.)

With the scholarly option and the pulpit forbidden, and the convents closed, the Reformation women were presented with one preferred option: marriage and motherhood, a calling equal to that of the priests and bishops, per Luther. Women seemed to have welcomed this new elevation in their traditional role. Some women, however, embraced marriage and motherhood as a calling beyond what was intended by the male preachers: marriage and particularly motherhood not only potentially emancipated women to enjoy their holy domestic roles as now theologically defined space or calling of highest value. In addition, women could have a more expansive vision of motherhood including authorization to speak to the matters of the world and church. As mothers women had an acceptable rationale to care for the dependents also beyond their households and with the power of the word. Letters were instrumental in this form of spiritual motherhood that had had a specific theological significance defined by women themselves.

Women effectively created an office for themselves as spiritual mothers, replacing the medieval female mystics. Without mystical visions, Lutheran women wrote theological works in their domestic calling and under the camouflage of private maternal or friendship letters.[19] These valuable sources, with other genres used by women (songs, poems, manuals to their children for Christian life, biblical interpretations, and diaries or other autobiographical pieces) have been discovered recently as theologically pertinent. Considering letter writing as women's theological forum is a step towards inclusivity in Reformation scholarship. Through them, scholarship gains theologically relevant insights from sixteenth-century women authors, and also important material for re-definition of women's activities and roles in the Reformation history: letters convey insights into the private and public worlds and identities of women, their mutual relationships, their activities in sharing news, educating, counseling, polemics, biblical interpretation

---

19. See Stjerna, *Women and the Reformation*; Bainton, *Women of the Reformation in Germany and Italy*.

and theological reflection, and proclamation of the Christian gospel. Just as they had originally use politically, theologically, spiritually and personally, the letters offer multi-layered information for scholarship today that seeks to be inclusive chronologically speaking, genre- and gender-wise.

Two best-selling pamphleteer female theologians of the reformation century offer a poignant case study: Argula von Grumbach from Ingolstadt, Germany, and Katharina Schütz Zell from Strasburg.[20]

Argula von Grumbach (1492?-1563?) from Bavaria is known by posterity because she wrote feisty letters to the University of Ingolstadt in defense of a student named Arsacius Seehofer. The student was accused of Lutheran heresy after his visit to Wittenberg[21] and Argula demanded the university men to prove to her with scripture, and in writing, why Arscacius—or Luther—would be heretical.[22] Argula was dismissed as a desperate "bitch" by the faculty, who indirectly punished her through husband: after losing his position, Argula's frustrated spouse "persecuted the Christ in her," in her words. Argula's letter campaign[23] in 1523-1524 made her a best-selling pamphleteer (with 30,000 circulation) and female author of the Reformation.[24]

Argula's letters chronicle a faith journey of a Lutheran woman who carved a specific vocation for herself, regardless of obstacles. They serve as a testament of her Word-centered Protestant theology.[25] With the authority she drew explicitly from scripture, which she thoroughly knew, she embodied priesthood of all believers in her bold confession of Protestant

---

20. Other examples: Marie Dentière from Geneva corresponded with Queen Marguerite de Navarra with an explosive "defense of women" and their rights in the church; she also wrote in defense of Calvin with biblical arguments. Lady Elisabeth von Braunschweig wrote a binding letter to her subjects about instilling the new faith with the Augsburg Confession; she defended Andreas Osiander's views with her bible and first-hand knowledge of Luther's works. (Her motto was that one should obey God, the Emperor and one's mother!)

21. See, e.g., von Grumbach, *Wie ein Christliche Fraw des adels / in // Beyern durch iren / in Gotlicher schrifft / wolgegrund // tenn Sendbrieffe/ die hohenschul zu Ingoldstat / // vmb das sie eynen Euangelischen Jungling / zu widersprechung des wort gottes. Betrangt// haben / straffet.*

22. See Matheson, *Argula von Grumbach. A Woman's Voice in the Reformation*, 86-87.

23. Argula's works include letters to the University of Ingolstadt (printed in 14 editions) and the Duke Wilhelm (IV) (1523); to the Mayor and the city council of Ingolstadt, the Count Palatine Johann von Simmern and to Fredrick the Wise, and Count Adam von Thering (1523); and a letter to the city of Regensburg (1524), and a poem in response to anonymous slander.

24. Matheson, *Argula von Grumbach*, 86-87.

25. Ibid., 101, also 108.

faith.[26] Argula defended Luther, who considered Argula a brave instrument of Christ and an exemplary confessor of faith.[27] Argula understood equality, she "included" herself and was empowered by her scripture-based spirituality and search for the truth as a woman. "What I have written to you is no woman's chit-chat, but the word of God; and (I write) as a member of the Christian Church, against which the gates of Hell cannot prevail. (...)" She envisioned reforms in the horizon and women taking the lead: "Yes, and whereas I have written on my own, a hundred women would emerge to write against them. For there are many who are able and better read than I am; as a result they might well come to be called 'a school for women.' (...) We have to confess publicly. (...)"[28]

In addition to her inclusion of women in her reformation vision, Argula's concern about justice is noteworthy. She considered it a Christian duty to fight with words for justice and against violence. She was compelled to use her voice in the face of human suffering.[29] The central Lutheran conviction of salvation as a gift of faith because of Christ's work entailed for her that the Holy Spirit was present both in and beyond the institutional church structures and that She called lay women like Argula to the proclamation task when situation so warranted; witnessing violence and injustice would qualify. With her radar on justice and Christian freedom, Argula's theology was compassionate and geared towards defending the vulnerable. Her theology involved risk-taking: "I am prepared to lose everything—even life and limb. May God stand by me!" Argula's story speaks about the importance of both religious experience and risk-taking in theological work.[30] She also reminds of the manifold importance of gender.

Argula stands in spirit with contemporary women who also feel compelled to speak up and yet are often ridiculed, attacked or marginalized for gender-related reasons. Global news report of life-and-death situations outspoken women face in different corners of the world. There is chilling continuity in women's experience in this regard. Reforms begin from exposing the roots of the problem in distorted gender notions and related power issues. The reformation women remind of the need for vigilance with the

---

26. Defense of Luther, see Matheson, *Argula von Grumbach*, 76–77.

27. On Luther and Argula, see Bainton, *Women of the Reformation in Germany and Italy*, 106–9; Luther, "Luther an Speratus," WABr 2, 509; Luther, "Luther an Spalatin," WABr 3, 706; Luther, "Luther an Spalatin," WABr 3, 709. Also Matheson, *Argula von Grumbach*, 18n48, 21n58; Luther, "Luther an Briessmann," WABr 3, 713; Luther, "Luther an Spalatin," WABr 3, 787.

28. See Matheson, *Argula von Grumbach*, 120–21.

29. Ibid., 75, 77.

30. Ibid., 149.

lingering sins of sexism, just as they model ways to make a difference with the word and compassionate commitment.

Katharina Schütz Zell (1498–1562), a pastor's wife from Strasbourg is another example.[31] Through her texts she offered manifold counsel and comfort to her contemporaries and critique on the church's failure to do "its job."[32] As a reformer, Katharina's first text was a forceful defense of marriage, clergy marriage—and her own. Katharina distinctly identified herself as a "church mother" and her marriage allowed her to fulfill that call.[33] For a woman with no surviving children of her own, "church motherhood" became an avenue in ministry and theology she confidently supported with her knowledge of the Scripture. In the end she even preached and officiated at funerals and escaped the otherwise inevitable punishment in death.

Katharina Schütz Zell employed a variety of genres to speak to people's spiritual concerns and to console and empower others with her protestant theology with a strikingly ecumenical approach. She also edited a hymnbook the first of its kind in German (the first edition of the Bohemian Brethren's hymns), with an expansive vision for empowering lay theology: "I found such an understanding of the work of God in this songbook that I want all people to understand it. Indeed, I ought much rather to call it a teaching, prayer, and praise book than a songbook. However, the little word 'song' is well and properly spoken, for the greatest praise of God is expressed in song."[34]

Katharina Schütz Zell's theology translated into concrete deeds of ecumenical charity. She visited the sick and the imprisoned, regardless of their confessional affiliation. She hosted representatives of different confessional sides, urging for concord (especially on the issue of Lord's Supper). With Protestant principles of "Word alone" and "justification by faith through grace," Katharina's theology underscored the importance of forgiveness, charitable love and active compassion as natural outcomes of justification.[35]

---

31. McKee, *Katharina Schütz Zell: The Life and Thought of a Sixteenth-Century Reformer*; McKee, *Katharina Schütz Zell: The Writings: A Critical Edition*; Schütz Zell, *Church Mother: The Writings of a Protestant Reformer in Sixteenth-Century Germany*.

32. See e.g., Schütz Zell, *Entschuldigung Katharina Schützinn/für M. Matthes Zellen/ jren Eegemahel/der ein Pfarrher und dyener ist im wort Gottes zu Strassburg. Von wegen grosser lügen uff jn erdiecht*; Schütz Zell, *Den leydenden Christglaubigen weyberen der gmein zu Kentzigen minen mitschwestern in Christo Jesus zu handen*.

33. McKee, *Katharina Schütz Zell: The Life and Thought of a Sixteenth-Century Reformer*, 224–25.

34. Ibid., 93, see 82–96.

35. Ibid., 128, 64, 82.

Both Katharina and Argula, brave in their actions as theologically outspoken and active publishing women, experienced the urgency to speak up on the basis of their faith experience and theology that both based on and led them to interpret scripture to address issues in their situation and to empower others. Freedom of conscience to them was far more important than doctrinal and confessional issues; eradicating justice was more important to them than being stuck with doctrinal arguments. Their Christian courage involved compassion, which in turn fueled their courage, based on their unfailing trust in God's loving omnipresence, justice, and truth.

To conclude: The sixteenth century writing women stretched their "acceptable" domestic calling of motherhood to include the task of caring of the world with the Word. Empowered by their biblical knowledge, the reformation mothers operated as situational biblically authorized lay theologians: they acted when witnessing injustice or suffering.[36] They applied Protestant theology most notably in their defense of the vulnerable and the suffering. Compassion characterized their theological approach. Working with the reformation mothers not only facilitates rewriting of the Reformation history that includes women appropriately, but also presents areas of renewed attention for contemporary Lutheran theology: Lutheran teaching of marriage and sexuality, and related, gender; countering gender-based exclusivism in Lutheran tradition; systematic inclusion of women's perspectives in all the areas of theology; the importance of experience in religious matters; violence, sexism and injustice as theological concerns imminently related to the relevance of the Lutheran spiritual theology.

The Reformation women invite scholars to engage in ongoing reforms. They give a courageous model for making a difference in the world as Protestant believers and (lay) theologians with a compassionate commitment to re-interpret the word in fresh ways relevant to new situations, with a focus on the integrity of human lives. Their personal stories enforce the necessity of the absolute commitment to ensure equality to all men and women. They speak to the transforming and emancipating power of faith and religious experience, and the centrality of spirituality. Lutheran spiritual theology has much promise today in the world where people continue to suffer from hurtful bondages, be they those of conscience or other. The study of the Reformation women leads Lutheran scholars to ask new questions and address with new sources the ongoing challenges for Lutheran theology with the timeless reformation concerns: inclusivity, equality, and spirituality.

---

36. Katharina Zell wrote "That is, it is proper to (and part of) being a Christian to suffer, but it is not at all proper for him [her] to be silent (. . .)" (ibid., 64, 62).

BIBLIOGRAPHY

Augsburg Confession. Die Augsburgische Konfession. Die Bekenntnisschriften der evangelisch-lutherischen Kirche. 6th ed. Göttingen: Vanderhoeck & Ruprecht, 1967.

Bainton, Roland. *Women of the Reformation in Germany and Italy.* 1971. N.p: Academic Renewal Press, 2001.

Cooper-White, Pamela. *The Cry of Tamar: Violence against Women and the Church's Response.* 2nd ed. Minneapolis: Fortress, 1995.

Gregory, Brad S. *The Unintended Reformation: How a Religious Revolution Secularized Society.* Cambridge, MA: Harvard University Press, 2012.

Guidelines for Inclusive Language. Evangelical Lutheran Church in Canada. Online: http://elcic.ca/Resources/Inclusive-Language.cfm (accessed 15/03/2014).

Forde, Gerhard O. *Justification by Faith: A Matter of Death and Life.* Eugene, OR: Wipf & Stock, 2012.

Hendrix, Scott. "Martin Luther's Reformation of Spirituality." In *Harvesting Martin Luther's Reflections on Theology, Ethics, and the Church*, edited by Timothy J. Wengert, 240–60. Grand Rapids, MI: Eerdman, 2003.

Hoffmann, Bengt R. *Theology of the Heart: The Role of Mysticism in the Theology of Martin Luther.* Minneapolis: Lutheran University Press, 2003.

Johnson, Elizabeth A. *She Who Is: The Mystery of God in Feminist Theological Discourse.* New York: Crossroad, 2002.

Krey, Philip D. W., and Peter D. S. Krey, editors. *Luther's Spirituality.* Mawhaw, NJ: Paulist, 2007.

Luther, Martin. *A Simple Way to Pray* (1535). LW 43. Philadelphia: Fortress, 1968.

———. *Cathechisms.* In the *Book of Concord*, edited by Timothy Wengert and Robert Kolb. Minneapolis: Fortress, 2000.

———. *Commentary on Galatians* (1535). LW 26. St. Louis: Concordia, 1963; LW 27. St. Louis: Concordia, 1964; WA 40, Erste Abteilung. Weimar: Hermann Böhlaus Nachfolger, 1911; WA 40, Zweite Abteilung. Weimar: Hermann Böhlaus Nachfolger, 1914.

———. *The Freedom of a Christian* (1520). LW 31. St. Louis: Concordia, 1957; WA 7. Weimar: Hermann Böhlaus Nachfolger, 1897.

———. *Lectures on Romans* (1515–1516). LW 25. St. Louis: Concordia, 1972; WA 56. Weimar: Hermann Böhlaus Nachfolger, 1938.

———. *Luther an Briessmann* (1524). WABr 3. Weimar: Hermann Böhlaus Nachfolger, 1933.

———. *Luther an Spalatin* (1524). WABr 3. Weimar: Hermann Böhlaus Nachfolger, 1933.

———. *Luther an Speratus* (1522). WABr 2. Weimar: Hermann Böhlaus Nachfolger, 1931.

———. *Personal Prayer Book* (1522). LW 43. Philadelphia: Fortress, 1968; WA 10, Zweite Abteilung. Weimar: Hermann Böhlaus Nachfolger, 1910.

———. *Two Kinds of Righteousness* (1519). LW 31. St. Louis: Concordia, 1957; WA 2. Weimar: Hermann Böhlau, 1884.

Mannermaa, Tuomo. *Christ Present in Faith.* Minneapolis: Fortress, 2005.

———. *Two Kinds of Love: Martin Luther's Religious World.* Minneapolis: Fortress, 2001.

Matheson, Paul, editor. *Argula von Grumbach. A Woman's Voice in the Reformation.* Edinburgh: T. & T. Clark, 1995.

McGinn, Bernard. *The Essential Writings of Christian Mysticism*. New York: Modern Library, 2006.

———. *The Foundations of Mysticism: Origins to the Fifth Century*. New York: Crossroad, 2004.

McGinn, Bernard, John Meyendorff, and Jean Leclercq. *Christian Spirituality: Origins to the Twelfth Century*. New York: Crossroad, 1985.

McKee, Elsie, editor. *Katharina Schütz Zell: The Life and Thought of a Sixteenth-Century Reformer*. Vols. 1–2. Leiden: Brill, 1999.

Rothenberg, Paula. *Race, Class, and Gender in the United States. An Integrated Study*. 3rd ed. New York: St Martin's, 1995.

Ruether, Rosemary Radford. *Sexism and God Talk. Toward a Feminist Theology*. Boston: Beacon, 1993.

Schneiders, Sandra M. "Spirituality in the Academy." In *Theological Studies* 50 (1989) 684.

Schütz Zell, Katharina. *Den leydenden Christglauben weyberen der gmein zu Kentzigen minen mitschwestern in Christo Jesus zu handen*. Strasbourg: W. Köpffel, 1524.

———. *Church Mother: The Writings of a Protestant Reformer in Sixteenth-Century Germany*. Chicago: The University of Chicago Press, 2006.

———. *Entschuldigung Katharina Schützinn / für M. Matthes Zellen / jren Eegemahler / der ein Pfarrher und dyener ist im wort Gottes zu Strassburg. Von wegen grosser lügen uff jn erdiecht*. Strasbourg: W. Köpffel, 1524.

Soelle, Dorothee. *The Silent Cry: Mysticism and Resistance*. Minneapolis: Fortress, 2001.

"Spirituality" in *Merriam-Webster*. Online: http://www.merriam-webster.com/dictionary/spirituality (accessed 20/12/2013).

Stjerna, Kirsi. "The Case of Women: New Perspectives, New Interests in Luther and Reformation Studies." *Lutheranism. Legacy and Future. Essays in Honor of Eric W. Gitsch on the 50th Anniversary of his Ordination*, edited by Holger Roggelin and Scott Gustafson. West Conshohocken, PA.: Infinity, 2012.

———. "Grief, Glory and Grace: Insights on Eve and Tamar in Luther's Genesis Commentary." *Seminary Ridge Review* 6/2, Spring 2004.

———. *No Greater Jewel: Thinking about Baptism with Luther*. Minneapolis: Fortress, 2010.

———. *Women and the Reformation*. Oxford: Wiley Blackwell, 2009.

Stjerna, Kirsi, and Brooks Schramm. *Spirituality: Toward A 21st Century Lutheran Understanding*. Minneapolis: Lutheran University Press, 2004

Trigg, Jonathan D. *Baptism in the Theology of Martin Luther*. Leiden: Brill, 1994.

Van Ness, Peter H. "Introduction." In *Spirituality and the Secular Quest*. World Spirituality 22. New York: Crossroad, 1996.

"Violence" in *Merriam-Webster*, Online: http://www.merriam-webster.com/dictionary/violence (accessed 20/12/2013).

Von Grumbach, Argula. *Wie ein Christliche Fraw des adels / in // Beyern durch iren / in Gotlicher schrifft / wolgegrund // tenn Sendbrieffe / die hohenschul zu Ingoldstat / // vmb das sie eynen Euangelischen Jungling / zu widersprechung des wort gottes. Betrangt // haben / staffet*. Actum Ingelstat. M D Xxiij. Erfurt: Matthes Maler, 1523.

Wiseman, James A. *Spirituality and Mysticism: A Global View*. Maryknoll, NY: Orbis, 2006.

Wood, Susan K. *One Baptism: Ecumenical Dimensions of the Doctrine of Baptism*. Collegeville, MN: Liturgical, 2009.

7

Liberating Aspects in Lutheran Theology for a Post-Gender Politics

ELSE MARIE WIBERG PEDERSEN

In this chapter, I will search out aspects in Lutheran theology, which have proven promising guidelines for a sustainable theology. As the title says, I am aiming at what I call a *post-gender politics*. By such a post-gender politics I aim at going beyond any specific gender theories and rather employ an approach of which *homo*, the human being, is the pre-eminent category from which I am arguing. Thus, *homo* in the sense of human equality and equal human dignity of all humanity in the widest sense will be my hermeneutical key for aspects from the past that can make the transition to the future. I will go back to basics and highlight aspects from a sixteenth century context I find promising, seen through the lenses of my context. One of my points will be that—despite all the faults and failures of the human being, the *homo*, Luther—it is possible to take out and highlight features of his theology that eventually, in all actuality, led to political and social improvements for the common people irrespective of sex, ethnicity, and social background. I acknowledge that different readers of the reformation will have very different reactions depending on their context. But that, in a Lutheran context, there is space for difference and for different perspectives, which are constantly tried out and debated without doctrinal anathemas, is in itself a basic liberating aspect.

In the genealogy of feminist studies since the 1960s, from the revisionist reconstruction of women's history and representation to gender studies in the 1990s, to the 2000s breakdown of the gender/sex distinction, focus shifted to the categories of difference and intersection in continuation of a poststructuralist and postmodern gender approach. With a further focus on the local-global perspective, the now well-known concepts of hybridity, mixture and the in-between used in post-colonial studies were integrated in most feminist studies. Today it is close to a truism that gender, ethnicity, and social status are not fixed categories but something found in diverse and intersected forms. In contrast to essentialism, many feminist scholars have realized how utterly complex history, including Lutheran history, is. Pertaining to Luther studies, with the stress on diversification and difference Luther's legacy as a reformer has been brought into question. Some claim that whether scholars do feminist studies and whether they are negative or positive to Luther's legacy has to do with confessional and/or national biases.[1]

When I choose *homo* as my hermeneutical key, it is to underline the significance of both the diversification of humanity and the individuality of each human being, yet simultaneously to claim some common ground for this diverse humanity. I find it important that we as theologians, feminist or not, do not simply translate a diversification into a value-free pluralist perception of theology, but that such a diversification take its point of departure on a firm and common ground from which the Lutheran gaze perceives. Hence, while recognizing the insights obtained by feminist, post-modernist and post-colonialist studies, I find the time mature to again speak from some sort of universal that goes beyond any form of gender, ethnicity or social setting. From this ground of a cosmic *homo*, without intending any anthropocentricism or speciesism, I will point to liberating ideas in Luther's theology that can make it for a democratic, post-gender politics of the twenty-first century.[2]

---

1. Wiesner-Hanks, "Women and the Reformations: Reflections on Recent Research," 1–27. Wiesner-Hanks postulates a split between particularly Lutheran church historians trained in Germany and social historians and literary scholars trained outside of Germany, arguing that women doing Luther studies in Germany are hindered in doing critical studies due to an old-fashioned confessionalism and a hostile attitude toward women's research. It is equally problematic though, if certain feminist scholars do not recognize colleagues who value certain Lutheran ideas positively and dismiss their studies as simply confessionalist, as Wiesner-Hanks seems to do.

2. The number of publications that search out Luther's reformatory ideas and how Luther's theology in general can be transformed to the twenty-first century global world is increasing, but let me point out two different types: Streufert, *Transformative Lutheran Theologies: Feminist, Womanist, and Mujerista Perspectives*; *Feminist Theology & Lutheran Thought: Dialog* 49/3, 190–247; Wiberg Pedersen, "Disciplined Freedom, or Free versus Slave? Recuperating Luther for Feminist Theology in an Age of Terror," 284–88.

Before I embark on my journey into the liberating aspects of Lutheran theology for a post-gender politics I will take a detour to some preliminary reflections on method and perception in order to remind us all of the complexity of our past.

READING THE PAST

In these years up to the 500th anniversary of the reformation in 2017, the old dispute who owns the Protestant Reformation and who best interprets Luther and Lutheran theology has again surfaced. Therefore the hermeneutical question how we read and use the past should concern us. We need to consider what it means when for example very different texts without regard of their different contexts are compared, or when texts from the past are being judged as if they were written in our own context, measurable on our ideals. The questions I want to raise here are: How do we read and understand the past without arrogant and easy perditions? How do we as scholars discern what to remit as signs of the times, signs of very diverse strata of society and culture of that past, and what to transmit as signs pointing to the future? What reader's perspective do we employ? Do we read the text as an entity in itself, ignoring that it was written under specific circumstances and with a specific address—politically, socially, historically, and theologically? Or do we read the text as part of a larger context of specific political and social conditions, historical circumstances, and theological disputes and feuds? Do we judge it from our own perspective and ideals, or do we judge a given text with respect for its own reality? The crucial question here is how we read the Reformation and the sixteenth century reformer Martin Luther and his theology today? Do we make Luther a hero, almost a God, or a scoundrel, almost a devil? Or do we recognize Luther as a man and theologian living in a specific time with particular ecclesiastical problems, which gave him a cause that he struggled for with all the errors that inevitably occur in a human life? Do we recognize that this struggle was not costless, fought as it was in the tumultuous sixteenth century Europe?[3]

Luther was not living in a modern democracy such as Sweden, but in a complex empire under the rule of both emperor and pope, and he was—due to his cause—excommunicated by the pope already in 1520 and outlawed by the emperor shortly after in the beginning of 1521 due to his criticism of abuses of the papal church. I.e., Luther was, in political terms, an outlaw in the entire German-Roman Empire, and, in ecclesiastical terms, declared a heretic by the transnational empirical Roman church institution from 1520

---

3. Oberman, *Luther: Mensch zwischen Gott und Teufel* provides nuanced answers to such questions.

onwards. Most of his time as a reformer, he was an outcast in relation to the empirical establishment. These special circumstances together with his initiating actions and writings provide him with a unique legacy as a reformer. Hence, can we judge all his views from a modern democratic view point? Of course, we cannot, as little as we can uncritically adapt all his views to a modern democratic society or any other society and culture of today. As German linguist, Michael Giesecke, points out, each cultural period develops its own ways of triadic perception that involves thinking, acting and communicating.[4]

Despite important insights from theology of the subaltern about the importance of context, there has been a tendency to forget about context in recent years when reading Luther—both of time, culture, and geography. Without consideration of the complexity of the German context in which he lived and operated, he has been accused of having extremely vulgar and at times even violent views on the pope, Jews, Peasants, Clergy, Women, and Princes. Important as language is, this should also be contextualized in view of specific semantic and rhetorical strategies in different cultural settings. Thus, Richard Glenn Cole, emeritus Professor of History, inspired by postmodern reading strategies has suggested to understand Luther's rhetorical intent in the context of early modern German culture and to read especially his satirical pamphlets as a "rhetorical use of 'masks' as metaphors."[5] When perceived in their historical-cultural context, it becomes obvious that Luther is writing political satire. His brusque vocabulary for Jews as "whores," violent peasants as "mad dogs," and bishops as "genitals" and "asses" should not be understood literally, but is a communicative strategy that was common in public debate and discourse from the Athenian Agora of Ancient Greece onwards[6] and still operative in Europe at least. Luther, who employed multiple styles and genres in his vast corpus, chiefly employed the classical political satire in the pamphlets. The problem is, according to Cole, that this genre is no longer accessible to twenty-first century academic readers. Besides, people tend to forget that Luther was also more sophisticated than that. Like his predecessors of the Middle Ages and his contemporaries, including his opponents, he wrote in all the diverse genres: satirical texts, sermons, letters, commentaries, lectures, and treatises that have each their address, particular style and semantics, though they would also compose hybrid forms. But his pamphlets, which became so widespread due to the

4. Giesecke, *Die Entdeckung der kommunikativen Welt: Studien zur Kulturvergleichen Mediengeschichte.*

5. Cole, "Martin Luther's Use of Rhetorical masks for Jews, Princes, Clerics, and other Enemies," 309–10.

6. Ibid., 310.

new printing press, are primarily satirical texts composed according to the style of the genre and written in the context of actual feuds taking place, not to be mistaken as academic or normative texts that we today in any way should adopt.

READING THE PAST THROUGH THE PRESENT FOR THE FUTURE: A POST-GENDER KEY

One of the liberating principles of Reformation theology that are of immense significance, and which in many ways reflects the different interpretations I have henceforth touched upon, is that the reformed church should always be in a process of reform (*ecclesia reformata semper reformanda*). This principle calls for theological interpretations that combine past and present. Interpretation is the new in light of the old, letting the present influence the understanding of the past, taking ever new phenomena that did not exist when the historical or normative texts were written (for instance a developed understanding of human equality and democracy) and combine them with the universe or core message that is expressed in the texts.

Gadamer understood this well. According to Gadamer, it is at the intersection between past and present that the "productive role" of interpretation arises as a fusion of horizons. Interpretation is a process where the interpreter puts his or her presuppositions into play, and in which phenomena and themes, considered to have a central and particularly important value, are sorted out and accentuated. Gadamer stresses the inevitable "distance between time periods, cultures, classes, races and even between persons" that can only be overcome by language: "The interpreter and the text each possesses his, her or its own horizon and every moment of understanding represents a fusion of these horizons."[7] In this process, arbitrary and subjective prejudices do not count. Rather, history delivers central points that become and remain part of theology's self-understanding. But history also delivers points that are not central of a theological self-understanding, and which may even become detrimental to the theological core.

For Lutherans, the core of unity or oneness of the church is guided by the central message of justification for all in Jesus Christ by grace through faith alone (CA 4). Having this core enables Lutherans to positively articulate unity in diversity in a global perspective and to constantly rethink and interpret Scripture and tradition in new ways that are adequate and timely. Even though we can easily find texts where Luther reflects thoughts and rhetoric of traditional exegesis inherited from Augustine and Augustinian tradition, his *sola scriptura* principle in fact goes against a totalitarian

7. Gadamer, *Truth and Method*, 45.

traditional way of reading scripture. Thus, the bible humanists' maxim of going to the sources, *ad fontes*, is at the bottom of the *sola scriptura* principle and points to an empowering of every person to read it and see what scripture says, understood as gospel not as a law book, as Luther explains in his introduction to his German translation of the New Testament.[8]

Concurrently, inasmuch as the extremely important *vernacularization of scripture* is indicative of the empowering of the common people, enabled as they are to read and interpret bible texts on their own, it is imperative that we as Lutheran theologians take serious the sound humanist principle of going back to the sources. It is not bible texts alone that may be "lost in translation," misinterpreted and distorted through translation and rendered in very different, at times dubious, versions. This is also true of Luther's texts. If we do not constantly go back to the sources, we are prone to uncritically adopt and render misrepresentations and distortions, deliberate or not, and run the risk of being unable to develop a Lutheran theology in its own right.

On this ground I shall try to sort out what I see as liberating aspects for human beings and politics in Lutheran theology. I will in this undertaking either leave out Luther's various ambivalences toward women or integrate them as self-contradictions of his higher ideals, exactly as we tend to do when we treat of the fathers of enlightenment and human rights.[9]

A HUMAN ECONOMY: THE THESES AGAINST ABUSE AND INDULGENCES

With his Ninety-Five Theses from 1517 Luther took up the fight against abuse of the common people and called for helping the poor and the needy (e.g. theses 43) instead of paying for the forgiveness of sins that Christ already paid for all humanity irrespective of class, sex, education, etc. Luther's critique of the church hierarchy is together with his *sola gratia* and *sola fide* principles a very strong signal of an egalitarian and inclusive view of humans: if you believe, you already have. With these ideals Lutheran theology evaluates the common people and the everyday life of each and every one as already graced and redeemed. But particularly, Luther's theses can be lifted up against any form of corruption and exploitation, as he was actually also fighting the new fiscal economy with its interest (usury) and speculations

---

8. Luther, *Eyn klein Unterricht, was man ynn den Euangeliis suchen und gewarten soll*, WA 10.I, 1:8–18.

9. For a more detailed treatment of Luther's ambiguities and ambivalences (compared with Thomas Jefferson), see Wiberg Pedersen, "A Man Caught Between Bad Anthropology and Good Theology? Martin Luther's View of Women Generally and of Mary Specifically," 190–200.

that the Roman church with the potentials of the new colonies took advantage of.[10] All resonated in the financial crisis that started in 2008 as a consequence of massive exploitation of common people by banks and tycoons.

THE HUMAN REALITY: THEOLOGY OF THE CROSS

This is a very risky aspect to highlight in this context, since it has been so vehemently critiqued from feminists and others.[11] But I take the risk, because I see humanizing features in it: From his basis of critique of the hierarchical church and papal sacramentality/sacral priesthood, Luther opposed a theology of glory and called for the true theologian who could identify with suffering and the cross.[12]

Besides addressing the abuse of indulgences and of the cross as a relic that was sold as wood taken from the historical cross of Christ, Luther called theologians to identify with real suffering and the real cross of Christ who suffered for all humanity, not with arbitrary merits. His calling should not be taken as a calling to seek suffering as a redeeming factor, but to see human life in its fullness of joys and sorrows as divinely embraced. The theologian of the cross envisages reality and real life, "calling a thing what it is," and does not explain away suffering. Directed toward the scholastics' rational and abstract explanations of divine mathematics, Luther's theology of the cross (as also his concept of *Deus absconditus*) is a non-explanation of real human life. God and the God-created life are not part of any petty human logic, but are completely theo-logic and as such highly complex. Luther's message is that life should not be rationalized, but accepted, experienced and lived in its fullness. Only when humans call suffering what it is and see what it does to the other, can they identify with this other in empathy, i.e. enter the *pathos*, the suffering, of others as did Christ on the cross.

Luther could not only identify with those in doubt from his own *Anfechtunge*, but as banned by both church and empire also with the excluded and marginalized, and as a father who lost some of his children with those in deep distress. As he stated when his beloved daughter, Elisabeth, died at 14 years old, he suffered "almost with a female spirit" (*animum paene*

10. For example Luther, *Sermon von dem Wucher*, WA 6, 1–8.

11. The theology of the cross has been one of the most debated themes in feminist theology during the past two decades because it has sometimes been abused in the victimization of women. But there are Lutheran feminists who have underlined the positive and constructive aspects of the theology of the cross, e.g. Solberg, *Compelling Knowledge: A Feminist Proposal for an Epistemology of the Cross*; Thompson, *Crossing the Divide: Luther, Feminism, and the Cross*; Guðmundsdóttir, *Meeting God on the Cross: Christ, the Cross, and the Feminist Critique*.

12. Luther, *Disputatio Heidelbergae habitat*, theses 19–20, WA 1, 354, 361–62.

muliebrem).[13] But he did not seek suffering or sacrifice. As he spells it out in his *Sermon on the New Testament*, the only sacrifice people should make is to "believe that Christ is a priest for them in Heaven" and thank him in prayer for the sacrifice he made for them. In that respect "all are equally priests for God," "all Christian men and women are priests, whether they are old or young, female and male masters of the house or female or male servants, learned or lay. Here is no difference—unless faith should not be the same for all."[14]

HUMANIZATION OF MINISTRY: THE PRIESTHOOD OF ALL BELIEVERS

Theologically Luther can but emphasize the equality of all human beings, women and men of faith. Everything else would contradict the substance of his reformation theology. This becomes particularly concrete in the texts where he explicates his idea of the priesthood of all believers: that all baptized as their priestly obligations have "to teach, preach and proclaim the word of God, baptize, consecrate and administer the Lord's supper, bind and solve from sins, pray for others, sacrifice oneself and judge all teachers and spirits,"[15] or as he states in a letter to Spalatin, referring to 1 Peter 2:10: "The apostle Peter drives me strongly when he says that we are all priests (*sacerdotes*),"[16] concluding that all are equal in the ministry of the word and sacrament and in human state. Luther's idea of the priesthood as a responsibility toward the neighbor and his rejection of an ontological distinction between lay and ordained in this letter as in writings from 1520 such as *To the Nobility* and *The Babylonian Captivity of the Church* opened avenues to common people, including women. Although nothing happened overnight because the Protestant churches were integrated in patriarchal states and principalities, we should not discard the fact that the potential of the idea— even spelt out in Luther's ambiguous-ambivalent statements in *On Councils and the Church*, in which he exempts women (and children) from his principle of the task and not the person doing the task being the issue[17]—did

13. Luther, *Luther an Nikolaus Hausmann*, WABr 4, 511 (Letter 1303).

14. Luther, *Ein Sermon von dem neuen Testament*, WA 6, 370.

15. Luther, *De instituendis ministris ecclesiae*, WA 12, 180. Cf. *De Captivitate Babylonica ecclesiae praeludium*, WA 6, 484–573.

16. Luther, *Luther an Spalatin*, WABr 1, 595 (Letter 231).

17. Luther, *Von den Konziliis und Kirchen*, WA 50, 633. Three things should be noted here: (1) Luther formulates his understanding of ministry in a universal way, before seemingly absolving this universality by stating that the Holy Spirit has exempted women (and children) from the ministry, except when in need. (2) Luther does not say, that it is not allowed women to be ministers. Instead he calls upon the Holy Spirit

not stay *in spe*, but eventually came out *in re* and still do so. In a fusion of horizons, Lutherans have aptly interpreted Luther against himself when it came to such ambivalences, which contradicted his own high ideals. It cannot be overstated that when Luther propounds his central theological principles, he always employs the generic term *homo* (or in German: *Mensch*), a human being, not the gender term *vir* (or in German: *Mann*), a (male) man. Thus, it is more than proper to free Luther from his Roman captivity in his ambivalence toward women and bind the ministry to the general liberating principles for all humans.

The texts propound the equality of believers in Christ through baptism, as in Luther's treatise *The Freedom of a Christian*, in which Luther, however, makes a significant differentiation within the priesthood of all believers.[18] Everyone is spiritual and a priest through baptism and faith in Christ, but to the ministry of the word (*ministerium verbi*; i.e. servant of the word) only some are called. For Luther the difference lies in the calling, which is not a secret inner calling but a public calling by the community of believers. Likewise, he clearly rejects a sacramental understanding of ordination as well as any special *character indelebilis* attached to such an ordination and the priesthood (of only males). An extremely liberating factor is also that simultaneously with perceiving the pastoral office as instituted by God, Luther humanizes it.[19] No pastor is more than a human being and no less a sinner than any member of the calling community.

Whereas the Catholic understanding of ministry is based on an ordination tied to a hierarchy of especially sacral males (*officium sacerdos*), Luther's understanding of ministry is based on baptism, the true ordination sacrament, and tied to the equality of all baptized believers. The minister is a follower (*succesor*) of the gospel and as such a servant of the word (*ministerium verbi*). While the Catholic *vicarius Christi* is a representation of Christ's divine nature, the Lutheran *ministerium verbi* is a representation of the incarnate Christ, the in-fleshed *Logos*. In Luther's perception, God wanted to be known in Christ in his humanity, as a human being, spelled out in *The Freedom of a Christian* as Christ's *similitudo hominis*, his likeness

---

to state an unclear exemption from his rule. (3) Text critically, the exemption in lines 12–24 stands as an interruptive interpolation parallel to Paul's in 1 Cor 14:34–35. It is in discord with the main discourse and immediately again absolved by Luther's statement that the efficacy of the ministry is independent on how and who the person in ministry is.

18. Luther, *De libertate christiana*, WA 7, 20–28.

19. Luther, *In epistolam S Pauli ad Galatas Commentarius*, WA 40.I, 59, here commenting on Gal 1:1 thus: "ministri sunt ex nobis electi (. . .) Deus vocat nos omnes ad ministerium vocatione per hominem estque divina vocatio."

to a human being. Therefore, the external word should be proclaimed orally "by humans, like by you and me."[20] The pastor must in all aspects be a human being, which is also the backdrop against which Luther's critique of celibacy and of monastic life as a *status perfectionis* should be perceived. All in all, Luther could be said to in fact secularize ministry and, quite adversary to its prior segregation from an ordinary life, place it in the midst of what he saw as a normal everyday life.

In my view, it is particularly liberating that this de-sacralization of ministry goes hand in hand with an actual sacralization of the everyday life of common people, as it comes to the fore in Luther's catechisms from 1529. In both the small and the large catechism, life is seen as part of a creational grace and sacredness that should never be suspended.[21]

THE COMMON HUMAN: *SIMUL IUSTUS ET PECCATOR*

In the same vein I suggest we understand the principle of every human being at once just and a sinner. It is important that both aspects are reflected in the right order: first just in the face of God, *coram Deo*, then sinner in the face of other humans, *coram hominibus*. The *simul* thus expresses Luther's understanding of the human being as a relational being in a dual perspective. In the eyes of God (*coram Deo*), the human being is already just due to both the creational grace and Christ's justifying act. In the eyes of other humans, the human being is always a sinner due to the fact that we constantly fail, even when trying to do good works. Luther does not speak ontologically as did Augustine, but relationally. He completely transforms Augustine's ontological concept to a relational concept: sin is no longer pride and desire, but unbelief. To be just is to believe in God's promises and forgiveness, to be a sinner is to not believe. Grace and sin are not substances gradually poured into the human like in a container as in Augustine's teaching, but two total perspectives—*coram Deo* and *coram hominibus*—denoting that humans are relational beings, always living in relation to other human beings and God as two simultaneous, yet different relationships. However, the *simul* also denotes that both are embraced by God's relation to the human, for God's grace as a favor and the justification of the sinner in Christ come first and are always present as a promise waiting to be received in faith as a gift.

---

20. Luther, *Von den Konziliis und Kirchen*, WA 50, 629.

21. Cf. Luther's exposition of the first of the Ten Commandments in *Der Grosse Katechismus*, WA 30.I, 132–39. Luther calls upon God's commandment to every human, irrespective of her position, to do good to her neighbor, for in the same way as a mother has been given breasts and milk to feed her child every creature is God's hand, channel, and means (136).

Hence, the *simul* is asymmetrical in that God's grace is so much greater than human sin.²²

Negative as particularly the last part of the *simul* principle sounds to some, reflecting a pessimistic anthropology, I have come to see it as an utterly liberating aspect pertaining to human life. What Luther is actually saying is that sin is a condition under which all creatures are living and that no creature can do anything to alter this condition. Sin is a human *conditio sine qua non*, for as humans we all fail in our inter-human enterprises. Sin is not bound to the body or sexuality, but to being human. This entails that no one human is more perfect or more sinful than others, the *simul justus et peccator* principle thus providing us with immense reconciliatory aspects. The principle says that humans as God's creatures are embraced by God's grace despite sin. The human deficit is divinely embraced, without anyone having to do special actions or pay special dues in order to be graced.

SHAPING THE HUMAN: THE EDUCATION OF ALL

Luther has been accused of reducing the educational options for girls and career options for women due to his stark criticism of monastic life. However, Luther's criticism should be seen against the backdrop of his own experience as an Augustinian friar and his understanding of human freedom as a gift of God that does not set divides between humans *coram Deo*, only different charismata to be lived out in service of the common faith.²³ Because monastic life claims to be an elite ranking higher than other estates, with celibacy as a *status perfectionis*, it is against evangelical freedom in Luther's perception. Only in one respect does the monastic life live out evangelical freedom, namely in the monastic schools that offered children of both sexes an education. But different from the monastic elite schools for the children of nobility and the affluent bourgeoisie, Luther emphasizes the importance of free Christian schools for boys and girls for the sake of a well-educated worldly regime with humanist standards. His advice is: "to establish the very best schools for both boys and girls at all places because in order to maintain its worldly estate outwardly the world must have good and capable men and women."²⁴ It is possible to interpret Luther's text as if he advices more schooling of boys than of girls regarding worldly ministries,²⁵ though this

22. Luther, *Rationis Latomianae confutatio*, WA 8, 103–15.
23. Luther, *De votis monastici iudicium*, WA 8, 612.
24. Luther, *An die Ratherren aller Städte deutsches Lands, dass sie christliche Schulen aufrichten und erhalten sollen*, WA 15, 44. Cf. Luther, *De votis monastici iudicium*, WA 8, 615: "et puellae quoque erudiebantur."
25. E.g., Karant-Nunn and Wiesner-Hanks, *Luther on Women*, 10.

is not at the heart of his message. Actually, Luther only explicitly requests more education pertaining to spiritual ministries and without making sex divides. His argument is that those who are to serve in the spiritual regime, such as male and female teachers, should learn more than others because they should be instrumental in elevating the cultural standard of the entire people. Hence, Luther recommends that those amongst capable people, both male and female, who are expected to hold spiritual ministries, "lerer und lereryn, prediger und andern geistlichen emptern," should be given more education.[26] Thus, Luther invited educated women to teach the little girls publicly and show their work as an example for others.[27]

By his call, Luther evoked a surge of building girls' schools in Protestant areas. The impact of this aspect of democratizing education, making it free for everyone, has been studied by e.g. social economists who found that a larger share of Protestants in Prussia in the nineteenth century decreased the gender gap in basic education (1816) as well as in literacy among the adult population (1871).[28] Limited as such a study may be, it points to the liberating and emancipating aspects of giving all children some education in common schools and not just the elite in convent schools. Besides, we know that the common school system has been a constitutive factor in the development of democratic societies.

HUMAN—NOT DIVINE: SEEING THE WORLD FROM BELOW

Luther has also been criticized for devaluating Mary and thereby discharging a female figure from the divine power center. But this is a huge misunderstanding of his eminent transformation of the role of Mary as supernatural being to a human being. Although he remains faithful to the confessing to Mary as virgin and the sinless Mother of God,[29] his most coherent and comprehensive interpretation of Mary's role is based on the lowly and poor maiden of Luke 1, who by her earthly humanity subverts inhuman earthly powers.[30] Luther utilizes his commentary on the *Magnificat* in his reforma-

---

26. Luther, *An die Ratherren aller Städte deutsches Lands, dass sie christliche Schulen aufrichten und erhalten sollen*, WA 15, 47; 15, 9–53.

27. Luther, *Luther an Else von Kanitz*, WABr 4, 236 (Letter 1133), a letter from 1527 in which he asks "the honorable and virtuous Maiden Else von Kanitz" to come and instruct the little girls in Wittenberg.

28. Becker, "Luther and the Girls: Religious Denomination and the Female Education Gap in Nineteenth-Century Prussia," 777–805.

29. E.g., Luther, *Epistel am Sonntag nach dem Christtage, Gal. 1–7*, WA 10.I, 352–69.

30. Luther, *Das Magnificat verdeutschet und ausgelegt*, WA 7, 538–604.

tion program by addressing it to his supporter, Prince John Frederick, Duke of Saxony, as a "Fürstenspiegel" written in the vernacular for laypeople.

Luther's choice of Mary's hymn to God is not arbitrary. It stems from a tradition in primarily the prophetic literature of the Old Testament called "the poor of Jahve," in which poverty is perceived the collective sin of a society unable to create justice in accordance with the purpose of God's creation. The *Magnificat* links the understanding of the history of Israel as God's history with his people and the message about Christ who liberates and saves all people, and it tells about real experiences of richness versus poverty and real hopes directed toward the savior of the wretched, thus weaving the ecclesiological experiences of God's people together with their eschatological hopes.

Luther takes this line of tradition and elaborates it. Furthermore, as the vernacularization of scripture is an important aspect to his church political purpose, he translates it from Greek into German. Thus, in his return to the German John Frederick's interest in the cause of the Reformation Luther combines his understanding of God's saving practice with his view on justice and princely power, contrasting the rich and powerful prince with the poor and powerless girl.[31] Luther is indeed writing about real and concrete poverty that cannot be beautified in any way in his reminder of how to employ worldly power rightly. Explicating the depth and reality of Mary's poverty, disgrace, and lowliness, Luther presents her hymn as a paradigm of God's just ruling from which the prince should learn: "God is the kind of Lord who does nothing but exalt those of low degree and put down the mighty from their thrones." In Luther's perception, God does his salutary work by subverting the ungodly social architecture, by healing the broken, and even breaking what is whole. This Mary has learned from the Holy Spirit and honors God for it, and Luther expects the prince to learn the same from Mary's God.

Hence, Luther employs *Magnificat* as a "program" for his ecclesio-political goals: to cleanse the God relationship from devotional amends that function as mere plaster without healing what is broken. Also a lord and ruler must love his subjects and have for his chief concern not how to live at ease but how to uplift and improve his people, or he rules only for the perdition of his soul. Such an understanding of government or governing propagated as the very creational and salutary program designed by God opens windows to a democratization program.

---

31. For a fuller exposition of this in contrast with a Mariology of glory, see Wiberg Pedersen, "'The Holy Spirit shall come upon you.' Mary—the Human 'Locus' for the Holy Spirit," 23–41. I am drawing on this earlier article here.

How Luther liberates his whole argumentation from any kind of ecclesial piety or sacramentality can hardly be overemphasized. His argument is theological. No doubt, the text will gain by being read intertextually with Luther's address to the nobility and related to his idea of the two realms. But the main point here is that Luther reminds those who are in rule that they have a special responsibility in taking care of God's creation. Mary represents the real human being as part of God's creation. Luther breaks with tradition by pulling down Mary from all pedestals and presents her—*sola scriptura*—as someone ordinary: "a poor and plain citizen's daughter." Mary is an ordinary woman who possesses the human characteristics, which enable her to experience divine grace and justice and to bear Christ.

Mary's lowly state is of immense importance in Luther's exposition not only as a contrast to elite worldly powers but also as a contrast to elite monastic and devotional piety. Hence, he makes a point of translating the Greek term for humility, *tapeinåsin teis douleis* (Luke 1:48), into "lowly estate" in a social sense "as that of human beings who are poor, sick, hungry, thirsty, in prison, suffering, and dying." Humility is not some deed that frees people of sin and perdition in the sight of God. Luther's focus is human beings living an ordinary and responsible human life together with other human beings. In that respect one might say that Luther is in fact propounding an everyday theology centered round the human being as God's graced creation.

Luther does not denigrate Mary but translates her role into liberating aspects that point toward a humanization and a democratization of the worldly regime.

CONCLUSION

However we study Luther's vast text corpus we get a multifaceted picture of a man who on his view of women (and so many other things) is torn between his own more modern ideas and the conventions and traditions of his time.[32] We should not be surprised that the texts and views of Luther reflect ambivalence or self-contradiction but use it constructively as deliberations from a (hu)man (being) whose own approach to theology was constructive and under process as in "reformation," not fixed and absolute. Luther's *opera omnia*, totaling more than 100 volumes in the *Weimar Edition* and encompassing such different genres as treatises, lectures, commentaries, sermons and letters (besides the table talks recorded by others), is evidence of a differentiating approach to theology and politics, including view of gender, ethnicity and social status. Hence, it is possible to constructively sort out the

---

32. Wiberg Pedersen, "A Man Caught Between Bad Anthropology and Good Theology," 190–200.

liberating aspects in Luther's theology that point forward to the future for us as humans in our post-secular global world. One must constantly return to the sources and simultaneously be aware of context and such hermeneutical questions as genre, rhetoric, addressee, situation and purpose.

I have here proposed what one could also label an ecumenical approach, namely that of taking as my point of departure a common ground for all humans by way of the category *homo*, and in this endeavor perceive Luther's ambivalences and self-contradictions, e.g. the ambivalence toward women and his own maleness (*Männlichkeit*) as a mode of *adiaphora*, the indifferent difference, or indifferent hybridity. I contend that by combining (or confronting) Luther's ambivalences with his clear cut good theology of justice and grace in which *homo*, the human being, is *the* central constitutive category, it is possible to lift up aspects that point to the future. When I suggest a post-gender politics, it is because there is a need for human beings to again search out a common ground beyond all the conflicts and differences that have become spiraling, hegemonic powers. From the cosmic *homo* as a common ground, we can then maintain our many differences, but as *adiaphora*, indifferent differences.

BIBLIOGRAPHY

Becker, Sascha O. "Luther and the Girls: Religious Denomination and the Female Education Gap in Nineteenth-Century Prussia." In *Journal of Economics* 4 (2008) 777–805.

Cole, Richard Glenn. "Martin Luther's Use of Rhetorical masks for Jews, princes, Clerics, and other Enemies: The Problem of Meaning in a Post Modern Age." *Journal of Religious History* 37/3 (2013) 309–21.

Feminist Theology & Lutheran Thought: Dialog 49/3, 2010.

Gadamer, Hans-Georg. *Truth and Method*. New York: Continuum, 2003.

Giesecke, Michael. *Die Entdeckung der kommunikativen Welt: Studien zur Kulturvergleichen Mediengeschichte*. Frankfurt am Main: Suhrkamp, 2007.

Guðmundsdóttir, Arnfriður. *Meeting God on the Cross: Christ, the Cross, and the Feminist Critique*. Oxford: Oxford University Press, 2010.

Karant-Nunn, Susan C., and Merry E. Wiesner-Hanks. *Luther on Women: A Sourcebook*. Cambridge: Cambridge University Press, 2003.

Luther, Martin. *An die Ratherren aller Städte deutsches Lands, dass sie christliche Schulen aufrichten und erhalten sollen* (1524). WA 15. Weimar: Hermann Böhlaus Nachfolger, 1899.

———. *Das Magnificat verdeutschet und ausgelegt* (1521). WA 7. Weimar: Hermann Böhlaus Nachfolger, 1897.

———. *De Captivitate Babylonica ecclesiae praeludium* (1520). WA 6. Weimar: Hermann Böhlau, 1888.

———. *De instituendis ministris ecclesiae* (1523). WA 12. Weimar: Hermann Böhlaus Nachfolger, 1891.

———. *De libertate christiana/Von der Freiheit eines Christenmenschen* (1520); WA 7. Weimar: Hermann Böhlaus Nachfolger, 1897.

———. *Der Grosse Katechismus* (1529). WA 30, Erste Abteilung. Weimar: Hermann Böhlaus Nachfolger, 1910.

———. *De votis monastici iudicium* (1521). WA 8. Weimar: Hermann Böhlaus Nachfolger, 1889.

———. *Disputatio Heidelbergae habita* (1518). WA 1. Weimar: Hermann Böhlau, 1883.

———. *Ein Sermon von dem neuen Testament* (1520). WA 6. Weimar: Hermann Böhlau, 1888.

———. *Epistel am Sonntag nach dem Christtage*, Gal. 1–7 (Kirchenpostille 1522). WA 10, Erste Abteilung. Weimar: Hermann Böhlaus Nachfolger, 1910.

———. *Eyn klein Unterricht, was man ynn den Euangeliis suchen und gewarten soll* (1521). WA 10, Erste Abteilung. Weimar: Hermann Böhlaus Nachfolger, 1910.

———. *In epistolam S Pauli ad Galatas Commentarius* (1535). WA 40, Erste Abteilung. Weimar: Hermann Böhlaus Nachfolger, 1911; WA 40, Zweite Abteilung. Weimar: Hermann Böhlaus Nachfolger, 1914.

———. *Luther an Else von Kanitz* (1527). WABr 4. Weimar: Hermann Böhlaus Nachfolger 1933.

———. *Luther an Nikolaus Hausmann* (1528). WABr 4. Weimar: Hermann Böhlaus Nachfolger 1933.

———. *Luther an Spalatin* (1519). WABr 1. Weimar: Hermann Böhlaus Nachfolger 1930.

———. *Rationis Latomianae confutatio* (1521). WA 8. Weimar: Hermann Böhlaus Nachfolger, 1889.

———. *Sermon von dem Wucher* (1520). WA 6. Weimar: Hermann Böhlau, 1888.

———. *Von den Konziliis und Kirchen* (1539). WA 50. Weimar: Hermann Böhlaus Nachfolger, 1914.

Oberman, Heiko A. *Luther: Mensch zwischen Gott und Teufel*, Berlin: Severin und Seitler, 1982.

Solberg, Mary M. *Compelling Knowledge: A Feminist Proposal for an Epistemology of the Cross*. New York: State University of New York Press, 1997.

Streufert, Mary J., editor. *Transformative Lutheran Theologies: Feminist, Womanist, and Mujerista Perspectives*. Minneapolis: Fortress, 2010.

Thompson, Deanna. *Crossing the Divide: Luther, Feminism, and the Cross*. Minneapolis: Fortress, 2004.

Wiberg Pedersen, Else Marie. "'The Holy Spirit shall come upon you.' Mary—the Human 'Locus' for the Holy Spirit." In *Cracks in the Walls: Essays on Spirituality, Ecumenicity and Ethics* edited by Else Marie Wiberg Pedersen et al., 23–41. Frankfurt am Main: Peter Lang, 2005.

———. "A Man Caught Between Bad Anthropology and Good Theology? Martin Luther's View of Women Generally and of Mary Specifically." *Dialog* 3 (2010) 190–200.

———, editor. "Disciplined Freedom, or Free versus Slave? Recuperating Luther for Feminist Theology in an Age of Terror." *Lutherjahrbuch*, 2013.

Wiesner-Hanks, Merry. "Women and the Reformations: Reflections on Recent Research." *History Compass* 2 (2004) 1–27.

8

Re-Embracing the Body of Jesus Christ

A Queer, Lutheran Theology of the Body of Christ

MARY ELISE LOWE

In the 1980s, many North American feminist theologians asked challenging questions about the salvific role and function of Jesus' "male" body. Today, lesbian, gay, bisexual, trans*, queer, and intersex (LGBTQI) theologians are asking closely-related questions about Jesus' gender, biological sex, and embodiment.¹ These theologians argue that historic claims that Jesus was male, had a masculine essence, was heterosexual and celibate have been theologically destructive and physically harmful for queer persons.² They offer portraits of Jesus as bisexual, indecent, trans*, cross-dressing, nomadic, Queer, Chalcedic, and displaced, and each of these images involve claims about Jesus' body.

Many queer theologians rely on the work of theorist Judith Butler to critique and reconstruct theological claims about bodies, sex, gender, and Jesus Christ. Three of her theoretical insights are heavily employed: (1) gender is repeatedly performed, (2) biological sex is constructed, and (3) the body is a process of materialization. I describe her approach as a textualist,

---

1. "Trans* . . . the asterisk is meant to show a more inclusive attitude towards the multitude of people under the transgender umbrella." See *Trans* 101*: Primer and Vocabulary*.

2. "'Queer,'(. . .) demarcates (. . .) a positionality that is not restricted to lesbians and gay men but is in fact available to anyone who is or who feels marginalized because of his or her sexual practices." Halperin, *Saint Foucault: Towards A Gay Hagiography*, 62.

materialized theory of the body.³ As a queer theologian, I am intrigued by the way Judith Butler helps LGBTQI Christians challenge heteronormativity in Christian theology.⁴ However, several queer Christologies which use her theories, seem to lay aside the physical, time-bound, suffering, and resurrected (yet wounded) body of Jesus Christ. And if we let go of Jesus' body, then liberating claims about the incarnation, human bodies, the Eucharist, and the church are in danger of being laid aside as well. This research challenges the dis-embodiment found in some queer Christologies and argues instead for a fully-embodied queer Christology that weaves in commitments from Martin Luther's theology, especially his radical view of the incarnation, his assertion that the finite can bear the infinite, his view of the human person as *totus homo*, and his theology of the cross. I also utilize biologist Anne Fausto-Sterling's research on the complexity of human sexual variation and the theory of embodied cognition developed by philosopher Mark Johnson, who uses cognitive science to argue that bodies profoundly shape identity, perception, reason, and how one experiences the world.

JUDITH BUTLER'S TEXTUALIST, MATERIALIZED THEORY OF THE BODY

The queer Christologies surveyed here rely on Judith Butler's textualist, materialized approach to the body and her interrelated theories on gender and sex. She avers that gender is repeatedly performed; it does not spring from an inborn essence, nor fall into the categories of masculine and feminine. Instead, gender is an ongoing performance that creates the illusion of a stable gender identity through constant repetition. She writes, "[N]o gender is 'expressed' by actions, gestures, or speech but (. . .) the performance of gender produces retroactively the illusion that there is an inner gender core."⁵ She also contends that biological sexual differentiation is not given: an individual's genitals do not create a particular type of person.⁶ Instead physical sexual differentiation is constructed in language, culture, and discourses, especially legal, medical, and religious discourses. Judith Butler's theories about gender and sex emerge from her view of the body. "What I

---

3. Susan Bordo calls Judith Butler's view of the body a textualist approach. Bordo, "Review Essay: Postmodern Subjects, Postmodern Bodies," 169.

4. Judith Butler's theory on gender is "fast achieving the status of dogma in some American women's studies and religious studies circles." Coakley, "The Eschatological Body: Gender, Transformation, and God," 61.

5. Butler, *Psychic Life of Power: Theories in Subjection*, 144.

6. Butler, *Bodies That Matter: On the Discursive Limits of Sex*, 2–3.

would propose (. . .) is a return to the notion of matter, not as a site or surface, but as *a process of materialization that stabilizes over time to produce the effects of boundary, fixity, and surface we call matter.*[7] Elsewhere she writes, "[T]he body becomes its gender through a series of acts. (. . .) one might try to reconceive the gendered body as the legacy of sedimented acts rather than a predetermined or foreclosed structure."[8] To better understand her proposal, think of the body as a blank piece of paper. It exists, but the paper does not carry meaning until something is written upon it. Likewise, although the body exists, it bears little meaning of its own until meaning is attached to it through the process of materialization.[9] Judith Butler's theories help queer theologians re-conceive of Jesus' sex, gender, and body.[10] However, the body seems to fade from view in these proposals, and they offer little reflection on how Jesus' body constituted his identity, reason, and ministerial vision.[11]

THE TEXTUALIST, MATERIALIZED BODY OF JESUS CHRIST IN QUEER CHRISTOLOGIES

Marcella Althaus-Reid's queer Christology is informed by queer theory and postcolonial critiques. She rejects the traditional "decent" images of Jesus Christ as male, celibate, asexual, and passive. Instead Marcella Althaus-Reid asks Christians to see Jesus as the "indecent" Christ who is in and with those whom many would call indecent today, such as sex workers and poor women. "If as the liberationists claim, Christ is neither male nor female in the sense that Christ represents the community of the poor, then Christ should be portrayed as a girl prostituted in Buenos Aires in a public toilet by two men."[12]

Marcella Althaus-Reid contends that there is no "real" meaning or body behind our interpretations of it in language, discourse, or history. And she applies this insight to Jesus Christ, stating that we have no access to the "coherent Jesus."

---

7. Ibid., 9.

8. Butler, "Performance Acts and Gender Constitution: An Essay in Phenomenology and Feminist Theory," 523.

9. Butler, *Bodies That Matter*, xi;

10. Cheng, *From Sin to Amazing Grace: Discovering the Queer Christ*; Cornwall, *Controversies in Queer Theology*.

11. Ministerial vision is an embodied way of describing Jesus' ministry, see Williams, *Sisters in the Wilderness: The Challenge of Womanist God-Talk*, 164–65.

12. Althaus-Reid, *From Feminist Theology to Indecent Theology*, 84.

> Traces of the obscene in Jesus (. . .) prevent us from falling into what Butler calls 'the illusion of the true body beyond the law' (Butler, 1990: 93). There is no pure, incorruptible and unique, coherent Jesus beyond the law of sexual regulation of heterosexual Systematic Theology. (. . .) God cannot be considered one body only beyond the law. God appears indecent.[13]

Marcella Althaus-Reid lets go of the coherent Jesus and offers an image of an Ultra or Bi Christ who represents and includes persons with a variety of sexual practices and gender identities. She writes, "[T]here is not just *The Christ* but a diverse Ultra Christ, incarnated (located) in our specific time and communities."[14] But in her desire to welcome all into Christ and locate Christ in the world today, has Marcella Althaus-Reid given up on the embodied and time-bound Jesus?

Tat-siong Benny Liew develops a queer Christology that resists hetero-masculinist interpretations of Jesus. His constructive work focuses on the portrait of Jesus found in the *Gospel of John*. He suggests that Jesus crosses socially-accepted boundaries about sex, gender, race, clothing, speech, and water. Tat-siong Benny Liew portrays Jesus as a cross-dresser or transvestite who performs, speaks, and acts like a woman.

> I want to suggest an illegibility or indeterminacy that displaces the male and/or female structure. Jesus' cross-dressing body in John is a truly porous and polysemous site-sight in which a collection or range of gender meanings converge, collude, collide and compete with each other. (. . .) John's cross-dressing Jesus shows that a so-called 'core' is but a(n significant) effect of bodily acts (Butler) 1990.[15]

Explicitly referring to Judith Butler's theories, Tat-siong Benny Liew argues that Jesus' body becomes a site-sight in which, on, and through Jesus transgresses borders of gender, sex, race-ethnicity, and nation. In John's gospel, Jesus relates to water the way a woman would. "John's constant references to Jesus wanting water (4:7; 19:28), giving water (6:35), and leaking water (19:34) speak to Jesus' gender indeterminacy and hence his cross-dressing and other queer desires that put out of place everything that the *Ioudaioa* treasure."[16] Although Tat-siong Benny Liew draws on the powerful image

---

13. Althaus-Reid, *Indecent Theology: Theological Perversions in Sex, Gender, and Politics*, 110.

14. Ibid., 117.

15. Liew, "Queering Closets and Perverting Desires: Cross-Examining John's Engendering and Trans-Gendering Word Across Different Worlds," 260.

16. Ibid., 278–79.

of Jesus leaking water from his pierced side at the crucifixion, he offers no reflection on how this piercing may have mattered to the embodied Jesus.

In Tricia Sheffield's Christology, she challenges how the body of Jesus has been read through dominant heteronormative (and Augustinian) lenses that support the dualistic theologies of imperial Christianity. She reflects on how transgendered individuals "destabilize the gender binary by their lived bodily experiences, reflecting the queer Chalcedic body of both/and."[17] Then she draws on the Council of Chalcedon's confession that Jesus Christ was/ is two natures (divine and human) undivided in one person. This Chalcedic transgendered Christ passes the boundaries between human and divine like trans* individuals pass sex and gender boundaries.

> What I argue is *this* body is a disruptive performance entity that queers the fallacy of dichotomous thinking through its refusal to be categorized as either/or: it is not human, it is not divine, yet it is both and none. (. . .) God is passing for human, and Jesus is passing for divine, and so they are both transgressively intertwined.[18]

Tricia Sheffield's critique and proposal are heavily indebted to Judith Butler. Gender is performed, biological sex is constructed, and the body—in this case, Jesus Christ's body—is ambiguous. "His body becomes a site that not only contains the gender binary but also exposes it as fictive by constructing a third, fourth, or fifth sex."[19] Although Tricia Sheffield's use of Judith Butler's theory produces a creative and trans* portrait of Jesus, she does not offer any significant reflection on the actual body of Jesus Christ nor explore how his bodily experiences shaped his ministerial vision. And I wonder if her suggestion that the human and the divine are *passing* for one another is consistent with the biblical witness that Jesus Christ *is* God and human and not just *passing* as God and human.

Graham Ward's view of the body is similar to Judith Butler's in that the body is a sign or process of materialization. But he argues that Jesus' body is different. "[O]nly the body of Christ (. . .) is the true body. (. . .) Christ's body as the true body is the pure sign—the only sign which is self-defining."[20] Ward then suggests that all bodies—even Jesus'—are transcorporeal because of their origin and destiny in God, not because of the way the body is

---

17. Sheffield, "Performing Jesus: A Queer Counternarrative of Embodied Transgression," 238.
18. Ibid., 243.
19. Ibid., 247.
20. Ward, *Cities of God*, 93.

materialized in language. And even Jesus' body takes on some meaning and identity in relationship to other signs and bodies.

> The body of Christ (. . .) is a body which constantly exceeds itself, figured forth in signs (. . .) the body (. . .) disseminates itself through a myriad of other bodies, which are themselves other signs where tissue is also a text. (. . .) 'To matter' is 'to materialise' and 'to mean', to return to Judith Butler's comment.[21]

Graham Ward proposes that the body of Jesus Christ also goes through a process of displacements at the incarnation, circumcision, transfiguration, Eucharist, crucifixion, resurrection, and ascension. At these moments, the body of Jesus is displaced and is continually refigured in the church. In physics, displacement defines where one point exists in relation to another, and Graham Ward uses displacement to connect the displaced body of Christ to Jesus' body. "What happens at the ascension, theologically constitutes a critical moment in a series of displacements (. . .) of the male body of Jesus Christ such that the body of Christ (. . .) become[s] multi-gendered."[22] Once again it seems fair to ask whether the body of Jesus Christ in this Christology is a time-bound, fleshy body like all others.

CHALLENGES TO THE TEXTUALIST, MATERIALIZED BODY OF JESUS CHRIST

All of these proposals help queer Christians hear echoes of their own stories in Jesus' story. However some of the substantive challenges put to Judith Butler's theory of the body can be brought to bear on these queer proposals. In her review of *Gender Trouble*, theorist Susan Bordo writes, "Butler's analysis of how gender is constituted and subverted takes the body as just such a 'text' whose meanings can be analyzed in abstraction from experience, history, material practice and context."[23] Disability theorist Ellen Samuels states, "the fragmented body parts littering the landscape are so firmly located within the imaginary that it is not even necessary for Butler to clarify at some point that she is not talking about actual bodies."[24] And though many trans* theorists applaud Judith Butler's work, Jay Prossser argues that, "transsexual autobiographies challenge theory's cynicism over identity's embodiment. (. . .) the transssexual does not approach the body as

21. Ibid., 92.
22. Ward, "Bodies: The Displaced Body of Jesus Christ," 163.
23. Bordo, "Review Essay: Postmodern Subjects, Postmodern Bodies," 170.
24. Samuels, "Critical Divides: Judith Butler's Body Theory and the Question of Disability," 70.

an immaterial provisional surround but, on the contrary, as the very 'seat' of the self."[25]

These queer portraits of Jesus Christ are also at odds with emerging scientific insights about human sexuality and the interconnectedness of mind and body. Anne Fausto-Sterling both echoes and challenges the textualist, materialized theory of the body. On one hand, her research regarding persons who are born intersex demonstrates that that there is a wide variety of sexual differentiation in humans, and it shows how sex is constructed by supposedly "objective" science.[26] "[S]ex and gender are best conceptualized as points in a multidimensional space. (. . .) What has become increasingly clear is that one can find levels of masculinity and femininity in almost every possible permutation."[27] On the other hand, she demonstrates that behavior and cognition are deeply rooted in the body and its environment. Some research shows that blind people who read braille "have recruited a region of the cortex that sighted people use to process visual information (. . .) and instead use it to process tactile sensations."[28] Their bodies have adapted in measurable ways to changes in vision, touch, perception, and cognition. Mind is inseparable from fingertips. Similarly, I argue that the body of Jesus Christ cannot merely be transgressed or displaced to the degree argued in some queer Christologies.

Research from cognitive science also counters the textualist, materialized theory of the body. Mark Johnson writes, "[T]*he ways our bodies work and the nature of our bodily encounters with our environments shape the nature of reason itself.*"[29] The body itself shapes an individual's abstract reason, perception, and identity. "Reason does not drop down from above like a transcendent dove; rather it emerges from the 'corporeal' logic and inference structure of our bodily, sensorimotor experience."[30] Mark Johnson explains that the human ability to see and categorize color is structured by the color cones in the retina, which allow most humans to perceive color through the color pairs of red-green, yellow-blue, and white-black. There is no category for "green" external to the human mind. Rather, "color catego-

25. Prosser, *Second Skins: The Body Narratives of Transsexuality*, 67.

26. "Estimates suggest that at least 1 in 2,500 children in Europe and North America is born with an intersex/DSD condition." Sharon Preves, *Intersex and Identity: The Contested Self*, quoted in Cornwall, *Sex and Uncertainty in the Body of Christ: Intersex Conditions and Christian Theology*, 2.

27. Fausto-Sterling, "The Five Sexes Revisited."

28. Fausto-Sterling, *Sexing the Body: Gender Politics and the Construction of Sexuality*, 241.

29. Johnson, "The Meaning of the Body," 20.

30. Johnson, "Embodied Reason," 86.

ries are a product of (1) our bodies and brains and (2) the reflectances of objects in the world."³¹ The matter of the bodies matters! The body of Jesus Christ mattered, and the environment in which he lived shaped Jesus' identity, perception, reasoning, and ministerial vision. Therefore christological proposals in which Jesus crosses over or transgresses his body need to be re-thought.

Finally, queer portraits of the textualist, materialized body of Jesus Christ may also echo the claims of ancient Docetism, which—believing that matter is opposed to spirit—argued that Jesus Christ only appeared human. In these queer proposals, the body of Jesus is so Ultra, cross-dressing, Chalcedic or displaced that his physical body almost disappears. If the body of Jesus can be *everything,* is it *anything*? Queer theologians may be laying aside the very body of Jesus Christ that grounds claims about the incarnation, human bodies, the Eucharist, and the body of Christ that is the church. And—although Luther may seem an odd ally—I suggest that his commitments to the radical incarnation, the presence of the infinite in the finite, *totus homo* (whole person), and the theology of the cross can help queer Christians re-embrace the physical, time-bound body of Jesus Christ.³²

QUEERING THE RADICAL INCARNATION

The reader will recall that Marcella Althaus-Reid suggests that Christ be reconceived of as indecent, Bi, or Ultra. She points to traditional claims that assume Jesus was celibate and straight, and possessed a male or masculine essence. The topic of essentialism—that one is born gay or straight or that one bears an essence of femaleness or maleness—is a complex issue. On one hand many find comfort in the assertion that they were born with a gay or lesbian essence. Others reject essentialism because it ignores the complexity of sexuality and gender and leads to the belief that there is one—usually-straight—way to be male or female. And trans* individuals often experience a strong sense of being male or female that is incongruent with their physical body. Surely Marcella Althaus-Reid's theology avoids essentialism, but I wonder if her proposal asks us to lay aside the fully-embodied Jesus Christ described in the gospels as time-bound, walking, and suffering. Here, Luther's radically incarnational theology woven together with Anne

31. Ibid., 87.

32. It may seem incongruous to employ Luther's theology. After all he wrote awful things about Muslims, "Italian marriages," and the Jewish people. But those of us who grapple with the historic, elite, "male" theologians, are tasked with drawing on their useful contributions, and then, separating their wisdom (wheat) from their dehumanizing theology (chaff).

Fausto-Sterling's insights can re-ground our christological claims in Jesus' body without re-inscribing an essentialist, male portrait of Jesus Christ.

Luther's incarnational emphasis counters the textualist, materialized view of the body. He wrote, "Christ (. . .) assumed true human nature, not the nature of an immaterial phantom, and that He became a natural man like any other man of flesh and blood. (. . .) He had eyes, ears, mouth, nose, chest, stomach, hands, and feet just as you and I do. He took the breast."[33] Luther taught that because of the incarnation, God and creation are connected in a new way. According to Kurt Hendel, Luther "was convinced that the physical and the spiritual, the material and the divine are not irreconcilable opposites but are intimately yoked in God's saving and life-giving work."[34] The incarnation is where this intimate yoking of God and creation is most evident. "I do not know of any God except him who was made flesh, nor do I want to have another. And there is no other God who could save us, besides the God incarnate. Therefore we should not suffer his humanity to be underestimated or neglected."[35]

Luther's incarnational perspective led him to reject any form of dualism that devalued the body. According to Hermann Sasse, "Over and against the Platonic separation of body and soul, he defended biblical anthropology."[36] Because the material (body) can bear the spiritual (Word or Son), Luther could say that Jesus Christ was fully human without repeating the metaphysical dualisms common in ancient and medieval thought which prioritized mind over body. Recall that I have argued that Christologies which employ the textualist, materialized view of the body may exhibit a related form of dualism.

For Luther, bodies matter and matter matters! His radical incarnational perspective helps him say that God in Jesus Christ is present in all creation, even now; and all flesh and matter are filled with God's presence and Spirit. Marcella Althaus-Reid's argues that the Ultra Christ in the world today is not bound to the "coherent" Jesus. In contrast, Luther's incarnational commitment allows him to say that God in Christ is in creation without leaving the body of Jesus behind. "Moreover, we believe that Christ, according to his human nature, is put over all creatures (. . .) and fills all things. (. . .) Not only

---

33. Luther, *The Gospel of Saint John*, LW 22, 113.

34. Hendel, "*Finitum capax infiniti*: Luther's Radical Incarnational Perspective," 427.

35. Martin Luther, "The Marburg Colloquy," quoted in Sasse, *This is My Body: Luther's Contention for the Real Presence in the Sacrament of the Altar*, 203.

36. Sasse, *This is My Body*, 150.

according to his divine nature, but also according to his human nature, he... has all things in his hand, and is present everywhere."[37]

Anne Fausto-Sterling's insights into the variety of human sexuality can also help queer theologians hold on to the body of Jesus Christ without falling into the traps of dualism or essentialism. Her research reveals more than two sexes, and that who counts as "androgynous," "intersex," "male," or "female" is not easy to discern. This work can help queer theologians to say that even though the tradition has taught that Jesus Christ was "male," we are no longer sure what "male" means. Thus, appeals to an essence that is masculine or feminine, male or female, or straight or gay, must be called into question as well. This means that the 'maleness' of Jesus Christ need no longer be used to support patriarchy and heteronormativity, and *hirs* sexed body no longer needs to be set aside because it valorizes male over female (hirs is a gender neutral possessive pronoun). And this affirmation of Jesus Christ's multidimensional, sexed body is an affirmation of the multidimensionality of our bodies as well.

QUEERING THE FINITE CAN BEAR THE INFINITE

Tricia Sheffield develops a transgendered Christ who crosses the boundaries between male and female and passes as human and divine. But if the body of Jesus Christ is Chalcedic and passing, then the incarnation may be compromised, as well as the accompanying promise that Jesus Christ is in the bread and wine, uniting believers in the body of Christ. Since many LGBTQI persons have been excluded from their families and congregations because of who they are, it is imperative that queer Christians hold on to the body of Jesus Christ as a source of identity and community.

In contrast to Tricia Sheffield's metaphor of passing, Luther appealed to the logic of the incarnation to show that the finite can bear the infinite—*finitum est capax infiniti*. According to Kurt Hendel, "The Reformer thus clearly differentiated himself from his sacramental opponents by insisting that (...) *finitum est capax infiniti*."[38] This occurs at the incarnation, in God's ongoing presence in creation, in the bread and the wine, and in the bodies of believers. Luther wrote, "Christ is God and man, and his humanity has become one person with God (...) so that he remains perfectly united with him. (...) If God and man are one person (...) so united that they belong together more intimately than body and soul, then Christ must also be man wherever he is God."[39] Luther pointed to the sacramental union of Jesus

37. Luther, *Confession Concerning Christ's Supper*, LW 37, 342.
38. Hendel, "*Finitum capax infiniti*," 430.
39. Luther, *Confession Concerning Christ's Supper*, LW 37, 228–29.

Christ and the elements in the Lord's Supper as a mystery accomplished through the Word. "It is enough for me to know that the word which I hear and the body which I take are truly those of my Lord and God. (. . .) The body which you take and the word which you hear are his who holds in his hands the entire world and who is everywhere."[40]

For those queer Christians who have been rejected by their families and congregations, the promise that Jesus Christ is present in the bread and wine and in the bodies of believers offers a way to envision intimate community. Hear Luther's words,

> And through the interchange (. . .) we become one loaf. (. . .) Again through this same love, we are to be changed and to make the infirmities of all other Christians our own; we are to take upon ourselves their form and necessity. (. . .) This is real fellowship, In this way we are changed into one another and are made into a community by love [41]

Luther sets aside the familiar boundaries of finite/infinite and self/other. The presence of the infinite God in Jesus Christ and in the world creates the basis for an embodied union that grounds Christian life and vocation. "[W]e permit all Christians to be partakers in us. (. . .) there is one bread, one drink, one body, one community. This is the true unity of Christian brethren."[42] If a principle task of queer theology is to cross boundaries, then bridging the chasm between self and other through the Lord's Supper is indeed transgressive and a resource for fully embodied community.

Finally, Luther's beliefs that the finite can bear the infinite, and that there is a sacramental union among believers resonates with what some emerging research shows regarding how human subjectivity, creativity, sexuality, and reason are constituted by a creature's environment, relations, and embodiment. Anne Fausto-Sterling's research shows that when mother rats do not groom (lick) male pups as much as they typically would, then as adults these male rats "[h]ad fewer spinal motor neurons in a region of the spinal cord associated with ejaculatory behavior. (. . .) Nature and nurture are not separate here."[43] The pups' environment and the way they were touched and raised actually changed their bodies. Mark Johnson's research into embodied cognition also demonstrates the way that environment and relations impact simple responses in single-celled organisms and more

---

40. Martin Luther, WA 11, 450:8, quoted in Sasse, *This is My Body*, 84–85.

41. Luther, *The Blessed Sacrament of the Holy and True Body of Christ, and the Brotherhoods*, LW 35, 58.

42. Ibid., LW 35, 67.

43. Fausto-Sterling, *Sexing the Body*, 229–30.

complex cognition in primates. In an experiment involving hand sensations in owl monkeys. When the monkeys' hands were altered so they could not process sensory information as they had done previously, the cortical areas "now lacking their previous sensory connections (. . .) were 'colonized' in a couple of weeks by adjacent neural maps with active sensory connections."[44] "Mind" was changed by "body." These scientific insights regarding the interconnections between bodies, environments, and relationships can be interwoven with Luther's emphasis on the presence of the infinite in the finite to provide a valuable resource for queer theologians to articulate new portraits of Jesus Christ, human creatures, and human communities.

QUEERING *TOTUS HOMO*

In Graham Ward's Christology, the transcorporeal body of Jesus Christ "constantly exceeds itself" and becomes "multi-gendered" through the process of displacement. And when reflecting on the crucifixion, he states that "body of Jesus is forgotten."[45] In contrast, Luther taught that every human being is *totus homo*—a whole person. From Luther's perspective, Graham Ward's Christology evinces a sort of dualism of spirit/mind *over* body/flesh that has been particularly harmful for LGBTQI Christians who have been told to cure, discipline, and control their bodies in order to conform to heteronormative demands.

Luther saw this *totus homo* anthropology in the *Letter to the Romans*. Luther wrote, "But because the spirit and the flesh are so intimately bound together into one, although they completely disagree with each other, therefore he [Paul] attributes to himself as a whole person [*totus homo*] the work of both of them, as if he were at the same time completely flesh and completely spirit."[46] According to Lewis Spitz, "Luther did not feel comfortable operating with the dichotomy of a body/soul division or the trichotomy of body/soul/spirit."[47] Luther's view of the human was shaped by his incarnational perspective. Since the Word became flesh, there is no need to view bodies negatively and separate body from spirit.

It is important to recognize what Luther means by "flesh." Kurt Hendel argues, "He [Luther] notes that when flesh and spirit are placed in opposition

---

44. Johnson and Rohrer, "We Are Live Creatures: Embodiment, American Pragmatism, and the Cognitive Organism," 29.
45. Ward, "Bodies: The Displaced Body of Jesus Christ," 169.
46. Luther, *Lectures on Romans*, LW 25, 333; see also LW 25, 336.
47. Spitz, "Luther's Importance for Anthropological Realism," 146.

in Scripture, flesh always refers to our sinful nature which is born of flesh."[48] Luther wrote:

> [T]hroughout Scripture body and soul (. . .) are called flesh. (. . .) The text 'The Word became flesh' supports our position. 'The Word,' that is, the eternal son of God, 'became flesh,' that is, became man, born of the Virgin Mary. In the German language the word 'body' does not denote a corpse; it denotes a living person in possession of body and soul.[49]

Luther is so committed to bodies that he even promises that they will enter heaven. "[T]he true and natural son of God, became man, with flesh and blood like that of any other human; that He became incarnate for our sakes in order that (. . .) our flesh and blood, skin and hair, hands and feet, stomach and back might reside in heaven as God does."[50] To queer persons who have been told that their bodies are sinful and polluting, a queer *totus homo* anthropology says that we are whole and we can be the body of Jesus Christ to one another.

The theory of embodied cognition also offers a way to see Jesus Christ as *totus homo*. Mark Johnson avers that an individual's body constitutes their identity and reason; there is no disembodied mind nor soul. He argues that repeated bodily movements contribute to the formation of image schemas (patterns of consciousness) which then form the basis for conceptual metaphors such as source-path-goal. For example, humans move through physical space in a particular way because of their bodies. This sensorimotor experience of motion through space forms the basis for the source-path-goal metaphor, which is then extended into cognitive processes about pursuing a goal, discovering something new, or going on a journey.[51] In the case of Jesus Christ, the recurring pattern of physically moving from one point to another provided the basis for the source-path-goal pattern in his ministerial vision. His preaching moved from one point to another along a reasoned path—consider the Sermon on the Mount (Matt 5–7). His teaching involved creative parables with a beginning, middle, and end—consider the Parable of the Good Samaritan (Luke 10:25–37). Even his self-understanding of his own ministerial vision was informed by the source-path-goal metaphor—consider his predictions of his passion, death, and return (Mark 8: 27–38). If Jesus' body had been different, he and his

---

48. Hendel "*Finitum capax infiniti*," 424.
49. Luther, *Sermon on the Gospel of John Chapters 1–4*, LW 22, 111.
50. Ibid., LW 22, 110.
51. Johnson, "Embodied Reason," 96.

message would not have been the same. In Johnson's words, "If our bodies were different (. . .) then we would have a different sense of self and different ways of understanding and reasoning."[52] This theory of embodied cognition challenges Graham Ward's Christology and any other proposals that separate Jesus Christ from his body. A queer *totus homo* anthropology offers LGBTQI Christians a word of grace: bodies are gifts from God, animated by God, and God is within flesh and bones. And, if persons are viewed as *totus homo*, then body *and* spirit are of equal precious value—both are gifts of the Word made flesh.

QUEERING THE CROSS

Should queer theologians incorporate Luther's theology of the cross into their liberating work? After all, the cross has often been used by the powerful to tell those with little power to endure their suffering. LGBTQI persons are frequently the victims of violence and told that they deserve to suffer.[53] In his cross-dressing christological proposal, Tat-siong Benny Liew reflects on the water that flowed from Jesus pierced body as he hung on the cross. Parts of Tat-siong Benny Liew's Christology are very persuasive, but where is the en-fleshed, time-bound body of Jesus Christ?

The cross was central to Luther's faith and served as an epistemological lens for theological reflection. In the *Heidelberg Disputation*, he wrote, "He deserves to be called a theologian, however, who comprehends the visible and manifest things of God seen through suffering and the cross."[54] Luther rejected what he called a theology of glory in which God is known from observing creation and humans establish a right relationship with God by performing good works. In contrast, Luther taught:

> The manifest and visible things of God are placed in opposition to the invisible, namely, his human nature, weakness, foolishness. (. . .) Because men misused the knowledge of God through works, God wished again to be recognized in suffering, and to condemn wisdom concerning invisible things by means of wisdom concerning visible things.[55]

Luther is clear that Jesus Christ physically suffered on the cross. "If you must do (. . .) what is distasteful to you: think, how Christ was led (. . .) bound and a captive. (. . .) think, how bitter it was for Christ to have his tender

---

52. Ibid., 99.

53. See Thompson, *Crossing the Divide: Luther, Feminism, and the Cross*.

54. Luther, *Heidelberg Disputation*, LW 31, 52; see also "That These Words of Christ, 'This is My Body,' Etc., Still Stand Firm Against the Fanatics," LW 37, 83.

55. Ibid.

flesh torn, pierced and beaten again and again."⁵⁶ Theologian Mary Solberg highlights the importance of the body in Luther's theology, and argues that the cross "announces God's solidarity with humankind and the value of embodied experience, especially through the incarnation and suffering and death of Jesus the Christ."⁵⁷ Ultimately the cross is empty, death does not have the final word, and Jesus Christ is raised—bodily (yet wounded).

If we embrace the textualized, materialist body of Jesus Christ, it could be that we will not encounter the suffering and water-bearing body that hung on the cross. And this may mean that some Christians will not be able to view their own pain in light of Jesus' story.⁵⁸ And surely most humans feel pain. When we experience tissue damage, nerve fibers carry stimulus through the spinal cord to the brain. Then this impulse is interpreted as pain. And even those individuals who are not persuaded by the theory of embodied cognition agree that pain occurs in body *and* mind. Surely Jesus felt physical discomfort and pain. He was circumcised (Luke 2:21–39), thirsty (John 19:28), hungry (Mark 11:12), tired (John 4:6), and he wept (John 11:35). If Jesus was like us in all things, surely he endured pain in the unity of body and soul.

The story of Jesus' passion and the theology of the cross are central to the faith and life of many queer Christians who want to embrace the body of Jesus Christ and their own bodies. Gay college student Matthew Shepard was beaten, tied to a fence, abandoned, and later died near Laramie, Wyoming in 1998. Afterward, the fence to which Matthew was tied became a pilgrimage site. Some visitors placed stones in the shape of a cross beneath the fence.⁵⁹ Perhaps they saw the cross as a symbol of martyrdom, or they sensed God's presence in that awful drama. Others may have reflected on Matthew's pain in light of Jesus' embodied suffering or they placed the cross of stones to witness to their hope in the resurrection. This is just one example of how the cross functions for many queer Christians who face their own crosses of violence and de-humanization.

Weaving Luther's theological insights into a queer, fully-embodied Christology offers LGBTQI theologians a way to re-embrace the body of Jesus Christ so that the incarnation of the Word made flesh can serve as the warp, weft, and direction of queer theological reflection. Drawing on Mark Johnson's theory of embodied cognition allows us to say that mind is inseparable from body, and that our identities, reason, and creativity spring from our bodies and our embodied experiences. The same can be said of

56. Luther, "Good Friday Sermon," in *Sermons of Martin Luther*, vol. 2, 191.
57. Solberg, "Cross Talk: A Feminist Appreciation of Luther's Theology," 46.
58. See Cone, *The Cross and the Lynching Tree*.
59. Kaufman, "A New Monument to Matthew Shepherd."

Jesus Christ, whose body shaped his perception, identity, reason, and ministerial vision. Finally, knitting Anne Fausto-Sterling's research about the multidimensional character of sexual differentiation into queer Christology helps LGBTQI theologians hold fast to Jesus body without clinging to essentialist ideas about bodies, gender, or sex. Hopefully this proposal will encourage other queer Christians to re-embrace body of Jesus Christ. For it is this very body that offers all the gifts of hope in the resurrection of the body, consolation in the reconciliation of God with creation, and joy in the celebration of our own blessed bodies.

BIBLIOGRAPHY

Althaus-Reid, Marcella. *From Feminist Theology to Indecent Theology*. London: SCM Press, 2004.

———. *Indecent Theology: Theological Perversions in Sex, Gender, and Politics*. New York: Routledge, 2000.

Bordo, Susan. "Review Essay: Postmodern Subjects, Postmodern Bodies," *Feminist Studies* 18.1 (Spring 1992).

Butler, Judith. *Bodies That Matter: On the Discursive Limits of Sex*. New York: Routledge, 1993.

———. "Performance Acts and Gender Constitution: An Essay in Phenomenology and Feminist Theory," *Theatre Journal* 40.4 (December 1988) 519–31.

———. *Psychic Life of Power: Theories in Subjection*. Stanford: Stanford University Press, 1997.

Cheng, Patrick S. *From Sin to Amazing Grace: Discovering the Queer Christ*. New York: Seabury, 2012.

Coakley, Sarah. "The Eschatological Body: Gender, Transformation, and God," *Modern Theology* 16.1 (January 2000) 61–73.

Cone, James H. *The Cross and the Lynching Tree*. Maryknoll: Orbis, 2011.

Cornwall, Susannah. *Controversies in Queer Theology*. London: SCM, 2011.

———. *Sex and Uncertainty in the Body of Christ: Intersex Conditions and Christian Theology*. London: Equinox, 2010.

Fausto-Sterling, Anne. "The Five Sexes Revisited." *Sciences*, 40, no. 4 (Jul/Aug 2000). Online: http://www.neiu.edu/~lsfuller/5sexesrevisited.htm (accessed 05/02/2013).

———. *Sexing the Body: Gender Politics and the Construction of Sexuality*. New York: Basic Books, 2000.

Halperin, David M. *Saint Foucault: Towards A Gay Hagiography*. New York: Oxford, 1995.

Hendel, Kurt. "*Finitum capax infiniti*: Luther's Radical Incarnational Perspective." *Currents in Theology and Mission* 35.6 (2008) 420–33.

Johnson, Mark L. "Embodied Reason." In *Perspectives on Embodiment: The Intersections of Nature and Culture*, edited by Gail Weiss and Honi Fern Haber, 81–102. New York: Routledge, 1999.

Johnson, Mark. "The Meaning of the Body." In *Developmental Perspectives on Embodiment and Consciousness*, edited by Willis F. Overton, Ulrich Miller, and Judith L. Newman, 19–43. New York: Lawrence Erlbaum Associates, 2008.

Johnson, Mark, and Tim Rohrer. "We Are Live Creatures: Embodiment, American Pragmatism, and the Cognitive Organism." In *Body, Language and Mind: Volume 1: Embodiment*, edited by Tom Ziemke, Jordan Zlatev, and Roslyn M. Frank, 17–54. New York: de Gruyter, 2007.

Kaufman, Moisés. "A New Monument to Matthew Shepherd." *SF Gate*, 12/07/ 2007. Online: http://www.sfgate.com/opinion/openforum/article/A-new-monument-to-Matthew-Shepard-2581901.php (accessed 05/02/2013).

Liew, Tat-siong Benny. "Queering Closets and Perverting Desires: Cross-Examining John's Engendering and Trans-Gendering Word Across Different Worlds." In *They Were All Together in One Place? Toward Minority Biblical Criticism*, edited by Randall C. Bailey, Tat-siong Benny Liew, and Fernando F. Segovia, 251–88. Atlanta: Society of Biblical Literature, 2009.

Luther, Martin. *The Blessed Sacrament of the Holy and True Body of Christ, and the Brotherhoods* (1519). LW 35. Philadelphia: Fortress, 1960.

———. *Confession Concerning Christ's Supper* (1528). LW 37. Philadelphia: Fortress, 1961.

———. "Good Friday Sermon," in *Sermons of Martin Luther*, vol. 2, edited and translated by John Nicholas Lenker. Grand Rapids: Baker, 1983.

———. *Heidelberg Disputation* (1518). LW 31. St. Louis: Concordia, 1957.

———. *Lectures on Romans* (1513–1515). LW 25. St Louis: Concordia, 1972.

———. *Sermons on the Gospel of St. John Chapters 1–4* (1537–1540). LW 22. St Louis: Concordia, 1957.

———. "That These Words of Christ, 'This is My Body,' Etc., Still Stand Firm Against the Fanatics" (1527). LW 37. Philadelphia: Fortress, 1961.

Prosser, Jay. *Second Skins: The Body Narratives of Transsexuality*. New York: Columbia University Press, 1998.

Samuels, Ellen. "Critical Divides: Judith Butler's Body Theory and the Question of Disability." *National Women's Studies Association Journal* 14.3 (Fall 2002) 58–76.

Sasse, Hermann. *This is My Body: Luther's Contention for the Real Presence in the Sacrament of the Altar*. Revised ed. Adelaide: Augsburg, 1977.

Sheffield, Tricia, "Performing Jesus: A Queer Counternarrative of Embodied Transgression." *Theology and Sexuality* 145.3 (2008) 233–58.

Solberg, Mary. "Cross Talk: A Feminist Appreciation of Luther's Theology," *Bangalore Theological Forum* 34.1 (June 2002) 43–57.

Spitz, Lewis W. "Luther's Importance for Anthropological Realism." In *Medieval and Renaissance Studies: Proceedings of the Southeastern Institute of Medieval and Renaissance Studies Summer 1968*, edited by John L. Lievsay, 134–70. Durham: Duke University Press, 1968.

Thompson, Deanna A. *Crossing the Divide: Luther, Feminism, and the Cross*. Minneapolis: Fortress, 2004.

Trans 101*: Primer and Vocabulary*. Rutgers Center for Social Justice Education and LGBT Communities. Online: http://socialjustice.rutgers.edu/trans-ru/trans-101 (accessed 05/02/2013).

Ward, Graham. "Bodies: The Displaced Body of Jesus Christ." In *Radical Orthodoxy: A New Theology*, edited by John Milbank, Catherine Pickstock, and Graham Ward, 163–81. New York: Routledge, 1998.

———. *Cities of God*. New York: Routledge, 2000.

Williams, Delores S. *Sisters in the Wilderness: The Challenge of Womanist God-Talk*. Maryknoll: Orbis, 1993.

9

Idolatry-Critical Justification and the Foreclosed Gendered Life

MARY J. STREUFERT

People suffer when we try to control each other. One way humans try to control each other is through the idea that people are opposites, physically, intellectually, and emotionally. Devastating racial, sexual, and gender binaries have proliferated over the last several centuries; at the same time, challenges to ideals of human binaries are not new. In 1928 Virginia Woolf wrote *Orlando*, an evocative exploration of gender through this title figure.[1] Orlando experiences what gender theorist Judith Butler calls a "foreclosed life."[2] Traversing time and place, Orlando moves from man to woman and in so doing, confronts the social meanings of gender from the experience of being the *same* person in each incarnation. After hundreds of years as a man serving as the ambassador of Great Britain to the Count of the Sultan in Constantinople, Orlando awakens from a coma to find that "he was a woman."[3] Now looking like a woman, Orlando leaves his ambassadorial post and joins a caravan of gypsies, with whom she is truly herself. With them, she displays courage, works hard physically, and finds delight in the contemplative and philosophical rooms of her mind.[4] Yet she longs for

---

1. Gender refers to meanings of sexed human bodies. See Jones, *Feminist Theory and Christian Theology*, esp. 7–8. For more on sex and gender manipulation and construction, see Mary Lowe in this volume, and Fausto-Sterling, *Sexing the Body*.
2. Butler, *Gender Trouble*, xxi.
3. Woolf, *Orlando*, 90.
4. Ibid., 92–95.

England, her homeland. While on board ship, she begins to realize through the clothing she must wear and interactions with the captain that life in England will be of little comfort; she will be expected to pour tea to men and be demurring. Because her body changed, who she is had also supposedly changed. Woolf narrates, "if [life in England] meant conventionality, meant slavery, meant deceit, meant denying her love, fettering her limbs, pursing her lips, and restraining her tongue, then she would turn about with the ship and set sail once more for the gipsies [sic]."[5] She would turn away from her own land, rather than face its foreclosed life.

Indeed, the heart of Butler's argument is that when we think gender expressions and roles are innate or must be upheld, we limit life, sometimes to death.[6] Through assumptions about gender, we advance particular standards of what it means to be human—of what is "real" and what "legitimate expression" is.[7] Sometimes these gender standards are "violently policed."[8] It is violent, Butler asserts, to create a "foreclosed life, the one that does not get named as 'living,' the one whose incarceration implies a suspension of life, or a sustained death sentence."[9] Orlando felt this foreclosed life, this death sentence within life, when she saw the edges of the British Isles, where her role was to pour tea.

JUSTIFICATION AND GENDER

The foreclosed life Woolf describes in *Orlando* continues to haunt humanity. During the late twentieth and into the twenty-first centuries, multiple Christian bodies have espoused theological anthropologies rooted in binaristic gender essentialism[10] and gender-based hierarchy. What it means to be human, these Christians argue, is to be hierarchically binaristic according to gender because God created humanity this way. They reflect some common elements. Women and men[11] are equal before God. Women are lower

---

5. Ibid., 106–7.
6. Butler, *Gender Trouble*, xxiv–xxv.
7. Ibid., xxv.
8. Ibid., xx.
9. Ibid., xxi.

10. Essentialism is the idea that there is an essence or root, biological, ontological, or otherwise, that is feminine or masculine. Numerous voices in the Christian tradition argue these essences are created by God and therefore are universal and eternal. Similarly, some feminists argue that women and men are "essentially" different and thus support various forms of separatism. See Jones, *Feminist Theory and Christian Theology*, esp. 22–48.

11. I acknowledge the tension in the vocabulary "women and men," for it can operate to support the idea of sex and gender binaries. Biological and genetic research

than men symbolically and in status. Women are different from men but special.[12] I argue that such theological anthropology suffers from: (1) an interpretation that hierarchy is God-ordained; (2) binaristic gender essentialism; and (3) a construal of vocation in male-female relationships that expects women to be obedient followers. Moreover, (4) any response to female oppression is the responsibility of individuals. Their manifest hierarchy and gender binaries foreclose human life.

This model of theological anthropology results in, for example, the foreclosed life of Woolf's fictional Orlando. Yet Orlando expresses a deep longing on the part of many people to be freed from the control of hierarchical gender binaries. When Christians claim a hierarchically binaristic gendered order of creation, they create foreclosed lives by claiming one particular construction of what it means to be human, with males in the superordinate position. Humans have put themselves in the place of God insofar as this expression of theological anthropology elevates the human male by being male-dominant, male-identified, and male-centered. As Martin Luther admonishes, it is idolatrous to put ourselves in the place of God.

Among a variety of keys in Lutheran theology available to address hierarchically binaristic gendered Christian theological anthropology, the doctrine of justification stands out. It stands out because it has been understood throughout the centuries of Lutheran reform as the most central and cogent expression of the Gospel: the promise of God's grace through Christ for all of creation. As many Lutheran theologians have long pointed out, the Lutheran confessional tradition aims to point Christians to the claim of the gospel, God's grace through faith. This is the interpretive key, the purpose of which is to serve the church catholic to witness to the gospel.[13]

The promise God gives through Jesus Christ is justification by grace through faith; the entire cosmos has been and is being saved. As theologian Lois Malcolm notes, the concomitant judgment that accompanies this promise is a judgment against "any human attempt at self-deification that would negate or refuse the very gift-like character of the promise."[14] From a Lutheran perspective, faith (through which we are justified) depends upon

---

reveals otherwise. See, e.g., Fausto-Sterling, *Sexing the Body*, esp. 45–56. Here I have chosen to use these terms, especially given their preponderant use in the theological anthropologies analyzed.

12. Despite efforts to the contrary, these theological anthropologies significantly mirror and are mirrored in cultural anthropology. For some initial analysis, see Streufert, "Gender and Justice within Empire: Toward a Christian Ethic of Gender Justice."

13. See, e.g., Braaten, *Principles of Lutheran Theology*, 4, 43.

14. Malcolm, "The Gospel and Feminism," 293.

the proclamation of the promise and the sacraments.[15] The promise comes to humans through witnesses, from the biblical canon to creeds and the rites of baptism and Eucharist. Although the *forms* of these witnesses have been criticized from a feminist perspective, Malcolm points out that what is central is the promise to which these varied witnesses *point*. This deeply Lutheran assertion guides readers to Malcolm's implicit argument that patriarchy is a sin:

> [I]nherent to the very witness itself, and this is precisely the insight informing the Lutheran reformation, is an ongoing denunciation—a kind of reflexive critique—of any and all ecclesial pretensions that would replace the promise with human-made laws that deify particular human persons or institutions.[16]

In other words, justification by grace through faith means that we are critical of any thinking or practice that sees Christian faith joined to "social structures and ways of thinking that sanction male privilege."[17] This is precisely the theological gift of Lutheran dogma to dismantling patriarchy and enlivening gender justice within God's world. Along with other keys in Lutheran theology,[18] feminist attention to justification helps to reorient theological anthropology towards the life promised in the Gospel, away from the literal and existential deaths provoked by idolatrous constructions of what it means to be human.

The doctrine of justification, despite its shortcomings from crucial feminist perspectives,[19] offers at least four benefits for theological anthropology. First, because the doctrine of justification is thoroughly theocentric and christocentric, it unseats idolatry. Second, the doctrine of justification declares freedom from bondage. Third, justification alters our sinful status and relations with each other through God's alien righteousness. Fourth, it clarifies human vocation. Moreover, this feminist reading of justification strengthens current arguments on Law and Gospel that challenge its juridical distinctions into God's acts as wrath as the first move and love as the second. This doctrine illuminates what three Christian theological anthropologies operative within the United States hold: the Roman Catholic Church, the Lutheran Church-Missouri Synod, and Promise Keepers.[20]

15. Ibid., 294.
16. Ibid.
17. Ibid.
18. On ethics, see, e.g., Wallace, "Hush No More!," 179–96, 258–60; on the cross, see, e.g., Guðmundsdóttir. *Meeting God on the Cross*; Thompson, *Crossing the Divide*.
19. See, e.g., Trelstad, "The Way of Salvation in Luther's Theology," 236–45.
20. These are three significant elements in Christianity in the United States. First,

Each of these theological anthropologies claims its faithful Christian identity, rooted largely in its interpretation of Scripture. Where Lutheran theology takes us to a different place is that the hermeneutical priority of Lutheran theology has been and continues to be the proclamation of the Gospel: How does Scripture show us God's promise of grace? The hermeneutical principle that determines the authority of Scripture, as Luther so famously put it, is "what carries Christ." Thus, any claims to a scripturally-based theological anthropology is best tested by the promise of God through Christ held in the doctrine of justification and its inherent challenge to Biblicism.

The theological anthropologies in question here deserve analysis from the viewpoint of this doctrine. I offer this work with the full knowledge that the doctrine of justification and consequent interpretations and applications are also highly problematic and deserve ongoing critical work. A body of such scholarship is already well under way.[21] I offer a critical application of a feminist interpretation of justification that adds to the ongoing constructive work in Lutheran theology—not as an isolated, retrospective historical theology or reform movement, but as a theology for the sake of Christ in and for the church and the world. This very world is filled with multiply-gendered bodies, many of whom long to know the meaning of God's grace *pro nobis* (for us)—and for the world. What sometimes stands in the way of this knowing—this "hearing"—is the foreclosed life which theology and the church create through hierarchically binaristic gendered theological anthropology.

GOD-ORDAINED HIERARCHY

Although each of these groups of Christians emphasizes human equality before God, they qualify gender equality as spiritual. For example, Pope John Paul II writes that everyone exists in "an essential 'equality'" because everyone receives an outpouring of the Holy Spirit.[22] Yet he qualifies equality, first, by the use of quotation marks around the word equality and second,

---

although global in scope, Roman Catholic theology and teaching has a far more pervasive influence in the United States than it does in Europe. Second, the Missouri Synod claims a confessional identity, along with the diverse member communions of the Lutheran World Federation, yet the differences among them on issues of sex and gender are significant. Third, the Promise Keepers represent a divergent span of American evangelicalism, given that Promise Keepers itself is not organized by a particular denomination. The organization evokes unity through its *Seven Promises* and has branches in Canada and New Zealand.

21. See, e.g., Malcolm, "The Gospel and Feminism"; Solberg, *Compelling Knowledge*.
22. Pope John Paul II, *Mulieris Dignitatem*, 16.3.

by calling it "*Gospel* 'equality.'"[23] The Missouri Synod and Promise Keepers follow suit with spiritual equality. The Missouri Synod affirms gender equality in God's image, but they qualify this equality as "a spiritual equality of man and woman before God."[24] The Promise Keepers also believe that women and men are equal before God, but the family is man's work and male headship in the family is ordained by God.[25] Ordinary human life is not equal, they argue, because God created humans in an order of gendered headship and subordination.

The idea that God intends gendered hierarchy lies in their interpretations of creation and redemption. One of the more famous expressions of a divinely ordained order rooted in an interpretation of creation comes from Pastor Tony Evans. Referring to familial leadership, he exhorted husbands, "TAKE IT BACK." And to wives he said, "*Give it back!* (. . .) [L]et your man be a man if he's willing. (. . .) God never meant for you to bear the load you're carrying."[26]

Although expressed differently, the Missouri Synod and Rome agree that humans are created in a hierarchy of headship. Pope John Paul II is a bit more subtle than Evans, yet he nevertheless argues in favor of God-ordained gender hierarchy. He refers to humans being entrusted to each other in creation, but men are implicitly in the primary role because "man [sic] was created male and female, and the woman was entrusted to the man with her feminine distinctiveness, and with her potential for motherhood."[27] Not only is the male primary in creation, as the pope expresses here, but the male is also primary in redemption, for the Bridegroom Christ is wedded to the bride, the Church, an analogy he makes clear fits with human man and woman. The bride is the "'feminine' element"[28] in all of humanity in its receptiveness to Christ's love, just as he implies that women are receptive. "*The symbol of the Bridegroom is masculine.* (. . .) [I]t is the model and pattern

---

23. Ibid., 16.4. Emphasis added.

24. See Lutheran Church—Missouri Synod, "Women in the Church," 17.

25. See Everton, "The Promise Keepers," 58–59. Other research highlights four or five gender ideals within Promise Keepers' writing and teaching, some of which nuances outright male elevation. However, male headship remains, despite the support of gender partnership in some instances. See Bartkowski. *The Promise Keepers*, 45–66.

26. See Tony Evans in Abraham, *Who are the Promise Keepers?*, 106. Although other Promise Keeper leaders do not advocate for male headship in this fashion, Evans does represent an operative theological anthropology among followers and leaders. For more, see Bartkowski, *The Promise Keepers*.

27. Pope John Paul II, *Mulieris Dignitatem*, 14.3.

28. Ibid., 25.3.

of all human love, men's love in particular."²⁹ At the same time, all humans "are called to respond—as a bride."³⁰ Just as humanity is called to respond to Christ, the giver, women are called to respond to men. In other words, humanity is called to act within the ideal of the Bridegroom and Bride.

Lastly, the Missouri Synod makes the clearest link between God-ordained hierarchy and creation and redemption. According to their interpretation of the Formula of Concord, God created a head-subordinate relationship between males and females before the Fall; God's intention is gendered, both in placement and in type, and it is unfaithful to ask for anything different.³¹ Headship should be maintained in the church and the family and is not redeemed through Christ because it needs no redeeming. However, *distortions* of the head-subordinate relationship are redeemed,³² they argue; redemption does not "annul" divisions in the world that reflect God's created intentions.

BINARISTIC GENDER ESSENTIALISM

Divine intention according to these anthropologies is binaristic; humans do not share sameness. These theological anthropologies hold that God wills us to be opposites. Redemption undoes the sinful *distortions* of binaristic headship created by God. Redemption does not "annul" divisions in the world that reflect God's created intentions. In other words, as the Missouri Synod writes, "[E]quality does not suggest the interchangeability of male and female identities."³³ Similarly, what it means to be human, John Paul II argues, is to give yourself, but "in accordance with the special qualities proper to each;" women should not act like men.³⁴ Such qualities stem from a hierarchically binaristic understanding of humanity, which he refers to as "the Creator's decision that the human being should always and only exist

---

29. Ibid., 25.5.

30. Ibid., 27.1.

31. See Lutheran Church—Missouri Synod, "Women in the Church," 47, 55n39, 57n56. Luther himself interpreted Genesis to mean that women were subordinate to men in marriage, the church, and society. See Luther, *Lectures on Genesis 1–5,*" LW 1. I am challenging his own reading of Genesis with the doctrine he held central to all others. For more on Luther as a ground-breaking theological anthropologist, see Kvam, "God's Heart Revealed in Eden," 57–67, 242–243; Kvam, "The Significance of Luther's Ideas for the Churches of the 21st Century," 71.

32. See Lutheran Church—Missouri Synod, "Women in the Church," 20–25.

33. Ibid., 24. In fact, "the order of redemption sanctifies [the order of creation]." See ibid., 36.

34. Pope John Paul II, *Mulieris Dignitatem*, 7.8.

as a woman or a man."[35] Women live for others best as virgin, spouse and mother, he argues, and their God-given femininity is given to them at creation.[36] He continues, "In the name of liberation from male 'domination,' women must not appropriate to themselves male characteristics contrary to their own feminine 'originality.'"[37] Acting outside of this script is sinful because God's intention is crossed. "*The inheritance of sin* (. . .)" he continues, "*can be conquered* only by following this path,"[38] one of gender binaries. In other words, be rightfully feminine and masculine and domination will end, he implies. Pope John Paul II wants no confusion, despite the vast multiplicity of bodies among humans.

Such redemptive gender appropriateness is also found in Promise Keepers. The personal relationships for which they advocate—with Jesus Christ, other men of all races, and their families—are the change agent that men are in charge of to fix national problems they name: divorce, crime, unemployment, and abortion. Male saviors need to step in and take up their roles of biblical manhood so that families and communities are healed. Within this male-identified relational system, men are to be attentive to their wives' needs as spouses, mothers, and even as workers outside the home.[39] Women and men are two aspects of the likeness of God in creation, argues one PK commentator; therefore, he counsels other men:

> In order to reflect God's diversity, we must allow our female counterparts to stand shoulder to shoulder with us. Headship does not designate rank or title. It simply refers to order and identifies the role that man serves.[40]

In other words, women and men are two parts of a binary. Humans are created differently; we "reflect differing opinions."[41] These differences are kept in place with the ideal of biblical headship. These theological anthropologies make a clear connection between distinct, gendered identities and God's creative and redemptive will.

---

35. Ibid., 1.3.
36. See ibid., 10.5.
37. Ibid., 10.4.
38. Ibid., 10.5. Italics in original.
39. See Everton, "The Promise Keepers," 60–61.
40. T. D. Jakes in ibid., 59.
41. Ibid.

VOCATION IN MALE-FEMALE RELATIONSHIPS

In fact, Promise Keepers clearly connects gender binaries and social salvation. The country is in crisis, according to Evans, due to "the feminization of the American male. (. . .) I'm trying to describe a misunderstanding of manhood that has produced a nation of 'sissified' men who abdicate their role as spiritually pure leaders."[42] For Promise Keepers, leadership is biologically male, and the family structure should reflect it. The relationships they advocate are all male-identified,[43] even though they support marital partnership.[44] Clearly, these anthropologies determine vocation through gender binaries.

For Promise Keepers, it is clear that men and women have different vocations in the male-female relationship. Men are to lead and redeem everyone and everything. Women are to follow and to reap the benefits of such fantastic men. Promise Keepers speak about a re-centered male-female life through the Christian terms of sacrifice, service, and giving, traditionally female-designated characteristics. In fact, it seems, men should take up their roles to be more than women, to be the great one in service in the male-female relationship. Feminist scholar Judith Newton notes, "[I]n general, PK participants were told to give *more* than women. For example, one PK speaker, Larry Jackson, said, '[I]t is my responsibility to give only and not to take,'" a sentiment Newton heard repeatedly at Promise Keepers events.[45]

While Promise Keepers want male giving to outstrip female giving in heterosexual marital relations, Pope John Paul II talks about the vocation of giving in a more gender essentialist fashion. Women are more naturally self-giving; woman is particularly dependent on the principle of self-giving;[46] in fact, the faithfulness of virginity and the self-giving of motherhood idealistically found in Mary, Mother of God, are "two particular dimensions of the fulfillment of the female personality."[47] He continues, "*Motherhood is linked to the personal structure of the woman.*"[48] Motherhood is God's

---

42. Tony Evans in Abraham, *Who Are the Promise Keepers?*, 106.

43. See Everton, "The Promise Keepers," 60–61.

44. See T. D. Jakes in ibid., 59. See Bartkowski, *The Promise Keepers*, for a nuanced analysis of Promise Keeper literature.

45. Newton, *From Panthers to Promise Keepers*, 222.

46. See Pope John Paul II, *Mulieres Dignitatem*, 10.2.

47. Ibid., 17.1.

48. Ibid., 17.4. Emphasis in original.

intent, he argues.⁴⁹ Motherhood is not simply pragmatic but is inherent to the essence of all females.

Although they differ from the Promise Keepers' urgency to outstrip women in self-sacrifice and Rome's emphasis on women's vocation as virgin, spouse, and mother, the Missouri Synod also holds to vocational headship and subordination. They are unequivocal about "an order of headship which endures,"⁵⁰ which both men and women need to "gratefully recognize and receive" because, they argue, such a structure serves others.⁵¹ Everyone is in a gendered relationship of priority. They quote Peter Brunner: "The 'head' is that which is prior, that which determines, that which leads. The head is the power that begins, it is principium, arche."⁵² God wills subordination, even if not abuse, and female vocation is to be subordinate "for the sake of orderliness and unity."⁵³ Another summary of this is: "The relationship between man and woman can also be defined as a headship structure of God-Christ-man-woman, each member of the order superordinated to the succeeding member. This is a theological and not merely a sociological relationship."⁵⁴ The implication is that particular gender roles are part of Christian life. Get it right, or be out of line with God.

INDIVIDUAL RESPONSIBILITY

No matter their divergences on gendered ideals of care, proponents of these theological anthropologies want women to take their "proper" roles gratefully —as mother and spousal and ecclesial subordinate. And, particular to the Promise Keepers' literature, some proponents of these theological anthropologies want men to be sensitive. While none of them advocate harm to women, the foreclosed life that hierarchically binaristic Christian theological anthropology produces is harmful. Feminists agree that females should not be hurt, and men should be sensitive. In part, where feminists diverge with these theological anthropologies is quite obvious: feminists argue that humans are created and exist in relationships of mutual egalitarianism.

Perhaps less obvious is an important critique. Responses to physical, economic, social, and emotional harms to women because they are women—a systemic analysis of patriarchy and sexism—are basically non-existent. We can see the harm in many systemic forms, from access to education and

49. See ibid., 11.8.
50. Lutheran Church–Missouri Synod, "Women in the Church," 26.
51. Ibid., 25–26.
52. Ibid., 25.
53. Ibid., 30.
54. Ibid., 36.

political and ecclesial authority to pandemic physical and sexual violence to global, gender-based economic disparities. The Missouri Synod remains silent. John Paul II says that women should not be objects of men or oppressed but gives no analysis of necessary change. He argues that due to the *"fundamental equality"* of creation, women should not be controlled by men, while he simultaneously emphasizes female dependence on self-giving for self-realization through the ideals of virgin-mother-spouse.[55]

Promise Keepers is more explicit in the kind of new masculinity they advocate for men so that women do not suffer from them. Simply put, if men could be nice to their wives, everything would be great. Granted, as Newton points out, personal change—learning to respect and care for women—is political work. And it is important work. What is striking, however, is that they make solid connections between the personal and the political in terms of racism. Being a real man involves not only forging personal relationships with men of other races and ethnicities, but also public activism in terms of racial justice. Promise Keepers makes no such connection between private relationships with their wives and public activism to advance women's equity.[56] Without a doubt, their unique focus on the emotional needs of women and children at home helps families and individuals, but as Newton concludes, they "had almost nothing to say about sexism or women themselves in relation to the public."[57] Promise Keepers were so successful in gaining men to embrace a kinder, gentler masculinity, in part, because the public sphere and the family are still male-identified, and they are still, albeit subtly, male-centered and male-dominated. They all fall short.

IDOLATRY-CRITICAL JUSTIFICATION

To repeat, a gift of Lutheran theology to the church catholic is the confessional reminder to begin with God's promise of grace, God's act towards us; care for neighbors, both individually and institutionally, springs from God's relationship with creation. The doctrine of justification challenges these theological anthropologies in the following ways. First, justification challenges the idolatry of male supremacy. Second, it declares freedom from the bondage of what gets in the way of the Gospel. Third, God's alien righteousness affirms human equality and alters human relationships. Fourth, the doctrine of justification clarifies human vocation in both individual and systemic realms. I offer a critique towards an egalitarian theological

---

55. See Pope John Paul II, *Mulieres Dignitatem*, 10.1.

56. Newton, *From Panthers to Promise Keepers*, 16. They have, however, spoken out against violence against women.

57. Ibid., 222.

anthropology of multiple gender legitimacies. Out of an idolatry of gendered hierarchy and binary, the doctrine of justification draws humanity towards the God-oriented future the Gospel promises. Thinking about theological anthropology from the perspective of justification also challenges the separation of Law and Gospel as two separate acts of humiliation and love, and as such, strengthens the growing work of feminist Lutheran scholarship.[58]

Once Luther came to clarity over the nature and centrality of justification, he never wavered from declaring God's radical freedom by grace through faith.[59] Any kind of work does not suffice a right relation with God. Paul's intention in Galatians, Luther explains, is "to defend the righteousness that comes by faith, and to refute the Law and the righteousness that comes by works."[60] Humans receive from God, Luther declares.[61] Indeed, Luther was certain, justification is the Gospel's primary focus. He states, "For if the doctrine of justification is lost, the whole of Christian doctrine is lost."[62] As the Gospel's primary focus, justification is thus the brain and the skeleton of all other doctrine. It is the brain, for we are to think through it in relation to all other doctrine; it is the skeleton, for it upholds and gives shape to all other doctrine. "[I]f this locus is securely retained," writes Martin Chemnitz, "all *idolatrous* (. . .) ravings, superstitions, and other corruptions are thereby destroyed under almost every locus."[63] Yet justification is brain and skeleton for one simple reason; as Melanchthon states, it "contains the sum and substance of the Gospel."[64] This is why Luther argued that the Church *exists* by the doctrine of justification.[65] Hierarchically binaristic Christian theological anthropology changes when it has justification by grace through faith for its brain and skeleton.

This central doctrine challenges the idolatry of male supremacy through its thoroughgoing theocentricity and christocentricity. The Book of Romans is a critique of *human* righteousness, a strong exhortation that God's righteousness does not equal human righteousness.[66] God's act, not ours, makes God's promise of love real; Luther declares that it is God who

---

58. See esp.Trelstad, "Putting the Cross in Context," 107–22, 248–50.
59. See McGrath, *Luther's Theology of the Cross*, 176.
60. See Luther, *Lectures on Galatians*, LW 26, 21. See also LW 26, 4.
61. Ibid., LW 26, 5.
62. Ibid., LW 26, 9.
63. Chemnitz, *Justification*, 12. Emphasis added.
64. Philip Melanchthon, *Loci communes*, in Chemnitz, *Justification*, 40.
65. See Luther, *Lectures on Galatians*, LW 26, 10.
66. See McGrath, *Luther's Theology of the Cross*, 135.

"regards" us righteous, which is done through Christ.[67] Furthermore, Melanchthon writes, "[T]he word 'freely' (. . .) transfers the cause of this blessing from ourselves to Christ."[68] To have God through Christ at the center of our human existence reveals human male supremacy for the idolatry that it is, for through it, the male is made a god, a good to be protected and even celebrated. Orlando experiences this when she realizes the limits placed on her as a woman. Luther expressed anti-idolatry particularly clearly in "The Freedom of a Christian," wherein he exposits Curial Law as works righteousness—humanly wrought grace. The law of patriarchy also stands in a class of human-made righteousness. Both Pope John Paul II and the Missouri Synod argue that the connection between creation and redemption is clear and pure when men and women adhere to hierarchical gender binaries. In short, humans sin if they act out of order with gender binaries. This seems to be what I would call "gender righteousness."

FREEDOM FROM BONDAGE

Even while the cause of blessing is not ours, Luther thinks justification relates to the whole person, turned in upon itself and open to God.[69] The entire person is freed from bondage to whatever stands in the way of the Gospel.[70] Luther button-holed the Curia for trying to define faith in relation to itself, rather than to God's promise of mercy and grace. He knew that the doctrine of justification mattered for human life. He thought, for example, that the hierarchy of human value held between lay and clergy perverted the grace and freedom of the Gospel because it is replaced with "an unbearable bondage of human works and laws."[71] Theologian Carl Braaten explicates the freedom Paul preached as the "core of justification." He writes, "This freedom is multidimensional; it has personal, ecclesial, and cosmic elements of meaning. It means freedom from the law, from sin, and finally from death. (. . .) This freedom in Christ has both an eschatological and an ethical aspect."[72] Malcolm continues this line of thought from a feminist perspective with a common feminist question: does the gospel really change humanity? Her answer is this: "The wager of the Lutheran

---

67. See Luther in ibid. Mc Grath is referring to WA 56, 287:16–21.

68. Melanchthon in Chemnitz, *Justification*, 18.

69. McGrath, *Luther's Theology of the Cross*, 133.

70. As some contemporary Lutheran scholars contend, freedom from bondage includes freedom from systems of oppression. See, e.g., Malcolm, "The Gospel and Feminism"; Pahl, *Empire of Sacrifice*; Thompson, *Crossing the Divide*.

71. Luther, *The Freedom of a Christian*, LW 31, 292.

72. Braaten, *Principles of Lutheran Theology*, 108.

movement is precisely that the heart of Jesus' gospel lies in its promise of liberation from oppression of all sorts and that this promise provides the church with a criterion for distinguishing what is Christian from what is not in its beliefs and practices."[73] Hierarchically binaristic gendered Christian theological anthropology is one such set of beliefs and concomitant practices that oppress people.

Orlando, for one, felt the weight of gender oppression, which separated her from herself and others. She is deeply startled by the expectations "the coil of skirts about her legs" carries.[74] Having never worn skirts before, Orlando realizes she is hemmed in by the meaning of the skirts; her clothing made her both dependent upon and desirable to—men. She is bound. Similarly, interpretations that God wills hierarchically binaristic gendered natures stand between people and the grace and freedom of the Gospel.[75] Imagine, for example, not matching Rome's feminine ideal of virgin, mother, spouse, which is connected to redemption in much the same way that the Missouri Synod connects proper gender behavior to the states of creation and redemption. Adhering to a hierarchical binary becomes a law to fulfill in order to be saved. In short, justification by grace through faith stipulates that nothing we do or do not do binds our relationship with God. No human law, no human standard or norm of acceptability, and no human will binds us to God in love. Faith is not in relationship to gender hierarchy. Only God's acts of love through Jesus Christ do this, and by this assurance, as Luther so vividly argues, do we live *un*bound, in freedom.

ALIEN RIGHTEOUSNESS AND VOCATION

As already noted, the doctrine of justification reminds Christians that humans are dependent upon God through Christ; this is the status of the God-human relationship. Humans are not in charge; neither are males. I have used this line of thinking to challenge the idolatry of male supremacy. Yet Luther's idea of God's alien righteousness turns us to collective human brokenness. God's alien righteousness is a reminder that we each and all receive from God equally. As McGrath points out, God's righteousness is given, not made possible by us.[76] In the eyes of God, *coram Deo*, Luther argues, there is not anything about us that makes us without brokenness, without sin. We are simply before God, imperfect. But God covers us. God's righteousness

73. Malcolm, "The Gospel and Feminism," 298.
74. Woolf, *Orlando*, 100.
75. Luther, for example, supports Paul's attacks on Peter for getting in the way of justification. See Luther, *Lectures on Galatians*, LW 26, 106.
76. See McGrath, *Luther's Theology of the Cross*, 132.

is alien, coming from outside of us, but it is nevertheless our righteousness because of God's promise to love us. We are covered—*coram Deo*. Being covered changes us. Much like the unwarranted love and care we receive from friends, who are bound to us neither by blood nor by law, changes us, so does God's alien righteousness—this love from outside of us—change us.

We are thereby simultaneously covered *coram hominibus*, face to face with each other, neighbors all. We all stand face to face, covered by God. When we remember this, it might be easier to ask different questions about Christian theological anthropology. For example, what do women and gender-queer persons think about binaries and hierarchy? God's alien righteousness ameliorates gender jostling because we see each other—stand face to face—nose to nose—by and through our existence *coram Deo*. Christian theological anthropology might then be less concerned with following gender-based "rules" and more concerned with seeing all people as we are, varied and not in relationships of headship and obedience. God's covering of us reminds us of human weakness and ennobles the church's search to speak apostolically in our own time, that is, to declare the meaning of the Gospel now.[77]

Lastly, idolatry-critical justification clarifies human vocation in both the individual and systemic realms. Justification leads to a particular kind of vocation, including vocation in male-female relationships, whether intimate, familial, ecclesial, or social. A Christian, Luther writes, "consider[s] nothing except the need and the advantage of the neighbor" because a Christian takes the form of Christ.[78] We live for others because Christ dwells within us.[79] As gendered individuals, we ask what our neighbor needs. The answers may surprise us, especially when we truly listen. When set in relation to each other, what is striking about *Orlando*, written in 1928, and the theological anthropologies analyzed in this chapter, written in the late twentieth century, is that in all instances, women are spoken for, are given rules about gender to follow, along with accompanying consequences. The vocation of service of which Luther writes, located within God's relationship with creation, compels Christian theology to "consider nothing except the need and the advantage of the neighbor." Individuals of many genders may need something very different from the theological anthropologies explored here. What does the neighbor say they need?

---

77. As Braaten argues, "What counts is not that the church replicate the past but that it become free to be apostolic for its own time, sometimes in contrast to the way of being apostolic in former times." Braaten, *Principles of Lutheran Theology*, 64.

78. Luther, *The Freedom of a Christian*, LW 31, 302, 303–4.

79. Ibid., LW 31, 309.

Nevertheless, service to the neighbor is not restricted to individual acts.[80] While changing patriarchy and sexism does not make us righteous before God, we are called to address systemic oppression because of faith, because such works serve others. Christians will know how much others need to be served when we put on everything our neighbor is, Luther reminds us, because of Christ.[81] Theologian Kristen Kvam's careful analysis of Luther's Lectures on Genesis strengthens the argument that vocation rooted in God's promise is egalitarian between the sexes and not limited to interpersonal relationships. She points out that when Eve and Adam hear God's curse of the serpent, Luther writes, "They even hear themselves drawn up, as it were, in battle against their condemned enemy, and this with the hope of help from the Son of God, the seed of the woman." Kvam contends further that Luther understood "that a dramatic transformation has taken place in the lives of the first man and the first woman because of God's promise to defeat sin. (. . .) Indeed, we see that their trust in God's promise instills them with the courage to contend against sin."[82] Vocation in male-female relationships can then more clearly be seen as less concerned with living in binaristic gender hierarchy and more concerned with working together "to defeat sin," which for the purposes of my argument is the sin of the foreclosed gendered life. So, for example, when a young woman in her first job is sexually harassed and paid less than her male peer, solutions will neither protect "God-given" gender roles nor rely exclusively on an individual man to correct the situation for her. Instead, policies, practices and laws must actually serve her. Whole bodies of people—institutions, churches, organizations—may find themselves in the form of Christ. In the form of Christ, individuals and bodies of people put on the neighbor and all that the collective "she" or "he" is (the neighbor) and challenge the ungodliness of bondage to a hierarchical binary of gender. In Christ we meet each other as whole bodies, covered in *God's* alien righteousness.

Implicit in any discussion of the doctrine of justification is the function of law and gospel. Lutheran theology espouses a long-standing practice, rooted in Luther's understanding of God's nature and Scripture, to speak of the necessary pairing of law and gospel. For example, theologian Hans Schwarz notes, "While they function quite differently, law and gospel are certainly the same word of God."[83] As noted above, Malcolm emphasizes the mutually inflected relationship between law and gospel when she argues

---

80. See *Church in Society: A Lutheran Perspective*.
81. Luther, *The Freedom of a Christian*, LW 31, 309.
82. Kvam, "God's Heart Revealed in Eden," 65–66.
83. Schwarz, "The Word," 273.

that God's promise of grace through Christ also brings a judgment against human elevation. Certainly, law and gospel both come from God, and both are necessary for humankind. However, Lutheran theologians express concern over the law being consumed by the gospel if we do not rightly experience the humiliation of the law—in order to hear the gospel. For example, Braaten writes, "The law terrifies, accuses, condemns, denounces, punishes, and kills. If this is not true, the gospel cannot comfort, strengthen, forgive, liberate, and renew. (...) [T]he law makes us realize our need for the gospel."[84] I suggest that the feminist reading of justification offered in this chapter builds upon and strengthens the argument that the law need not be underscored by humiliation as God's first move and redemption as God's second move. Although Lutheran theologians emphasize the simultaneity of law and gospel, to speak of the nature of God as wrathful and the function of the law as humiliating seems to lose, from a feminist perspective, the very heart of justification by grace through faith. As Trelstad argues, "judgment emerges from love."[85] It is God's relationship of promise, of love, that allows the law to function. This is exactly what I have attempted to demonstrate in this chapter: the christocentricity, freedom from bondage, alien righteousness, and human vocation of the doctrine of justification emerge from God's love. And out of this love emerges God's judgment on hierarchical gendered binaries.

CONCLUSION

The story of Orlando brings the foreclosed life of hierarchical gender binaries to our imaginations, yet this reality of control manipulates many lives, individually and systemically. As demonstrated here, a number of Christian theological anthropologies advance a particular understanding of what it means to be human that is closely linked to creation and redemption. A feminist use of the doctrine of justification serves in both critical and constructive functions towards an egalitarian theological anthropology of multiple gender legitimacies. The far-reaching effect is that, true to its catholic intent, a Lutheran interpretation of justification challenges both worldly and religious beliefs that stand in the way of the gospel.

Thus I conclude that Lutheran theology, specifically the doctrine of justification, does the following. It points us away from the regulation and control found in the idolatry of male-oriented theological anthropologies. It likewise points us towards physical and psychological variability among

84. Braaten, *Principles of Lutheran Theology*, 139. See also, Schwarz, "The Word," 273.

85. Trelstad, "Putting the Cross in Context: Atonement Through Covenant," 120.

humans, with no binaries and no hierarchy. It points us towards a variety of expressions of human vocation. And the doctrine of justification points us towards a serious affront to systemic patriarchy and sexism. For the global Lutheran church to think, talk, and act as if it is true that we are justified by grace through faith—we say it is, after all—casts God's freedom from bondage to millions who suffer from thinking, talking, and acting as if it were not true.

BIBLIOGRAPHY

Abraham, Ken. *Who Are the Promise Keepers? Understanding the Christian Men's Movement*. New York: Doubleday, 1997.

Bartkowski, John P. *The Promise Keepers: Servants, Soldiers, and Godly Men*. New Brunswick: Rutgers, 2004.

Braaten, Carl E. *Principles of Lutheran Theology*. 2nd ed. Minneapolis: Fortress, 2007.

Butler, Judith. *Gender Trouble: Feminism and the Subversion of Identity*. New York: Routledge, 1990.

Chemnitz, Martin. *Justification: The Chief Article of Christian Doctrine as Expounded in Loci Theologici*, edited by Delpha Holleque Preus. St. Louis: Concordia, 1985.

Church in Society: A Lutheran Perspective. Chicago: ELCA, 1991.

Everton, Sean F. "The Promise Keepers: Religious Revival or Third Wave of the Religious Right?" *Review of Religious Research*. 43.1 (2001) 51–69.

Fausto-Sterling, Anne. *Sexing the Body: Gender Politics and the Construction of Sexuality*. New York: Basic Books, 2000.

Guðmundsdóttir, Arnfríður. *Meeting God on the Cross: Christ, the Cross, and the Feminist Critique*. Oxford: Oxford University Press, 2010.

Jones, Serene. *Feminist Theory and Christian Theology: Cartographies of Grace*, Guides to Theological Inquiry. Minneapolis: Augsburg Fortress, 2000.

Luther, Martin. *The Freedom of a Christian* (1520). LW 31. St. Louis: Concordia, 1957.

———. *Lectures on Galatians* (1535). LW 26. St. Louis: Concordia, 1963.

———. *Lectures on Genesis 1–5*. (1535–1545). LW 1. St. Louis: Concordia, 1958.

Lutheran Church—Missouri Synod. "Women in the Church: Scriptural and Ecclesial Practice." St. Louis, 1985.

Kvam, Kristen E. "The Significance of Luther's Ideas for the Churches of the 21st Century." *Lutherjahrbuch* 71 (2004) 65–71.

———. "God's Heart Revealed in Eden." In *Transformative Lutheran Theologies: Feminist, Womanist, and Mujerista Perspectives*, edited by Mary J. Streufert. Minneapolis: Fortress, 2010.

Malcolm, Lois. "The Gospel and Feminism: A Proposal for Lutheran Dogmatics." *Word & World* 15.3 (Summer 1995) 290–98.

McGrath, Alister E. *Luther's Theology of the Cross*. Malden, MA: Blackwell, 1995.

Newton, Judith. *From Panthers to Promise Keepers: Rethinking the Men's Movement*. Lanham, MD: Rowman & Littlefield, 2005.

Pahl, John. *Empire of Sacrifice: The Religious Origins of American Violence*. New York: New York University, 2010.

Pope John Paul II. *Mulieris Dignitatem: Apostolic Letter of the Supreme Pontiff John Paul II on the Dignity and Vocation of Women on the Occasion of the Marian Year.* Rome, 1988.

Solberg, Mary M. *Compelling Knowledge: A Feminist Proposal for an Epistemology of the Cross.* Albany: State University of New York Press, 1997.

Streufert, Mary J. "Gender and Justice within Empire: Toward a Christian Ethic of Gender Justice." *Journal of Lutheran Ethics*, Vol. 13, no. 5. Online: www.elca.org/What-We-Believe/Social-Issues/Lutheran-Ethics.aspx (accessed 12/09/2013).

Schwarz, Hans. "The Word." In *Christian Dogmatics*, vol. II, edited by Carl E. Braaten and Robert W. Jenson, 257–88. Philadelphia: Fortress, 1984.

Thompson, Deanna A. *Crossing the Divide: Luther, Feminism, and the Cross.* Minneapolis: Fortress, 2004.

Trelstad, Marit, "Putting the Cross in Context: Atonement Through Covenant." In *Transformative Lutheran Theologies: Feminist, Womanist, and Mujerista Perspectives*, edited by Mary J. Streufert. Minneapolis: Fortress, 2010.

———. "The Way of Salvation in Luther's Theology: A Feminist Evaluation." *Dialog* 45.3 (Fall 2006) 236–45.

Wallace, Beverly "Hush No More!" In *Transformative Lutheran Theologies: Feminist, Womanist, and Mujerista Perspectives*, edited by Mary J. Streufert. Minneapolis: Fortress, 2010.

Woolf, Virgina. *Orlando: A Biography.* 1928. New York: Signet, 1960.

PART THREE

Lutheran Theology and Politics

10

Luther, Wittgenstein, and Political Theology

TAGE KURTÉN

A FRESH EXAMPLE FROM FINLAND

In the summer 2013 the Finnish Minister of the Interior, Päivi Räsänen, took part in a summer meeting of one of the leading conservative Christian inner-Church movements, Kansanlähetys (Folk Mission). Räsänen, a physician by profession but for a long time a full time politician, is also the chairwoman of the Christian Democratic Party in Finland. She gave a speech where she, among other things, criticized the fact that Finland and Sweden, as the only countries in the world, do not grant health care professionals the right to refuse to take part in the practice of abortion. According to her, this kind of violence against the individual conscience is problematic. In connection to this, she also took up the Biblical principle that one should obey God more than humans (she referred to the Acts in the New Testament).[1]

Her speech awoke a huge debate in Finnish media. She was interpreted to have encouraged, not to say exhorted, people to act against the law. As a consequence, a large number of members of the Lutheran Church left it.[2]

Afterwards Räsänen felt that she had to explain her position. She thereby had to admit that in countries like Finland the rule of law is arranged in a way that makes it almost impossible to think that anyone could

---

1. Räsänen, Päivi, "Kristittynä maallistuneessa yhteiskunnassa—kristillinen ihmiskuva haastettuna," 4, 8–9.
2. *Kouvolan Sanomat* 12/7/2013.

be entitled to actually act against the written law. She further stressed that she had given her speech not as a Minister in the state of Finland, but as a Christian member of the church. However, she noted that her office as a Minister could not be totally excluded when she was speaking in public. In a way she admitted that her wordings had been careless.[3]

The case was felt to be embarrassing by the church authorities. The Archbishop of the Lutheran church, among others, found it necessary to underscore publicly that the view expressed by Räsänen could not be seen as an official stand taken by the church.[4]

This case is interesting and it raises a large number of questions. I will return to this example several times below. I think that the example is an expression of the transitional times we all are in the midst of.

In my chapter, I will primarily focus on the modern, secular state and society in relation to religion and the church, and upon the radical change which our societies undergo when the secularism, which is taken for granted in modernity, is being questioned. The changes open up for a post-secular way of understanding society and politics.

My context is primarily the Nordic societies with their strong Lutheran tradition. Almost 80 percent of the populations still belong to the Lutheran Church in all countries although the number is decreasing.

THE POST-SECULAR IN A LUTHERAN TRADITION

Professor Brad S. Gregory, professor at the University of Notre Dame, published an important book in 2012 where he tries to show how important traits in the Reformation must be seen as having contributed to the coming to be of the modern secularized society.

According to him Martin Luther and other church reformers started a process resulting in something quite different from what they had intended. The result was a modern society where the understanding of the Church and the state, the religious and the secular radically changed. Belief in God lost its influence over ordinary life. The language used outside a religious sphere slowly lost all transcendent connotations. Finally this modern secularism has also colored the general understanding of religion.[5]

3. *Päivi Räsäsen blogi*, 10/7/2013.

4. *Helsingin Sanomat* 11/7/2013.

5. Gregory, *The Unintended Reformation: How a Religious Revolution Secularized Society*, 1–14, 382–87. Charles Taylor makes a similar point, see Taylor, *A Secular Age*, 19–22, 75–84, 767–72. I am not convinced by Gregory's optimism regarding religious truth claims and their ability to overcome the relativism of a secular, liberal modern culture. (Gregory, *The Unintended Reformation*, 384–85.) However, his picture of the modern development is convincing to most other parts.

Gregory and, before him, Charles Taylor have both offered us important interpretations of the becoming of the modern secular societies where religion is marginalized, and a clear split between the secular and the religious emerges. Eventually they both suggest the possibility of a radical critique of an ideological secular spirit. I will take such a post- secular view of secularism as my starting point, adopting the following words by a third important interpreter, Jeffrey W. Robbins.

> With the postsecular reconfiguration of the proper role of religion within the public sphere, it is no longer a question of whether religion and politics mix, but how. More specifically, since the postsecular indicates a change in mindset about the enduring nature of religious beliefs and practices and, consequently, a change with regard to the secularist self-understanding of the state, then how might religion contribute to making our politics more democratic?[6]

I take the emerging of a post-secular condition today as a fact. My interest is in how this change could be understood, and what a Lutheran tradition may contribute to this ongoing change in contemporary Western societies. Consequently the Lutheran idea of two kingdoms becomes central.[7]

I take it that the main idea of the two kingdoms is well-known. Roughly it draws a line between church authorities and political authorities. In his rule over mankind God uses law and gospel. In the spiritual realm, God rules through the gospel, while God in the worldly realm uses politics and the written law. By Luther himself the political understanding of the law could be a matter both for the Prince and for church theologians. However, the proclaiming of the gospel belonged only to the church, while the worldly, secular, matters (the political use of the law) concerned things outside the spiritual realm of the church. In these latter matters both church and state authorities could have something to say. This was due to a commonly held belief in God.

In the era of the reformation, the distinction between the two realms, or regiments, was applied within a cultural frame where belief in God was taken for granted, and God-talk (religious language) was a natural part of people's understanding of their daily life and of the political authorities.

---

6. Robbins, *Radical Democracy and Political Theology*, 180.

7. The following paragraphs lean on a more detailed presentation I have made in Kurtén, "Political theology in a Nordic post-secular setting," 90–95. For a good presentation of the original view by Luther, but a slightly different interpretation from mine of the current Lutheran position, see Andersen, "Can We Still Do Lutheran Political Theology?," 110–27.

Religiously colored deliberations played a part in the way political power was understood and talked about. People in Northern Europe lived in a *monolithic Christian society*, where church authorities had a great influence on the organizing of life in society and the state.

From the seventeenth century onwards things slowly changed. Sociologically, these changes were caused by the growing functional differentiation of the Western societies. The change was also mirrored in moral philosophy. A strictly secular ethical reflection on rational grounds developed relatively early (by Immanuel Kant, "Anglosachs utilitarians," etc.). Contractarian philosophers like Thomas Hobbes, John Locke, Jean-Jacques Rousseau, among others, formulated the foundations for much of social philosophy that is still relevant today.[8]

As a consequence of the factors mentioned, the separation between religion and politics has been a quite typical feature of the Nordic societies over the past fifty years. The Lutheran churches have not had any difficulties adjusting to this secularized political discourse. Due to the idea of the two kingdoms, Lutheran social ethics has understood moral life and the political realm as belonging to the part of life that human beings have in common, whereas the special competence of the church deals with the spiritual part of life.

The problem with this modern secular situation lied in the way a secular mentality became an all embracing framework. Where formerly a Christian belief in God had been a stabilizing factor in a monolithic Christian society, now a mentality totally independent of the church shaped *a monolithic secular society*. Thereby, the understanding of the idea of the two kingdoms underwent a huge change. Secular reason, which was in every respect uninfluenced by the idea of a God, was the kind of reason that defined the language which everyone, including all Christians, used in their daily life, also in politics.

In such a context political theology could hardly develop. Theology, besides social ethics on purely humanistic grounds, had no part to play in political life.

The position taken by minister Räsänen could be seen as one not fully accepting such a situation. I think she can be interpreted as wishing to say that, in fact, abortion is against the law of God and therefore abortion should not be accepted—on the grounds of biblical arguments. And I suggest that the reaction by those leaving the church was a reaction to this position that Räsänen took on religious, moral grounds, and to the idea

---

8. Suffice it to mention the rational social philosophy by Jürgen Habermas and John Rawls.

that such moral deliberations ought to be publicly accepted and put into a political framework. As a Christian person she may have any opinions she likes, but in public she is not allowed to express them with any claim for general acceptance.

The present talk of "post-secularity" takes us a step outside of both the monolithic Christian, and the monolithic secular society. The views that people in the current Nordic societies take for granted can neither any longer automatically be perceived to depend upon a belief in God, nor on a belief in secular reason. A common language suitable for the discussion of public matters has lost part of its validity. The question then arises: How does this influence the way a Christian view of life (on Lutheran grounds) can be expressed?

THE RETURN OF RELIGION—HABERMAS AND TAYLOR

The idea, primarily within the sociology of religion, of the secularized society, and of an inevitable development in Western societies towards totally non-religious societies, has been seriously questioned ever since the 1990s. Especially since the turn of the century, sociologists have talked about two phenomena that are different but interrelated: the return of religion and the post-secular society.[9]

Both of these concepts are of importance when we try to understand what is going on in Western countries just now.

Jürgen Habermas has awoken much interest for his changed view on public discourse. Due, among other things, to the phenomena of 9/11 and the growing presence of Islam in Western democracies, Habermas began to rethink his idea of the conditions for political public discourse. There must be room also for voices stemming from religious contexts to take part in political life, on their own premises, he now wishes to say. However, (and this is the key problem) we must, according to him, presuppose a kind of *lingua franca* on the political arena. And this shared language must be a secular, "neutral," one.

In an article published in 2011, Habermas explicitly sticks to the idea of a secular language common to all citizens. In addition, religious people bring in a language that is meaningful only to a smaller group. Such a language has therefore to be translated when it enters a political discourse.[10]

---

9. One starting point was a book edited by Peter Berger in 1999: Berger, *The Desecularization of the World : Resurgent Religion and World Politics*.

10. Habermas, "'The Political'. The rational Meaning of a Questionable Inheritance of Political Theology," 23–25.

In the same book where the article by Habermas is published, Charles Taylor also notices the return of religion, but draws different conclusions. Taylor sees the difference between religious and non-religious arguments and use of language. But he claims that they ought to be equally treated as valid ways of arguing on the same level that secular arguments do work.[11]

When replying to Habermas' idea of a neutral political language, Taylor points out the impossibility of translating certain religious beliefs. Habermas' request that every religious argument ought to be translated is met by Taylor saying: "You can't have translation for those kinds of [religious] references [Habermas' example is Gen. 1] because they are the references that really touch on certain people's spiritual lives and not others."[12]

Taylor's point is understandable within a post-secular frame where priority of a secular perspective is not taken for granted. In an adequate way he thereby manages not only to question the primacy of a secular viewpoint. He also underlines the impossibility of translating some religious expressions into something else.

We can again return to minister Räsänen from Finland. The point that one should obey God more than humans is of course nonsense to a non-religious person. And it is difficult to see how it could be translated into a language in which this interlocutor would really understand Räsänen. It is not enough to say that Räsänen embraces a theory of an invisible being called God who demands that she does not take part in abortion practices, which Habermas perhaps could accept. The weight of the religious position includes much more. It includes, as Taylor could be inclined to say, a whole life, lived in a Christian community and led by ponderings over the will of God given, among other things, through the Bible.

The return of religion thereby makes it urgent to dig deeper into the conditions for a public discourse in present societies and for the idea of a political theology. The concept of the post-secular takes us a step forward.

POST-SECULAR POLITICAL THEOLOGY—ROBBINS

The argument of Taylor, given above, touches upon a question which is important for any idea of political theology. What exactly are the conditions for a theopolitical discourse in a multicultural society? What can be done when a shared language cannot be taken for granted? How could we reach agreement? And what would it mean to reach agreement? The answers are not obvious.

---

11. Taylor, "Why We Need a Radical Redefinition of Secularism," 49–51.
12. Habermas and Taylor, "Dialogue," 64.

Jeffrey W. Robbins has tried to express a theological view on politics in the present post-secular context. Robbins develops a democratic political theology adjusted to a multicultural society. He presents a way of understanding politics in opposition to a possible modern understanding of political sovereignty in democracies. The view of political power expressed by the German philosopher Carl Schmitt in the 1930s expressed ideas that are still considered to be valid within the political discourse, on the left and the right wings of the political field. Schmitt defended a legitimate, absolute power of the state. Thereby the political sovereign has the mandate to stop the democratic discussion on some point. In such a tradition also the democratic ruler can represent an absolute power. The only alternative seems to be an acceptance of different views where no one is allowed to attain absolute power. Robbins welcomes a post-secular political arena where citizens are allowed to enter on religious as well as on non-religious grounds.[13] The view has bearings on how the relation between church and state can be understood, which we see from the following quotation.

> Returning to my argument in its schematic form, recognizing the inherently political dimension within any an [sic] all religious formulations should not be misconstrued as a denial either of the process of secularization or of the continued political commitment to the separation of church and state. Instead, what we have with the postsecular is a rejection of a rigid, modernist, secular ideology that would extend a particular political commitment—namely, the separation of church and state, which only emerged and makes sense within a particular, historical, cultural, and religious matrix—into a generalized rule regarding the separation of powers.[14]

Looking at the post-secular condition Robbins at the same time sees a risk in the return of religion to the public: it opens up for a transcendent voice undermining the democratic discourse as a discussion between equals.[15]

The solution is not to deny religion the return to the public. However, an inherent possibility in every view on religious grounds, to make the view absolutely compelling, must be critically attended to. Robbins therefore argues that a fundamental task of political theology is to continuously remind the democratic leaders that democracy is an open process, and that the idea of sovereignty is a threat to every democratic state. The contribution

---

13. Robbins, *Radical Democracy and Political Theology*, 14–15, 70–74, 97.
14. Ibid., 85–86.
15. Ibid., 81–86.

of political theology is not primarily some religiously colored policy apart from secular politics. His main concern is in the form rather than in the content.

> Thus, the democratic political theology envisioned here is neither an ideological argument for restoring religion to a place of centrality for what is otherwise feared to be a nihilistic culture nor a positioning of some transcendent base of authority by which a more potent form of political resistance might be developed and deployed. It is instead only a supplement to a much larger effort at rethinking the conceptual bases for democratic theory and practice.[16]

The task of political theology is to be a necessary supplement to an ongoing process of finding new forms for democratic decision-making. In a post-secular situation the political realm cannot afford to be blind to a religious element that necessarily is part of the political. It is the task of political theology to remind of the danger of a religious element (a dimension of something absolute) in every policymaking, both religious and non-religious. Robbins thereby underscores that the political power belongs to humanity, not to a transcendent God.

> Democracy as the theological affirmation of the power particular to humanity is 'the decision of the multitude over itself'. So understood, the political potency that is key to radical democracy's resistance to all forms of hegemony comes not by way of a transcendent authority—by an appeal to some power outside ourselves—but by way of an exodus emanating from within: 'In postmodernity', [the Italian philosopher Antonio] Negri writes, 'the eminent form of rebellion is the exodus from obedience, that is to say, from participation in measure, i.e., as the opening of the immeasurable.'[17]

The task that Robbins thus gives to political theology seems to be quite limited. It is concerned with the form rather than with the content. However, I find that his position in an important way points to the impossibility of forming a policy which one could claim that everybody ought to accept, on an argumentative basis.

Robbins does not deny that politics concerns substantial questions. However he tries to overcome the distinction between a secular and a religious context by stressing a common humanity so to say beyond this

---

16. Ibid., 190.
17. Ibid., 191.

dichotomy. He seems to be saying that no part, in a political discussion open to all citizens, must claim monopoly of the truth.

> As a radical democracy that insists upon the immanence or our common life together and the generative power that comes from our modes of cooperation, both already present and still to come, this is a project that is theopolitical as well. A valorization of the City of Man as our home, a grappling with the nature of sovereign power as it has become radically transformed by its divestment and diffusion, and an affirmation of humanity's own creative capacities and political potency—this alternative political theology proves itself both possible and a necessary supplement to radical philosophy's project at rethinking the conceptual bases of democracy itself.[18]

I think this position by Robbins contains both a formal and a substantial task for political theology. I can agree to his view. However, I want to elaborate a little more both the conditions and the more precise nature of a Christian contribution to politics in a post-secular situation. And I want to make plausible that the position so viewed is the one that must currently be taken also by a Lutheran church.

I will take up some points by the American theologian Stanley Hauerwas in a later section. However, I want already now to point to Hauerwas' affirmative comment to radical democracy.

> I hope therefore that it might be possible to tell the story of the church across time and space as the story of conflict that makes possible a political alternative otherwise not available. No doubt the church has often betrayed this 'politics' by imitating the diverse forms that the politics of fear can take. Yet Christians rightly believe that God has never left the church without faithful witnesses capable of identifying and challenging our accommodation to the powers. If it is useful to call this process 'radical democracy', I certainly have no objections.[19]

MANY LANGUAGES, ONE HUMANITY—GAITA

As we have seen, the playgrounds of both a pre-modern Lutheranism and a secular modernity are currently put aside. This makes it necessary, both for individual Christians and for a Lutheran Church, to become theologically

---

18. Ibid., 191.

19. Stanley Hauerwas in Hauerwas and Coles, *Christianity, Democracy, and the Radical Ordinary: Conversations between a Radical Democrat and a Christian*, 30.

conscious in political matters in a way which is different both from the premodern reformation period and the modern secularist one.

How can a Lutheran theology meet that challenge? Is it possible to find a common language in spite of some profound differences over important points? In a previous article I expressed *the hope* that a sense of a common humanity could be found. In addition, my point was that such a sense cannot rest on certainty, offered by a shared rationality. Together with Taylor we have to reject Habermas' idea of a secular, "neutral" language, common to all.[20] Are there other ways to get hold of something common to all humankind?

In order to answer that question I will turn to philosophers and theologians inspired by Ludwig Wittgenstein. I will suggest that we find some important insights, that take us a step forward, in a contextual understanding of language in line with the thoughts by Wittgenstein.

The Australian philosopher Raimond Gaita gives a good expression of the dilemma we are presently facing. In his book *A Common Humanity* (1998), he tries to show something commonly human which would draw us humans together. As far as I can see, Gaita, who is working in a tradition very much formed by Wittgenstein, refuses to build upon the modern idea of rationality common to us all. He does this, among other things, by arguing for a concept of "humanity" based on an understanding of love. In the important preface of the book, he writes the following:

> Later I argue that improbable though it may seem at first, placing the weight that I do on our humanity and on love rather than on, say, the obligated acknowledgement of rights is more hardheaded than the longing to make secure to reason what reason cannot secure, all the while whistling in the dark.[21]

In a tight way Gaita here criticizes modern rational thinking for its tendency to look for comfort in a reason that, after all, is incapable of giving security. Instead he wishes to investigate whether not something like love could better constitute our moral and political life.

Gaita perceives of humanity as a concept that may bring us people together. However, it is not humanity in the shape of Human Rights that comes to his mind. He searches for something more profound which he thinks could be found in a talk of love in terms of relations. He implicitly criticizes "Human Rights" and "Human Dignity" as characteristics which

---

20. Kurtén, "Political theology in a Nordic post-secular setting," 107–9.
21. Gaita, *A Common Humanity: Thinking About Love and Truth and Justice*, xxi.

can be stated independent of the way fellow humans relate to a concrete human person.

> Treat me as a human being, fully as your equal, without condescension—that demand (or plea), whether it is made by women to men or by blacks to whites, is a demand or a plea for justice (…) conceived as equality or respect. Only when one's humanity is fully visible will one be treated as someone who can intelligibly press claims to equal access to goods and opportunities.[22]

The emphasis is here put *on the way we humans relate* to "the other."

Gaita's analysis continues by his pointing to the importance of love for our ability to see the humanity in every fellow human being. In a very intense sentence he expresses a view where the idea of the possibility to look at a person with love is a precondition for our whole way of relating to that other person.

> We have obligations to those whom we do not and could not love, but that does not mean that we would find it intelligible that we should have those obligations if we did not also find it intelligible that someone could love them, and more fundamentally, if we did not see them as having the kind of individuality I elaborate in this book and which, I claim, is in part constituted by our attachments, of which the forms of love are the most important.[23]

Gaita finds that love has an epistemic role to play. Love reveals what he calls "the preciousness of individuals." Then he adds "Often we see something as precious only when we see it in the light of someone's love."[24] In the love of saints, Gaita sees the paradigm example of love. It deepens our language of love to a point where even the worst of evil-doers will be seen as our fellow human beings. A talk of human rights or of unconditional respect for others becomes empty if such a language of love ceases to affect us.

Gaita, himself a non-religious philosopher, wants to think that the kind of love he tries to explicate is possible to keep up independent of any religious sentiments. His paradigm example of the deepest kind of love is a case where a nun he once met showed her love for a most miserable human being. Gaita himself was able to observe her actions of love in a psychiatric hospital where he once worked as a young boy. He, however, thinks that this

---

22. Ibid., xxi.
23. Ibid., xxii.
24. Ibid.

kind of life is not necessarily constituted by a religious context like the one the nun lived in.

Here we meet a most important passage. Gaita relates a discussion he once had with Stanley Hauerwas. Hauerwas had asked him "whether the kind of love shown by the nun could exist in the prolonged absence of the kind of practices that were part of her religious vocation." And Gaita remarks "I don't know the answer."[25]

I think this illustrates the current dilemma we are facing when we try to express the conditions for political theology today: We cannot be sure that a standpoint stemming from one religious or cultural context could be fully understood and be meaningfully put into practice by people stemming from quite different contexts.

There are at least two important lessons one can learn from this: the first one is that the moral point in question is *something that is shown* in a life of actions, not anything that can be put in words of theory. And the second lesson is the one taken up by Hauerwas' remark: *Is it possible* to imagine the coming-to-be of the self-sacrificing love in the example *without the kind of community which supports* the whole life of the nun?

The position of Gaita is one way to approach the future of social ethics. What he can teach us, among other things, is that the classical Lutheran idea of human reasonableness as constituting our common humanity must be put under debate. Human morality is not, according to him, manageable by reason. Reasonableness has limits which are not the limits of morality. Furthermore Gaita's position invites us to look for concrete ways of life, not for principles regulating such life.

If we return to our Minister-story, we get a totally different perspective through Gaita. What becomes central is not an idea of what should be the right way of handling abortion cases. What becomes central is a more holistic understanding of the persons involved. What does the actions of Räsänen say concerning her moral outlook? And what do we learn from the church members leaving the church on this occasion? The answers will be many. However, they all contribute to an understanding of what a Christian existence in Finnish society today might embrace. As far as Räsänen is concerned, a closer analysis could perhaps take up the significance of her being a member of the government in relation to her eventual rejection of the Finnish law on abortions, and what it means that she, despite this fact, has seen it fit to become a minister in the first place.

---

25. Ibid., 17, xxiv.

OVERCOMING FIDEISM—WITTGENSTEIN AND HAUERWAS

The next thinker I wish to present has been mentioned in passing in the previous sections. The theological ethicist Stanley Hauerwas, professor emeritus (he retired in November 2014) at Duke University, USA, is a well known and much criticized moral theologian.

Hauerwas has been labeled a tribalist and a *fideist*, both of which characteristics he does not feel fitting. I agree with him. However, the accusation of being a fideist brings us to the question which occupies us here. And this is also a point where the influence of Wittgenstein upon Hauerwas becomes clear. Hauerwas himself has declared his intellectual debts to Wittgenstein several times.[26]

Within the philosophy of religion there has been a continuing discussion of fideism in the view of Wittgenstein and his followers—most important of which is Dewi Z. Phillips. The view of Wittgenstein was labeled "Wittgenstein fideism" by the Canadian philosopher Kai Nielsen in 1967. To a great extent, Nielsen builds his concept of "fideism" on some terms found in the writings of Wittgenstein. The most important concept is that of "language game." According to Nielsen, a language game is by definition an activity that consists of language and connected actions in a closed context. Within a certain language-game such concepts as true or false, right or wrong and so forth, can be applied. But there is no archimedian point, Nielsen observes, outside this game with the help of which the game with its grammar could be justified or philosophically criticized.[27] In other words, talking of religious language in the way Wittgenstein suggests makes it, according to Nielsen, into a language that is meaningful only within a closed context, like a church.

The precondition for Nielsen is of course a modern secular rationality. The picture resembles the view of Habermas. In Nielsen's case, the requirement for critique primarily concerns "religious" views. Religious God-talk should be discussed publicly on a basis of shared rational presuppositions, Nielsen claims.[28]

What the late D.Z. Philips patiently tried to explain during his last forty years, was that the problematic point in the view of Nielsen lies in the

---

26. See for example Hauerwas, *The Peaceable Kingdom: A Primer in Christian Ethics*, xix–xxi. One of the most thorough studies of Hauerwas in relation to Wittgenstein is made by Brad Kallenberg, see Kallenberg, *Ethics as Grammar: Changing the Postmodern Subject*.

27. Kai Nielsen in Nielsen and Phillips, *Wittgensteinian Fideism?*, 22–23, 100–101.

28. Kai Nielsen in ibid., 122–23.

idea of some neutral observer position, entitling the philosopher to make judgments on universal rational grounds.[29] As we can see, this objection by Phillips resembles Taylor's critique of Habermas.

During the later part of the twentieth century, Phillips' position was not understood by many of his interlocutors.[30] This can be seen as an example of the modern, rationalist, and secular framework which was taken for granted. According to the modern mind, there simply must be a position from outside where language can be used independent of any context, or where you can presuppose a universal context common to all of mankind. Religious language must be possible to understand outside a very limited religious context in order to avoid a fideistic position. That is the essence of Nielsen's argument.

However, Phillips' understanding of religious language does not imply the idea that this language would have a bearing only upon a small Christian context—within the church or something like that. A Christian view of life concerns every part of human life.[31] This is easily seen, for example, in the wordings of prayers. Its meaning is embedded in the daily life of people, as also Luther was eager to teach his fellow Christians.

Phillips' position may be seen as representative of post-secular thought, be it that it was adopted at a much earlier stage than the ideas of the post-secular writers of today. Phillips denies that a religious language could be meaningfully taken out of its concrete context in real people's lives, and inserted into a philosophical context of general principles and ways of justification. However, the concrete context must not be mistaken to consist only of a private sphere, or of an isolated life in the church. The concrete context is constituted by the life the religious person leads, both in the church and in the world outside the church. And a religious language can have bearings upon every part of human life, and upon every part of society.

According to me, the same point may, *mutatis mutandis,* be applied to Stanley Hauerwas' whole program for theological ethics. In his view we meet a heavy critique of the modern liberal society and state (he thinks mainly of the United States and the way in which the USA have been built up). If you study his enormous production, you will find a (for the most part) coherent expression of what I here have named a post-secular political theology. As a theologian he finds his primary context in the Christian church. And every Christian life must, by definition, be a life in the church.

---

29. Dewi Z. Phillips in ibid., 80–82.
30. See for example the discussions in Runzo, *Is God Real?*
31. See for example Phillips, "Wittgenstein's Full Stop," 186–87.

However, that does not mean that a Christian would live an apolitical life.[32] On the contrary; as we have seen Hauerwas can find a Christian politically at home in radical democracy.

Only when we are able to see such features in Hauerwas' position we can see how he illuminates our problem in this chapter. The ethical position of Hauerwas is a radical *no* to the possibility of finding a common ethical and political language on modern secular grounds. But that does not mean that he deems it impossible to communicate a Christian political position in the larger society. He pleads for theological ethics built upon a Christian life in the church. His, perhaps somewhat idealistic, view is that the church *is* a social ethic. That is, the community of the church gets a central political role.[33]

You don't have to be a "Hauerwasian" in a narrow sense to see the point he is trying to make. With his stressing of the church, of virtue ethics, and of a narrative understanding of how to pass on an ethical point of view in language, he provides the means for a theological and a Christian ethic with political implications. It is a position that accepts the difficulties to imagine a common political (secular) language in a multi religious and a multicultural world. The political view is primarily communicated through practical actions, through a way of life, not through theoretical deliberations.

For my part I find it important to focus on the individual citizen within a democratic state. In our attempts to explicate the possible political role of an individual Christian in current Nordic societies, Hauerwas offers a view that is not building on pre-modern Christian, nor on modern secularistic, presuppositions. Under post-secular conditions a Christian may anchor his whole life in the tradition of the church and he may express his ethical position in a virtual life taking shape in concrete political engagement. Through his way of life he communicates his religious life-view. Instead of modern morally normative deliberations leaning on a supposedly common rationality he expresses his political and social ethical views in narratives.

CONCLUSIONS

I agree with Robbins' remark that the post-secular situation gives rise to the question of *how* the religious and the political mix. If we accept the

---

32. Suffice it to point at the view presented in one of Hauerwas's earlier books, mentioned above: Hauerwas, *The Peaceable Kingdom*.

33. See Tolonen, *Witness is Presence: Reading Stanley Hauerwas in a Nordic Setting*. For another Nordic study of the political theology by Hauerwas, see Rasmusson, *The Church as Polis. From Political Theology to Theological Politics as Exemplified by Jürgen Moltmann and Stanley Hauerwas*.

view presented by me in this chapter, the traditional ways of understanding Lutheran social ethics must be abandoned. The traditional interpretation of the two kingdoms presupposes the idea of a common political and ethical language that unites all members of a society. When this presupposition is questioned, Lutheran theology must understand the identity of the church and the task of Christian theological ethics in a new way. I have only sketched what this might imply.

Much can be learnt from the voices I have referred to in my chapter. At the end of the day I think that the most important thing to be learnt from them is that a Christian cannot take for granted that her/his fellow humans would actually share her/his personal moral views. And, as Robbins firmly underscores, this should challenge everyone to be humble, and to give room for "the other" to represent a way of life different from one's own. The most important factor when it comes to one's own view, will not be the linguistic expressions of one's standpoint, but the way every person (Christian or non-Christian) through her/his way of life shows what she/he means by language as it is used.

What about minister Räsänen? If Päivi Räsänen had lived in a monolithic Christian society, then a well informed Lutheran position would have been to publicly discuss, for example abortion, as a question of the will of God, involving all citizens. If she had lived in a modern monolithic secular society, then a solution to the abortion question would entail discussions on rational and purely secular grounds concerning right ways to handle such questions. However, when she lives in a multi religious and multicultural society she has to take her stand in moral, and political, questions on the basis of her personal (Christian) view of life. This is the only possible solution even for a good Lutheran. And this position-taking cannot presuppose that every other citizen will agree. She has to make her point, live according to it, and *hope* that fellow humans would see her point as valid.

BIBLIOGRAPHY

Andersen, Svend. "Can We Still Do Lutheran Political Theology?" *Studia Theologica* 67 (2013) 110–27.

Berger, Peter, editor. *The Desecularization of the World: Resurgent Religion and World Politics*. Washington, D.C. and Grand Rapids, MI: Eerdmans, 1999.

Gaita, Raimond. *A Common Humanity: Thinking About Love and Truth and Justice*. London and New York: Routledge, 2000.

Gregory, Brad S. *The Unintended Reformation: How a Religious Revolution Secularized Society*. Cambridge, MA: Belknap of Harvard University Press, 2012.

Habermas, Jürgen. "'The Political'. The rational Meaning of a Questionable Inheritance of Political Theology." In Judith Butler et al., *The Power of Religion in the Public Sphere*, 15–33. New York: Columbia University Press, 2011.

Habermas, Jürgen, and Charles Taylor. "Dialogue." In Judith Butler et al., *The Power of Religion in the Public Sphere*, 60–69. New York: Columbia University Press, 2011.
Hauerwas, Stanley. *The Peaceable Kingdom: A Primer in Christian Ethics*. Notre Dame: University of Notre Dame Press, 2002.
Hauerwas, Stanley, and Romand Coles. *Christianity, Democracy, and the Radical Ordinary. Conversations between a Radical Democrat and a Christian*. Theopolitical Visions. Eugene, OR: Cascade, 2008.
Helsingin Sanomat. 11/7/2013.
Kallenberg, Brad J. *Ethics as Grammar: Changing the Postmodern Subject*. Notre Dame: University of Notre Dame Press, 2001.
Kouvolan Sanomat. 12/7/2013.
Kurtén, Tage. "Political theology in a Nordic post-secular setting." *Studia Theologica* 67 (2013) 90–109.
Nielsen, Kai, and Dewi Z. Phillips. *Wittgensteinian Fideism?* London: SCM, 2005.
Päivi Räsäsen blogi, 10/7/2013. Online: http://paivirasanen.puheenvuoro.uusisuomi.fi/144338-suomen-lakia-on-noudatettava (accessed 14/02/2014).
Phillips, Dewi Z. "Wittgenstein's Full Stop." In *Perspectives on the Philosophy of Wittgenstein*, edited by Irving Block. Oxford: Blackwell, 1981.
Rasmusson, Arne. *The Church as Polis. From Political Theology to Theological Politics as Exemplified by Jürgen Moltmann and Stanley Hauerwas*. Lund: Lund University Press, 1994.
Robbins, Jeffrey W. *Radical Democracy and Political Theology*. New York: Columbia University Press, 2011.
Runzo, Joseph, editor. *Is God Real?* Basingstoke: Macmillan, 1977.
Räsänen, Päivi. "Kristittynä maallistuneessa yhteiskunnassa—kristillinen ihmiskuva haastettuna." Online: http://on.fi/sites/default/files/bilagor/rasanens_tal.pdf (accessed 10/02/2014).
Taylor, Charles. *A Secular Age*. Cambridge, MA: Belknap of Harvard University Press, 2007.
———. "Why We Need a Radical Redefinition of Secularism." In Judith Butler et al., *The Power of Religion in the Public Sphere*, 34–59. New York: Columbia University Press, 2011.
Tolonen, Miika. *Witness is Presence: Reading Stanley Hauerwas in a Nordic Setting*. Åbo: Åbo Akademi University, 2012.

11

The "Communitarian" Critique of Luther's Ethics

LEIF SVENSSON

Martin Luther's ethics have been widely criticized in modern theology. As is well-known, the critique after the Second World War can in part be understood as a reaction against the way some influential Protestant theologians connected Luther's thinking on the two kingdoms and orders of creation to an emphasis on the German Volk—in order to legitimize the National Socialist regime—in the 1930s and 1940s.

I will argue that Ernst Troeltsch is also important to recent critique of Luther's ethics. Troeltsch is often connected with objections raised against Luther in the early twentieth century. However, elements of his analysis have been further developed by community- and tradition-oriented theologians, who make up a very influential strand of contemporary Luther critique. The result of their critique is that Luther's ethics is often conceived by Christian theologians today at best as irrelevant, and at worst as deeply problematic. Furthermore, there is, to some extent, an unfortunate lack of attention paid to the critique among Luther scholars, which has helped to cement simplified notions about Luther and also contributed to the isolation of Luther research from critical questions.

In this chapter, I will describe the main features of Troeltsch's critical interpretation of Luther's ethics and analyze the direction it has taken in a contemporary "communitarian" critique of Luther. The aim is to highlight this critique as a major challenge for Lutherans today. I will end it by presenting David S. Yeago's research as a way to take up the gauntlet. Yeago points to interesting aspects of Luther's ethics that are often neglected by defenders and critics of Luther alike.

ERNST TROELTSCH'S INTERPRETATION OF LUTHER'S ETHICS

Troeltsch was famous for his role in what was known as the History of Religions School. His work was very wide in scope and can be described as a mixture of theology, philosophy, sociology, and history. One of the aims of Troeltsch's research was to understand the role of the Reformation in the development of the modern world view. His fundamental answer was that the Reformation was a reformulation of the medieval cultural synthesis or *corpus christianum*. As in medieval theology, he thought a single vision of truth unified both the church and the state in early Protestant thinking.[1] His interpretation of Luther was important to the argument that early Protestantism stands in continuity with medieval theology. Luther's thinking, says Troeltsch, must be understood as a response to medieval problems. However, he transformed medieval concepts of, for example, grace and faith and thereby introduced indirect elements of importance to the formation of the modern world.[2] According to Troeltsch, the idea of autonomy is the determining factor of the modern world view. But he thought only some beginnings of this principle can be connected with Luther. So in the end it seems that Troeltsch identified a tension between medieval supernaturalism and modern religious individualism in Luther.[3]

The main features of Troeltsch's critical understanding of Luther's ethics[4] become especially visible in his most famous work, *The Social Teaching of the Christian Churches* (1912). For Luther, writes Troeltsch, Christianity is mainly about faith, that is, religious individualism and inner community with God. This is reflected in Luther's understanding of the church. The preaching of the Word, the sacraments, and the office of the ministry make the church visible, but the church's influence is restricted to a purely spiritual sphere. The Word's inner and personal influence is what constitutes

---

1. See Danz, "Reformation, Neuzeit und die ethische Bestimmtheit des Glaubens. Überlegungen zur Lutherdeutung von Ernst Troeltsch und Friedrich Gogarten," 262-63; Drescher, *Ernst Troeltsch: His Life and Work*, 134-35.

2. Troeltsch, "Protestantisches Christentum und Kirche in der Neuzeit," 481-94; Troeltsch, *Protestantism and Progress: A Historical Study of the Relation of Protestantism to the Modern World*, 191-199; Troeltsch, *The Social Teaching of the Christian Churches*, Vol. II, 465-494. See further Danz, "Reformation, Neuzeit und die ethische Bestimmtheit des Glaubens," 260-70; Drescher, *Ernst Troeltsch*, 135-36, 139-41, 144, 235-36; von Loewenich, *Luther und der Neuprotestantismus*, 132-34.

3. Cf. the analysis of Troeltsch's final verdict upon Luther's theology in Drescher, *Ernst Troeltsch*, 142-43; von Loewenich, *Luther und der Neuprotestantismus*, 139-40.

4. Troeltsch was not critical of all aspects of Luther's ethics. But even though he also see features he considered positive in Luther's understanding of morality, it still seems correct to identify a critical tone in much of what he had to say about it.

the church and the true community of Christians.[5] The Christian ethic developed by Luther, argues Troeltsch, tends towards a spiritual Christianity. What is most important is to carry out one's calling in a new inner spiritual disposition of obedience and love. Good works flow naturally from faith.[6]

Troeltsch also emphasizes Luther's conservatism, which leads to an unconditional respect for secular authority and its harsh methods for preserving order and dealing with sin. The secular and natural order contributes to welfare, represses evil and is instituted by God. To obey the authorities in society is therefore of the highest importance and the main way to serve one's neighbor is through the secular institutions. God has established nature as the sphere in which good values are to be realized.[7] Furthermore, Troeltsch identifies a double morality in Luther. In personal and private matters a Christian should follow the radical ethic of the Sermon on the Mount. However, the Christian also has the obligation to participate in and submit to the secular order, which is instituted by God. The Christian ethic is on the one hand radical and personal and on the other hand natural and controlled by secular reason.[8]

The impact of Troeltsch's interpretation of Luther was considerable. The way he connected Luther and the Reformation to the Medieval Age was at an early stage much criticized in Germany, where his understanding of Luther lost in influence because it called into question a common assumption in the German Protestant historiography of the time about Luther as a spiritual ancestor to modern Protestant theology and culture. However, Troeltsch's understanding of Luther's ethics met another fate in the English-speaking world, where it was used to criticize the nationalistic interpretation of Luther in Germany during the Weimar era and the rule of the National Socialist regime.[9] So Troeltsch's Luther analysis has continued to be important in the Anglo-Saxon theological debate since the Second World War.

---

5. Troeltsch, *The Social Teaching of the Christian Churches*, Vol. II, 470, 477–84.

6. Ibid., 494–95, 509–11; Troeltsch, "The Dispositional Ethic," 168–69; Troeltsch, "Stoic-Christian Natural Law and Modern Secular Natural Law," 333–34.

7. Troeltsch, *The Social Teaching of the Christian Churches*, Vol. II, 499–500, 529–35, 539–43, 547–53; Troeltsch, "Stoic-Christian Natural Law," 334–35.

8. Troeltsch, *The Social Teaching of the Christian Churches*, Vol. II, 499–500, 503–11.

9. I am following Thomas Kaufmann's account of the impact of Troeltsch's Luther interpretation in Kaufmann, "Luther zwischen den Wissenschaftskulturen. Ernst Troeltschs Lutherdeutung in der englischsprachigen Welt und in Deutschland," 457–58.

THE "COMMUNITARIAN" CRITIQUE OF LUTHER'S ETHICS

There are connections between Troeltsch and what I will call the "communitarian" critique of Luther's ethics in contemporary theology. Communitarianism is usually described as a movement in moral and political philosophy, which started in the 1970s and 1980s when a number of mainly political philosophers in America criticized what they considered to be the excessive individualism of liberal political theory. In contrast with contemporary individualist political reasoning, the communitarians emphasize the importance of tradition, social context, and community for moral and political thinking. Human behavior can never be understood in isolation from the different contexts that form individual lives.[10]

There are, however, certain problems connected with the communitarian label. To begin with, most of the main philosophers associated with the movement have rejected the term as an inadequate way of describing their positions. One objection to the label is that it gives the impression of an appeal to community in the abstract, but the philosophers described as communitarians are usually much more interested in what kinds of communities we should defend and support and which ones we should not. They do not consider community as a good in itself. Another objection is that the term is often associated with an alternative to liberalism, but this is problematic since several of the important thinkers usually included in the movement can describe their own political theory as a sort of chastened liberalism.[11] The situation is quite similar when it comes to theologians identified as communitarians. They are often critical of the term and point out that they are not appealing to community in a general sense. Instead, they are emphasizing the importance of the concrete community of the church to Christian ethics.[12]

Nevertheless, it is not uncommon to classify certain theologians as communitarians. A frequently expressed view is that the works of the Protestant theologian Stanley Hauerwas, who is influenced by some philosophers usually included in the communitarian movement, is a good example of a communitarian position in theological ethics. He is critical of modern individualism, among other things, and emphasizes the importance of, for example, the church, discipleship, virtues, and also the narrative tradition to Christian life. Hauerwas can describe the task of Christian ethics thus:

---

10. See Avineri and de-Shalit, "Introduction," 1–11; Bell, *Communitarianism and Its Critics*, 4–8.

11. See Beiner, *Liberalism, Nationalism, Citizenship*, 66–69.

12. See Rasmusson, "Justice and Solidarity in a 'Communitarian' Perspective."

> Theologians (...) have something significant to say about ethics, but they will not say it significantly if they try to disguise the fact that they think, write, and speak out of and to a distinctive community. (...) Our task as theologians remains what it has always been: namely, to exploit the considerable resources embodied in particular Christian convictions which sustain our ability to be a community faithful to our belief that we are creatures of a graceful God.[13]

As far as I know, Hauerwas does not criticize Luther's thinking on morality to any great extent in any of his texts.[14] Even so, one of the most influential currents of contemporary Luther critique is developed by Christian thinkers who can be connected with "Hauerwasian" ethics. This critique is based, at least partly, on an emphasis on community and tradition, and I will use the name "communitarian" critique as an abbreviation for it. The political theorist Jean Bethke Elshtain, the Catholic philosopher Alasdair MacIntyre, and the Mennonite theologian John Howard Yoder have much—though of course not everything—in common with Hauerwas' views, and they can also illustrate a "communitarian" critique of Luther's ethics.[15] Elshtain, MacIntyre, and Yoder are often depicted, though not by themselves, as communitarians. However, it is important to note that I am not using the label "communitarian" as a designation of a movement in political or moral philosophy but as a helpful term in describing a certain orientation in contemporary Luther critique.

Elshtain, MacIntyre, and Yoder share Hauerwas' critique of a modern prioritizing of the individual and his insistence on the formative role of tradition and community. Christian moral convictions and ethical reflection are, in their view, bound up with a distinctive, historical community. This, of course, set their own constructive theological and ethical positions apart from Troeltsch, who was an advocate of an idealistic morality which emphasized personal conscience and valued individual freedom and responsibility highly.[16] These differences in theological perspective also have an effect

---

13. Hauerwas, "On Keeping Theological Ethics Theological," 73–74.

14. Hauerwas' positive remarks on Luther's ethics might even outnumber his more negative one and he uses Luther constructively in a couple of books written together with William H. Willimon. See Hauerwas and Willimon, *Lord, Teach Us: The Lord's Prayer and the Christian Life*; Hauerwas and Willimon, *The Truth About God: The Ten Commandments in Christian Life*.

15. It should be noted that the main object of Yoder's critique is modern Lutheran ethics and not Luther, but it seems quite likely that this critique approximates his verdict on Luther's ethics.

16. For an informative description of Troeltsch's ethics, see Chapman, *Ernst Troeltsch and Liberal Theology: Religion and Cultural Synthesis in Wilhelmine Germany*, 138–186.

on their respective Luther interpretations. Elshtain, MacIntyre, and Yoder concentrate their criticism, in a way that Troeltsch does not, on what they identify as the strong individualism and neglect of community and tradition in Luther's ethics. Nevertheless, from the point of view of content, their descriptions of Luther are reminiscent of Troeltsch's. It might, therefore, be possible in a sense to call the "communitarian" critique Troeltschian.[17] Similarly to Troeltsch, this critique understands an emphasis on the individual, obedience to secular authority, and a double morality as characteristic features of Luther's ethics. It is now time to take a more detailed look at the critical Luther analyses of Elsthain, MacIntyre, and Yoder.

As we saw above, Troeltsch argues that Luther's thinking on Christian life is characterized by inwardness. The most important thing is the individual's inner community with God. Good works follow after the transformation of one's inner dispositions through faith. So Christian ethics is reduced to inner motivation. What is important is to impregnate natural activities with love and religious trust in God. This restriction of ethics to an inner spiritual sphere by Luther is emphasized by Elsthain and Yoder.[18]

They also follow Troeltsch's identification of a conservative stress on obedience to secular authority in Luther's thinking. God has instituted the secular and natural order as a necessary barrier to human sin and it is therefore necessary to subordinate oneself to the authorities in society. Temporal authority must be shown almost unconditional respect. They argue that this Lutheran emphasis on obedience to secular authority leads to a neglect of the importance of specific Christian norms and community to social life. Yoder thinks that many Lutherans fail to take due notice of the way the New Testament makes Christ central to social ethics.[19] He also says that this leads to a neglect of the role of the Christian community, the church, which the apostle Paul, according to Yoder, understands as

---

17. There are examples of a sort of Troeltschian Luther critique among theologians not constructively oriented to community and tradition. Important in this regard are the well-known brothers and theologians Reinhold Niebuhr and H. Richard Niebuhr. Their theologies are influenced by Troeltsch, and it is plausible that the same is the case with their critical Luther interpretation, which has many similarities with Troeltsch's. See their descriptions of Luther in Niebuhr, Reinhold, *The Nature and Destiny of Man: A Christian Interpretation*, vol. II, 187-98; Niebuhr, H. Richard, *Christ and Culture*, 170-79.

18. See Elshtain, *Meditations on Modern Political Thought: Masculine/Feminine Themes from Luther to Arendt*, 80-82; Elshtain, *Public Man, Private Woman: Women in Social and Political Thought*, 80-82; Elshtain, *Sovereignty: God, State, and Self*, 80-81; Yoder, *The Politics of Jesus: Vicit Agnus Noster*, 134-36; Yoder, *The Priestly Kingdom: Social Ethics as Gospel*, 140-41.

19. Yoder, *The Politics of Jesus*, 193-94, 198-99, 209-10.

> the primary social structure through which the gospel works to change other structures (...) Here, within this community, people are rendered humble and changed in the way they behave not simply by a proclamation directed to their sense of guilt but also by genuine social relationships with other persons who ask them about their obedience; who (in the words of Jesus) "bind and loose."[20]

Elshtain is critical of how Luther's emphasis on inner faith and celebration of temporal authority "depoliticizes" the church—it is stripped of its institutional authority, and political authority is transferred to secular rule instead:

> [A] (partially) sovereign self confronts a sovereign state that is limited by its place in God's orders of creation, although it is no longer hemmed in institutionally, the medieval Church having been stripped of its institutional authority. (...) In depoliticizing the Church, Luther does not so much break the bonds of authority as draw these tighter by providing for the flow of all political authority over to secular rule.[21]

Furthermore, Troeltsch stresses the appearance of a double morality in Luther's theology. There is, on the one hand, a radical Christian ethic, and, on the other hand, an autonomous secular ethic. In private matters, the ethic of the Sermon on the Mount is normative, but when exercising public office one must act in accordance with natural reason and not follow the radical Christian ethic. So there is a gap between God's commandments and the natural ethics of the social realm. The economic and political order has its own natural norms separate from the divine commandments. The individual is subject to both God and the secular order. MacIntyre argues that this means that the individual is not related to the secular order and God through a web of social relations. Instead, the individual stands alone before God and the state. The individual's social identity cannot provide a criterion for moral choice.[22] MacIntyre writes:

> From the facts of [the individual's] situations as he is able to describe them in his new social vocabulary nothing at all follows

---

20. Ibid., 153–54.

21. Elshtain, *Sovereignty*, 80–81. See also Elshtain, *Meditations on Modern Political Thought*, 13–15; Elshtain, *Public Man, Private Woman*, 83–84; Elshtain, *Sovereignty*, 77–85; Elshtain, *Women and War*, 135–36.

22. MacIntyre, *A Short History of Ethics: A History of Moral Philosophy from the Homeric Age to the Twentieth Century*, 121–26.

about what he ought to do. Everything comes to depend upon his own individual choice.[23]

I think the "communitarian" critique identifies several connected weak spots in much of modern Lutheran ethics, namely how it has often amounted to both a strong individualism and the irrelevance of Christian community, norms, and authorities to social life. The issue of problematic individualism becomes very apparent when Luther's so-called two kingdoms doctrine is interpreted in terms of a double morality. If there is a radical Christian ethic and an autonomous secular ethic that are separated from one another, a fundamental question arises: when should one follow the Christian ethic and when the secular one? It might be argued that in many cases this could be decided easily. However, it is often not so apparent if something should be understood as a private matter or as belonging to the duties of one's public office. This problem becomes more acute since the institutional authority of the church tends to be downplayed by Lutheran theologians. Furthermore, moral life is abstracted from the Christian social community. Moreover, the individual agent receives no guidelines and no help but needs to choose which of the competing policies to follow. It all depends on one's own choice.

However, did Karl Holl, the initiator of the Luther Renaissance, not, as is often asserted, decisively refute Troeltsch's charge of moral dualism?[24] Holl's answer to Troeltsch is also interesting since it is characteristic of much modern Luther scholarship. He agrees with Troeltsch that Luther maintains that reason should regulate civil affairs. However, Holl argues, Troeltsch has failed to observe that Luther demands of believers that they lift their reason to a higher level by the guiding force of love. The effects of Christian love must manifest themselves in society.[25] Love—and not natural law, the Bible or the gospel—is the rule by which it is possible, according to Luther, to distinguish the sinful estates and social structures from those ordained by God, writes Holl. He goes on to argue that Luther also understands love as the principle uniting the kingdom of God and the state. In the proper light, the state's coercive practice, when used correctly, is a work of love because its final purpose is to protect the weak, and the Christian community. Holl emphasizes, against Troeltsch, that Luther views the secular orders as institutions capable of improvement by the exercise of love. Furthermore, the ruling motive of actions must be love in both private and public life. How

23. Ibid., 126.
24. William H. Lazareth is one of those who argue thus, see Lazareth, *Christians in Society: Luther, the Bible, and Social Ethics*, 6–7.
25. Holl, *The Cultural Significance of the Reformation*, 28–29.

love should be expressed varies. Sometimes voluntary self-sacrifice is called for, and at other times even violent coercion. It is part of the freedom of a Christian to decide which course of action to take. What must be constant is a Christian attitude of love of one's neighbor and the absence of egoism.[26]

Holl, of course, subtly refined Troeltsch's analysis of Luther in many ways. Nevertheless, Holl's Luther interpretation fails to solve the problem of individualism highlighted by the "communitarian" critique. At the end of the day, Holl's emphasis on the spontaneous character of love and the freedom and the necessity of choosing what to do with love as a guiding motive still leaves the individual with little help and few concrete guidelines for moral actions. Holl's Luther—and therefore also the Luther of many modern Luther researchers—seems to leave it to individual choice. To a significant degree, the problem of individualism arises because the Christian community, norms, and authorities are irrelevant to social life in Holl's Luther understanding.

A POSSIBLE RESPONSE TO THE CRITIQUE: REREADING LUTHER WITH DAVID YEAGO

The "communitarian" critique is shared, at least partly, by many theologians today and it therefore provides an important clue as to why Luther's ethics often fail to gain a hearing in contemporary debate. The objections raised by this critique therefore amount to challenges to Lutherans today. Historically, the question about the content of Luther's thinking has been very important to Lutheran theologians owing to Luther's central role in the Lutheran tradition. It is true that his authoritative role in contemporary Lutheran theology is somewhat unclear, but the problems and resources in his ethics should still be of interest to Lutheran theologians wanting to take their own tradition seriously. So it seems a good idea to try to get to grips with the "communitarian" critique if one is interested in using Luther's ethics constructively. Two primary ways to do this are to argue the point that the features that the critics highlight are not problematic, or to show that there are sides of Luther's thinking not taken into account by the critics.

The latter approach to the critique is more promising, in my view, and one recent, but not uncontroversial, research trend, which indirectly questions the accuracy of the "communitarian" critique of Luther's ethics, is the emphasis on the catholic Luther by some Lutheran theologians in America.[27] Yeago is one of the most important representatives of this trend and

26. Holl, *The Reconstruction of Morality*, 102–3.

27. The conference held on this theme was important to the emergence of this tendency to stress the catholic Luther in America. The following book contains

his Luther research shows that it is possible to find resources in Luther's theology that could be used fruitfully to respond to this critique.

Yeago would probably say that it is more correct to apply the "communitarian" critique to trends in modern Lutheran theology than to Luther.[28] It should also be noted that Yeago's own constructive theology and ethics have similarities with the thinking of Hauerwas.[29] This fact helps to explain his interest in highlighting aspects of Luther's thinking that seem to contradict what Yeago considers to be the problematic individualism of much contemporary Lutheranism. To this end he has, for example, stressed the importance of the church and law to Luther's ethics. Yeago highlights two aspects of Luther's thinking on the church as especially important to ethics, namely his emphasis on the sanctifying practices of the Christian community and the public discipline of Christians. According to Yeago, Luther also has a more positive view than is usually imagined on the role of the law as the form of Christian life.

It is undeniable that the importance of church, law, and authority is emphasized by Luther in many texts. This poses a challenge for any interpreter because there seems to be a tension between these themes and another strand of Luther's thought—also undeniably present in some texts—that emphasize the "inner" dimensions of spiritual life. One notable strength of Yeago's interpretation is that it aims at reconciling these two strands by highlighting Luther's own idea that "the inward follows the outward," meaning that "the spiritual grace is inseparable from and dependent for its presence on the bodily and sacramental."[30] This seems to me to be a very fruitful approach, and one that should have priority in relation to approaches that conveniently neglect problematic texts. It can be argued that such neglect has helped to produce the image of Luther that is targeted by the "communitarian" critique. A fruitful research program, therefore, would explore whether the individualistic and spiritualized image of Luther can be modified by a broader and more attentive reading of Luther's texts along the lines sketched by Yeago.

---

contributions to the conference: Braaten and Jenson, *The Catholicity of the Reformation*.

28. A central theme in Yeago's research is the attempt to highlight the ways modern Lutheranism has distorted Luther's theology. See, for example, Yeago, "Gnosticism, Antinomianism, and Reformation Theology: Reflections on the Costs of a Construal"; Yeago, "The Church as Polity? The Lutheran Context of Robert W. Jenson's Ecclesiology"; Yeago, "The Office of the Keys: On the Disappearance of Discipline in Protestant Modernity."

29. See Yeago, "Modern but Not Liberal."

30. Yeago, "'A Christian, Holy People:' Martin Luther on Salvation and the Church," 107.

In *Against the Heavenly Prophets* (1525), Luther clearly expresses the thought that inner faith and spiritual gifts are given to us by God through that which is outward:

> Now when God sends forth his holy gospel he deals with us in a twofold manner, first outwardly, then inwardly. Outwardly he deals with us through the oral word of the gospel and through material signs, that is, baptism and the sacrament of the altar. Inwardly he deals with us through the Holy Spirit, faith, and other gifts. But whatever their measure or order the outward factors should and must precede. The inward experience follows and is effected by the outward. God has determined to give the inward to no one except through the outward.[31]

Yeago's main point, in stressing the idea that the inward follows the outward, is to pay attention to the fact that Luther understands the public sacramental practices of the church as necessary to inner faith and love. This is in line with Luther's tendency—even though he never denies the Holy Spirit's inner working—to connect the sanctifying work of the Spirit to external means. So what Yeago does is to call attention to the fact that the practices of the church are fundamental to how Luther understands the sanctifying work of the Spirit.

Luther's most important treatment of ecclesiology in his later years is probably found in *On the Councils and the Church* (1539). In the treatise, Luther describes the church as a holy Christian people and says that the church can be identified by means of different marks. These signs can, as Yeago emphasizes, be understood as distinctive, public practices. Luther lists seven marks or practices in the text: the public proclamation of the Gospel, baptism and the sacrament of the altar, the public exercise of the keys, the calling of ministers, the public liturgy of prayer, praise, and thanksgiving to God, and also the bearing of the cross, that is, suffering and persecution. These signs or practices distinguish the church from other groups of people in the world. They also constitute and sanctify the church in the sense of being the things through which the Holy Spirit makes Christians a holy people.[32] "These are," writes Luther, "the true seven principal parts of the great holy possession whereby the Holy Spirit effects in us a daily sanctification and vivification in Christ."[33]

---

31. Luther, *Against the Heavenly Prophets in the Matter of Images and Sacraments*, LW 40, 146.

32. Luther, *On the Councils and the Church*, LW 41, 143–67. See also Yeago, "'A Christian, Holy People,'" 107–10.

33. Luther, *On the Councils and the Church*, LW 41, 165–66.

It should also be noted that external preaching of the gospel, correct administration of baptism and Communion, public exercise of the keys, the existence of called ministers, public prayer and thanksgiving, and also outward suffering and persecution are not enough, according to Luther. Christians must also, as it were, live these things. It is important to believe and openly profess the gospel. The sacraments must be received in the right way. Reproved Christians must mend their ways. It is important to learn from prayers and songs. Suffering and persecution must be endured in the right way. The list continues. Christians must actively participate in the life-transforming marks of the church, which the Holy Spirit uses to sanctify them. Moreover, this practice is included in the very signs by which it is possible for the world to note the existence of the true church.[34]

Yeago also highlights Luther's thoughts (perhaps shocking to a modern audience) on church discipline in the treatise *The Keys* (1530) and also in *On the Councils and the Church*. Luther calls the keys "extremely necessary in Christendom, so that we never can thank God enough for them."[35] The office of the keys is, as Yeago rightly says, not only important to Luther as an office of consolation, but also as a means for the public discipline of Christians. The exercise of the keys is used to warn and judge public sinners so that they can be made holy again or, if they do not submit themselves to that authority, be excluded from the church. It is therefore an instrument of the Spirit's work of sanctification. So public sin must be met with open resistance. Coercion is, of course, not to be used. It is rather a question of the church mediating God's no to sin. It is also clear that the keys must not be used to bind just any type of sin. What is not to be tolerated in the Christian congregation is public or open sin. The keys are also a means of honoring God since God's glory is denied and the church is a false sign when it tolerates public sinners in its midst. Christians bear false witness of God when they do not live according to God's will.[36]

Finally, it is time to turn to how Yeago interprets Luther's understanding of the role of the law in Christian life in the direction of a third, didactic or positive use of the law. Generally, the third use means that God uses the law to teach and to tell Christians about good works. God's commands become a pattern for their behavior. The question about the existence of a didactic use of the law in Luther's theology is a very controversial issue. During the last 60 or so years many Luther scholars have denied that there is such a use. But perhaps the tides are turning. It at least seems as though

---

34. Ibid., LW 41, 149–53, 164–65.
35. Luther, *The Keys*, LW 40, 373.
36. Ibid., LW 40, 366–77; Yeago, "The Office of the Keys," 103–6.

nowadays more interpreters of Luther are willing to defend a positive use of the law.[37] Yeago's research is one such example. Due to the controversial nature of Yeago's Luther interpretation on this point, I will take the time to describe it.

Setting out from Luther's late and extensive *Lectures on Genesis* (1535–1545) and Luther's analysis of God's command to Adam not to eat of the tree of knowledge of good and evil, Yeago emphasizes that Luther thinks the divine law was present in "the state of innocence," that is, in the world before sin entered it. Luther writes, as Yeago notes, that it was not only Adam before the fall who was given commandments to obey; the good angels were as well:

> The angel Gabriel (. . .) is without sin, a very pure and guiltless creature. And yet he accepts from God the command to instruct Daniel about very important matters (Dan. 8:16) and to announce to Mary that she will be the mother of Christ, who had been promised to the fathers (Luke 1:26). These are in truth commands which were addressed to a guiltless being. Likewise, Adam is here commanded by the Lord before sin to refrain from eating the tree of the knowledge of good and evil.[38]

The law was not given to Adam so that he, by keeping it, could turn into a person who loves God. This is the case, as Yeago says, because Luther thinks of the innocent Adam as an already deified human being. He was created for community with and participation in God.[39] Instead, the purpose of the law given to Adam was to make possible for his love of God to take a specific form. Yeago concludes: "The fundamental significance of the law is thus (. . .) to give concrete, historical form to the 'divine life' of the human creature deified by grace."[40]

After sin, however, according to Luther we are no longer united with God and in a state of grace, Yeago writes. The meaning of the law changes for the human being. The law can now be misunderstood as an external code or be experienced spiritually and truthfully. To the sinning human being the law is distorted, resulting in the commands being experienced as an

---

37. See, for example, Engelbrecht, *Friends of the Law: Luther's Use of the Law for the Christian Life*; Murray, *Law, Life, and the Living God: The Third Use of the Law in Modern American Lutheranism*.

38. Luther, *Lectures on Genesis*, LW 1, 109. See also Yeago, "Martin Luther on Grace, Law, and Moral Life: Prolegomena to an Ecumenical Discussion of Veritatis Splendor," 175–76.

39. Yeago, "Martin Luther on Grace, Law, and Moral Life," 167–68. See also Luther, *Lectures on Genesis*, LW 1, 55–65.

40. Yeago, "Martin Luther on Grace, Law, and Moral Life," 177.

external code that easily becomes abused as a means of self-justification. However, the law can also be spiritually experienced after the fall, meaning a truthful understanding of the law that has in view that the fulfillment of God's commandments requires a subject who is deified by the grace of God. The spiritual law accuses because it demands a type of person that we cannot become on our own. What the law really calls for is a person who is filled with love of God and love of the world, that is, it calls for Christ. He is the doer and the fulfiller of the spiritual law.[41] The notion of Christ as the fulfiller of the law occurs frequently in Luther's texts. Here is one illuminating example in *Theses Concerning Faith and Law* (1535):

> 67. Whoever wishes to enter life must keep God's commandments.
> 68. But none of the saints keep God's commandments.
> 69. Therefore none of the saints can enter life.
> (...)
> 74. We truly hold forth a certain and trustworthy example of the fulfilment of the law, but it is to be found in that unique man who was Mediator between God and man.
> 75. Of this one and only person God says, "He has done no sin and there was no deceit in his mouth" [Isa. 53:9]; that is, he fulfilled the law.[42]

Yeago's interpretation of Luther's doctrine of justification follows the much debated Finnish Mannermaa School's stress on the union with Christ. The believer and Christ are joined together and one's righteousness is dependent on this union, on the righteous Christ dwelling in one's heart. In faith a new person is constituted and the form of this person is the present Christ, who lives and acts in the believer.[43] Two classic passages in which Luther expresses the idea of union with Christ in faith are the following in *Lectures on Galatians* (1535):

> [H]e [Paul] says: "Not I, but Christ lives in me." Christ is my "form," which adorns my faith as color or light adorns a wall. (...) "Christ," he says, "is fixed and cemented to me and abides in me. The life that I now live, He lives in me. Indeed, Christ

---

41. Ibid., 178–83.
42. Luther, *Theses Concerning Faith and Law*, LW 34, 118–19.
43. Yeago, "Martin Luther on Grace, Law, and Moral Life," 184–86. On the Mannermaa School, see Braaten and Jenson, *Union with Christ: The New Finnish Interpretation of Luther*; Vainio, *Engaging Luther: A (New) Theological Assessment*.

> himself is the life that I now live. In this way, therefore, Christ and I are one."⁴⁴

> [S]o far as justification is concerned, Christ and I must be so closely attached that He lives in me and I in Him. What a marvelous way of speaking! Because He lives in me, whatever grace, righteousness, life, peace, and salvation there is in me is all Christ's; nevertheless, it is mine as well, by the cementing and attachment that are through faith, by which we become as one body in the Spirit.⁴⁵

This also means, says Yeago, that Luther thinks that in faith we have what the law demands, namely Christ. The gospel therefore puts an end to the "old" forms of the law—the law as mere code and as accusation. However, the believer who has died under this "old law" is not lawless. On the contrary, the life of the Christian begins to be ordered in accordance with the law's original intention because the deified subject demanded by the law of God is present in faith.⁴⁶ And so, writes Yeago, the commandments once again become for believers

> what they were for Adam in the state of innocence, neither a means of self-justification, nor a terrifying accusation, but a divinely granted opportunity to give concrete historical form to their identity as God's children and images.⁴⁷

Christians can therefore take delight in the law as the historical form of existence corresponding to their identity as children of God. This changed experience of the law is described by Luther as follows in a sermon on the Gospel of John in 1537:

> He [Christ] supplies grace and truth, and the means which enable me to keep the First, the Second, and the Third Commandment. Thus I acquire a trust and a faith in God as my Father, and I begin to praise His name with a cheerful heart and to hallow His name. (...) Now I take delight in the command to trust God above all things. I sense that I can do it; I have started with the lesson and have already mastered the ABC's. The grace of God, which Christ has bestowed on me because I believe in Him, now makes the First Commandment a pleasure for me.⁴⁸

44. Luther, *Lectures on Galatians*, LW 26, 167.
45. Ibid., LW 26, 167–68.
46. Yeago, "Martin Luther on Grace, Law, and Moral Life," 185–88.
47. Ibid., 189.
48. Luther, *Sermons on the Gospel of St. John*, LW 22, 144.

CONCLUSION

Troeltsch's influence on the reception of Luther's ethics in modern theology is considerable. Even today many theologians take his objections against Luther, the most famous of which being the charge of a double morality, for granted. There is also, as I have tried to show, a connection between Troeltsch and some recent critics. In contrast to him, they aim their blows at what they regard as Luther's problematic individualism together with his neglect of the church, norms, and authorities.

The "communitarian" critique presents difficult obstacles for any theologian wanting to use Luther constructively today. I have highlighted the research by Yeago as showing the way forward to an understanding with great potential to refine the widespread, bleak picture of Luther's ethics. There is a lot said by Luther that stands in obvious contradiction with his alleged individualism. This is made clear by Yeago when he sheds light on what Luther has written about the marks of the church, public discipline of Christians, and the role of the law in Christian life. The practices of the church are necessary for sanctification. Believers are responsible for their actions before the Christian community. Christians are to take delight in the law as the form of their existence. Many today might not like what Luther has to say about these things. Still, one should take note of these thoughts if the aim is a faithful description of Luther's ethics because they are found in many of his most important texts. Exploring the insights of Yeago further is therefore a most interesting and pressing task for future Luther research.

Lastly, a warning. Luther undeniably has many things to say about the inner and individual dimensions of Christian life and spirituality. However, and as Yeago points out, Luther's general approach is to connect the inward to the outward, that is, to the bodily and sacramental. A comprehensive description of Luther's thinking on Christian life must therefore not separate these two sides—the inner and the outer—from each other and also not focus one-sidedly on one of them. That is, perhaps, an even more difficult task for future research.

BIBLIOGRAPHY

Avineri, Shlomo, and Avner de-Shalit. "Introduction." In *Communitarianism and Individualism*, edited by Shlomo Avineri and Avner de-Shalit, 1–11. Oxford, New York: Oxford University Press, 1992.

Bell, Daniel. *Communitarianism and Its Critics*. Oxford, New York: Oxford University Press, 1993.

Beiner, Ronald. *Liberalism, Nationalism, Citizenship: Essays on the Problem of Political Community*. Vancouver: UBC Press, 2003.

Braaten, Carl E., and Robert W. Jenson, editors. *The Catholicity of the Reformation*. Grand Rapids: Eerdmans, 1996.

———. *Union with Christ: The New Finnish Interpretation of Luther*. Grand Rapids: Eerdmans, 1998.

Chapman, Mark D. *Ernst Troeltsch and Liberal Theology: Religion and Cultural Synthesis in Wilhelmine Germany*. Oxford, New York: Oxford University Press, 2001.

Danz, Christian. "Reformation, Neuzeit und die ethische Bestimmtheit des Glaubens. Überlegungen zur Lutherdeutung von Ernst Troeltsch und Friedrich Gogarten." In *Erinnerte Reformation: Studien zur Luther-Rezeption von der Aufklärung bis zum 20. Jahrhundert*, edited by Christian Danz and Rochus Leonhardt, 259–79. Berlin, New York: Walter de Gruyter, 2008.

Drescher, Hans-Georg. *Ernst Troeltsch: His Life and Work*. London: SCM, 1992.

Elshtain, Jean Bethke. *Meditations on Modern Political Thought: Masculine/Feminine Themes from Luther to Arendt*. New York: Praeger, 1986.

———. *Public Man, Private Woman: Women in Social and Political Thought*. Oxford: Robertson, 1981.

———. *Sovereignty: God, State, and Self*. New York: Basic Books, 2012.

———. *Women and War*. Chicago: University of Chicago Press, 1995.

Engelbrecht, Edward. *Friends of the Law: Luther's Use of the Law for the Christian Life*. St. Louis: Concordia, 2011.

Hauerwas, Stanley. "On Keeping Theological Ethics Theological." In Stanley Hauerwas, *The Hauerwas Reader*, edited by Michael Cartwright and John Berkman, 51–74. Durham: Duke University Press, 2001.

Hauerwas, Stanley, and William H. Willimon. *Lord, Teach Us: The Lord's Prayer & the Christian Life*. Nashville: Abingdon, 1996.

———. *The Truth About God: The Ten Commandments in Christian Life*. Nashville: Abingdon, 1999.

Holl, Karl. *The Cultural Significance of the Reformation*. New York: Living Age, 1959.

———. *The Reconstruction of Morality*. Minneapolis: Augsburg, 1979.

Kaufmann, Thomas. "Luther zwischen den Wissenschaftskulturen. Ernst Troeltschs Lutherdeutung in der englischsprachigen Welt und in Deutschland." In *Luther zwischen den Kulturen: Zeitgenossenschaft—Weltwirkung*, edited by Hans Medick and Peer Schmidt, 455–481. Göttingen: Vandenhoeck and Ruprecht, 2004.

Lazareth, William H. *Christians in Society: Luther, the Bible, and Social Ethics*. Minneapolis: Fortress, 2001.

Luther, Martin. *Against the Heavenly Prophets in the Matter of Images and Sacraments* (1525). LW 40. Philadelphia: Fortress, 1958.

———. *Lectures on Galatians* (1535). LW 26. St. Louis: Concordia, 1963.

———. *Lectures on Genesis* (1535–1545). LW 1. St. Louis: Concordia, 1958.

———. *On the Councils and the Church* (1539). LW 41. Philadelphia: Fortress, 1966.

———. *Sermons on the Gospel of St. John Chapters 1–4* (1537–1540). LW 22. St. Louis: Concordia, 1957.

———. *The Keys* (1530). LW 40. Philadelphia: Fortress, 1958.

———. *Theses Concerning Faith and Law* (1535). LW 34. Philadelphia: Fortress, 1960.

MacIntyre, Alasdair. *A Short History of Ethics: A History of Moral Philosophy from the Homeric Age to the Twentieth Century*. London: Routledge & Keegan Paul, 1967.

Murray, Scott R. *Law, Life, and the Living God: The Third Use of the Law in Modern American Lutheranism*. St. Louis: Concordia, 2002.

Niebuhr, H. Richard. *Christ and Culture*. New York: HarperCollins, 2001.
Niebuhr, Reinhold. *The Nature and Destiny of Man: A Christian Interpretation*. Vol. 2. Louisville: Westminster John Knox, 1996.
Rasmusson, Arne. "Justice and Solidarity in a 'Communitarian' Perspective." *Societas Ethica. Jahresbericht 1997*, 68–85.
Troeltsch, Ernst. "The Dispositional Ethic." In *Religion in History*, by Ernst Troeltsch, 168–172. Minneapolis: Fortress, 2007.
———. "Protestantisches Christentum und Kirche in der Neuzeit." In *Die Kultur der Gegenwart*, I.VI.1, edited by Paul Hinneberg, 431–792. Berlin, Leipzig: B.G. Teubner, 1909.
———. *Protestantism and Progress: A Historical Study of the Relation of Protestantism to the Modern World*. Eugene: Wipf and Stock, 1999.
———. "Stoic-Christian Natural Law and Modern Secular Natural Law." In *Religion in History*, by Ernst Troeltsch, 321–42. Minneapolis: Fortress, 2007.
———. *The Social Teaching of the Christian Churches*. Vol. 2. Louisville: Westminster John Knox, 1992.
Vainio, Olli-Pekka, editor. *Engaging Luther: A (New) Theological Assessment*. Eugene: Cascade, 2010.
von Loewenich, Walther. *Luther und der Neuprotestantismus*. Witten: Luther-Verlag, 1963.
Yeago, David S. "'A Christian, Holy People:' Martin Luther on Salvation and the Church." *Modern Theology* 13.1 (1997) 101–20.
———. "The Church as Polity? The Lutheran Context of Robert W. Jenson's Ecclesiology." In *Trinity, Time and Church: A Response to the Theology of Robert W. Jenson*, edited by Colin E. Gunton, 201–37. Grand Rapids, Cambridge: Wipf & Stock, 2000.
———. "Gnosticism, Antinomianism, and Reformation Theology: Reflections on the Costs of a Construal." *Pro Ecclesia* 2.1 (1993) 37–49.
———. "Martin Luther on Grace, Law, and Moral Life: Prolegomena to an Ecumenical Discussion of Veritatis Splendor." *The Thomist* 62.2 (1998) 163–91.
———. "Modern but Not Liberal." *First Things* (June/July 2012) http://www.firstthings.com/article/2012/06/modern-but-not-liberal.
———. "The Office of the Keys: On the Disappearance of Discipline in Protestant Modernity." In *Marks of the Body of Christ*, edited by Carl E. Braaten and Robert W. Jenson, 95–122. Grand Rapids, Cambridge: Eerdmans, 1999.
Yoder, John Howard *The Politics of Jesus: Vicit Agnus Noster*. Grand Rapids, Cambridge: Eerdmans, 1994.
———. *The Priestly Kingdom: Social Ethics as Gospel*. Notre Dame: University of Notre Dame Press, 1984.

12

Reconfiguring Church-State Relations

Toward a Rwandan Political Theology

VICTOR THASIAH

John Rutsindintwarane, a Rwandan Lutheran community organizer, embodies a political theology both responsive to a problematic history of relations between church and state and expressive of alternative possibilities in the context of civil society. After considering the dominant, historical patterns of interaction between church and state in Rwanda and lessons proposed for Christians post-genocide, we turn to Rutsindintwarane and a critical, theological description of the political form of Christian love communicated through his organizing across Rwanda. If one lesson Christians need to learn there, as elsewhere, has to do with maintaining a critical distance to government, then setting out the theological intelligibility of Rutsindintwarane's practices contributes to the education. Crucial to maintaining such critical distance is the development of political capacities for holding public officials accountable. This distance, however, is not without certain proximities. The vocation of the church includes critically cooperating with the same political authorities to address areas—social, economic, and ecological—of mutual concern, especially those affecting one's own community.

Research conducted in Rwanda during the summer of 2013 serves as the basis of the material in this chapter on Rutsindintwarane, the executive director of the community and leadership development organization PICO Rwanda (People Improving Communities through Organizing).[1] The inves-

---

1. I would like to thank the many people across Rwanda who kindly and patiently

tigation involved: observation of adults and youth participating in the various stages of organizing in rural and urban settings; attendance at meetings with staff, leaders, various constituencies, and public officials; participation in organizing and leadership training sessions; reading project reports from 2006 to the present; and interviewing either formally or informally an estimated fifty Rwandans associated with one or more of Rutsindintwarane's projects. The informants comprised people from rural and urban contexts either participating in or affected by community organizing; local, regional, and national-level public officials; field staff and executives of local and global, faith-based, non-governmental organizations (NGOs) working in development; and lay, clergy, and national leaders from several different Christian denominations. Since little is known about the history and mission of the Lutheran Church of Rwanda (LCR) beyond the nation's borders, we pay special attention to the LCR in relation to Rutsindintwarane's efforts. Most scholarly and popular interest in Rwandan Christianity deals either directly or indirectly with the nature of Christian responsibility for the 1994 Rwanda genocide.[2] Founded after the genocide in 1995, the LCR usually escapes notice.

THE ROLE OF CHRISTIANITY IN RWANDA

The complicity of churches in the genocide continues to call for examination, as does the question concerning what the term complicity means in this context.[3] The devastating contradictions to what many people imagine religious communities to be generate the need for explanation, understanding, and, if appropriate, the recognition of extenuating circumstances. Pre-colonial, colonial, and post-colonial historical accounts of Rwanda are important responses.[4] Theological criticism of church discourse, structures,

---

shared their stories with me, and helped me understand community organizing, development, and what I call "Rwandan political theology," especially Rev. John Rutsindintwarane, Robin Strickler, Gerard Gerardson Muvunyi, Bishop Mugabo Evalister, Father Innocent Rugaragu, Emmanuel Ngoga, Ezra Nkubana, Rev. Seburikoko Celestin, Rev. Ntidendereza David, Veronica John Mwakasungura, and Emmanuel Luena. I would also like to thank Father John Baumann, PICO founder and director of special projects, and Ron Snyder, PICO director of international organizing, for their interest and insights regarding my research.

2. See, for example, Rittner, Roth, and Whitworth. *Genocide in Rwanda: Complicity of the Churches.*

3. Carney, *Rwanda Before the Genocide: Catholic Politics and Ethnic Discourse in the Late Colonial Era*; Katongole, *Mirror to the Church: Resurrecting Faith after Genocide in Rwanda*; Longman, *Christianity and Genocide in Rwanda.*

4. Vansina, *Antecedents to Modern Rwanda: The Nyiginya Kingdom*; Mamdani, *When Victims Become Killers*; Prunier, *The Rwanda Crisis: History of a Genocide.*

and practices is imperative, as is honoring Christians who resisted fear, hatred, and violence, crossing ethnic and political lines to protect people's lives during the genocide.[5] "The large-scale participation of Christians in the killings," Ian Linden notes, "is to some degree, of course, a simple reflection of the fact that about 90 percent of the population were Christians of one denomination or another, with 62 percent baptized Catholics."[6] While numbers do not always directly correlate with social, economic, or political power, in Rwanda's case they did. Peter Uvin remarks:

> the church—foremost the Catholic Church, but also a variety of Protestant denominations—is the largest nonstate actor, with enormous resources and social clout (. . .) It suffices to be in Rwanda's countryside on a Sunday morning—or in Rwandan refugee camps any day—to observe the strength of Christianity (. . .) After the state, the church is, and has been for decades, Rwanda's prime employer, landowner, and investor and is very well connected with European aid agencies and political parties. (. . .) Local church groups, NGOs associated with the church, and parish priests are all important elements of civil society.[7]

Rwandans continue to ask questions about the compatibility of Rwandan faith and mass atrocity, and, with regard to a genocide authorized by political and military leaders, about the default settings of church-state relations. The latter question is our immediate concern.

It is not that the church collapsed in the face of the state; rather, the church helped to consolidate it. "An analysis of the historical role of Christianity in Rwanda," Timothy Longman claims, "reveals that, far from simply adapting to and reflecting Rwandan society, the churches actively shaped ethnic and political realities that made genocide possible by acting to define and politicize ethnicity, legitimizing authoritarian regimes, and encouraging public obedience to political authorities."[8] The White Fathers, the first missionaries to construct Catholicism in Rwanda during the early twentieth century, like missionaries elsewhere, forged ideological, institutional, and instrumental alliances with successive regimes to facilitate large-scale conversions to Christianity. Their work with colonial personnel was likewise at

---

5. Carney, *Rwanda Before the Genocide*; Longman, *Christianity and Genocide in Rwanda*; Longman and Rutagengwa, "Religion, Memory, and Violence in Rwanda," 132–149; Katongole, *Mirror to the Church*; Katongole, *The Sacrifice of Africa: A Political Theology for Africa*.

6. Linden, *Church and Revolution in Rwanda*, 51.

7. Uvin, *Aiding Violence: The Development Enterprise in Rwanda*, 166–67.

8. Longman, *Christianity and Genocide in Rwanda*, 10.

once inextricable and consequential. "The missionaries," Longman argues, "regarded Hutu, Tutsi, and Twa as clearly distinct, homogeneous, and mutually antagonistic racial groups, and this erroneous interpretation became a basis for colonial policy and, ultimately, shaped the nature of ethnic identity in the country."[9] Dissolving, re-imagining, or otherwise negotiating these identities is still a challenge for both church and society in Rwanda today.

Though church-state relations evolved with society from the colonial era through independence in 1962 to the genocide in 1994, the default settings remained unchanged. Churches, Catholic and Protestant, tended to legitimize state power, encourage obedience to political authority, promote ethnic divisions, practice ethnic discrimination, and ignore ethnic scapegoating and massive human rights violations, even when the victims were their own members.[10] Regarding the elimination of Tutsi and moderate Hutu, Longman comments on the nature of Christian complicity, "Churches played an important role in helping to make participation in the killing morally acceptable (...) While Tutsi were never defined as heretics or infidels, the churches were extremely powerful and influential institutions in Rwanda, and their majority voice gave moral sanction to the killings as an acceptable form of political engagement."[11] Thus, many Christians understood and perpetrated genocide as the continuation of politics by other means.

Some Rwandan Christians, however, prior to the nightmare of 1994, mobilized with other citizens for democratic reform. Acknowledging their activism is important, even if religious elites with vested interests in maintaining the ecclesial and political status quo effectively suppressed their efforts. "The churches," Longman documents, "played an important role in encouraging the growth of civil society—human rights groups, the media, women's associations—out of which eventually emerged challenges to established structures of power, not only within the state but within churches as well."[12] There is strong continuity between these associations and democratic reform on the one hand, and Rutsindintwarane's community organizing and political participation on the other, as we will see. Balancing the church's contributions directly to democratic reform and indirectly to genocide, Longman further elaborates on the nature of Christian complicity in relation to the preservation of personal privilege, "Ultimately the genocide served the interests of church leaders who felt their own power was

---

9. Ibid., 28.
10. Gatwa, *The Churches and Ethnic Ideology in the Rwandan Crises 1900–1994*.
11. Longman, *Christianity and Genocide in Rwanda*, 306–7.
12. Ibid., 28.

being threatened by the movement for reform and were, thus, not willing to condemn the violence once it had begun."[13] This sense of entitlement helped turn what were two, church sanctuaries and church graveyards, into one.

How could churches in Rwanda reconfigure their complex relations with the state to contribute more consistently to democratic reform and community development rather than to the dispossession of place, property, and community, and—if not directly, then indirectly—to rape, torture, and murder?[14] James Carney concludes his history of the late colonial-era Catholic Church in Rwanda with a set of lessons, briefly outlined, for the church to consider. As a Catholic theologian, his archival work demonstrates the kind of self-interrogation and theological criticism, what he calls "the purification of memory," necessary for the integrity of the church's witness to and vocation of reconciliation.[15] While the urgency for interpersonal forgiveness, reconciliation, and restoration among Rwandans will continue into the foreseeable future, understanding of the church's own formation and deformation on the way to genocide is equally pressing. Carney's lessons are few and concentrated, but formidable and comprehensive, calling for a politics of ecclesial repentance, prophetic distance, and non-violence, and the critical-theological practices of social description and identity performance.

The hierarchy representing the Catholic Church in Rwanda has neither confessed responsibility nor publicly repented of its role in the genocide. Whether it should or not remains controversial. "Part of this reluctance," Carney explains, "has stemmed from tensions between the contemporary Catholic Church and the Rwandan government, as well as the church's fears concerning the political manipulation of any institutional confession."[16] Rwandan Christians across denominations, as do people elsewhere implicated in other genocides, debate the nature of institutional responsibility and its relationship to individual responsibility. Carney's response combines sociological and theological views: "To limit repentance to individuals is to

---

13. Ibid., 28.

14. Des Forges, *Leave None to Tell the Story: Genocide in Rwanda*.

15. Willie Jennings's perspective on reconciliation is helpful: "The concept of reconciliation is not irretrievable, but I am convinced that before we theologians can interpret the depths of the divine action of reconciliation we must first articulate the profound deformities of Christian intimacy and identity in modernity. Until we do, all theological discussions of reconciliation will be exactly what they tend to be: (a) ideological tools for facilitating negotiations of power; or (b) socially exhausted idealist claims masquerading as serious theological accounts. In truth, it is not at all clear that most Christians are ready to imagine reconciliation." Jennings, *The Christian Imagination: Theology and the Origins of Race*, 10.

16. Carney, *Rwanda Before the Genocide*, 202.

lose sight of the communal, social, and institutional nature of the Catholic Church. It is also to ignore the structural nature of sin."[17] It is not enough to object to violence rhetorically without countering it politically. "Rwanda's history reminds Christian leaders of the dangers of condemning generic violence," Carney remarks, "while failing to hold state leaders accountable for their own abuses."[18] A theologically-determined conception of the vocation of political authority norms such accountability, with reference to constitutionally-established roles when compatible.

Other lessons pertain to the critical-theological practices of performing one's identity, and identifying and describing others. These practices, loaded with personal, social, historical, and political meaning, and resistant to revision, shape much of the human experience. Carney observes, "while ethical and political debates often center around the question of 'what should we do,' the Rwandan case reminds us of the importance of social descriptions and theological imagination—namely the question of 'who are we.'"[19] Both Christian liturgies and theologies identify Christians as members of the body of Christ, and describe them as loved by God and called to love God and others, including their enemies. The lesson, easier to state than learn, is to retrieve this identity and perform it socially, while acknowledging both past and present failures to do so. Emmanuel Katongole examines these identity matters by interrogating determinative narratives. He views politics "as dramatic performance grounded in a particular story that requires, and in the end shapes, particular characters."[20] Thus, narratives shape political ecologies, and political ecologies in turn shape the constituents of these environments. "Stories, therefore, are not simply fictional narratives meant for our entertainment; stories are part of our social ecology. They are embedded in us and form the very heart of our cultural, economic, religious, and political worlds. This applies not only to individuals, but to institutions and even nations."[21] Critically interpreting the narratives that shape identities and vocations in Rwanda is one important way to practice the kind of social description and identity performance Carney suggests. Such work, Katongole argues, involves Christians repositioning their bodies in relation to the dominant ideologies of politics and economics and the ways they socially identify, separate, and discipline people.[22] Rutsindintwarane's community

17. Ibid.
18. Ibid., 205.
19. Ibid., 201.
20. Katongole, *The Sacrifice of Africa*, 3.
21. Ibid., 2.
22. Ibid., 95.

organizing repositions marginalized bodies in relation to public officials, reconfiguring church-state relations in the process, as we will see.

One final lesson, and the focus of this chapter, concerns the nature of Christian engagement with political authorities. The church should maintain what Carney calls "prophetic distance" from the state. Crucial to this prophetic positioning in Rwanda involves coming to terms with the church's deformed identity and distorted views of others.[23] In other words, the maintenance of critical distance depends on the church's retrieval of its own identity and vocation. "The church is called to be a prophetic herald of the common good," claims Carney, "calling the state away from its tendencies toward self-love and national pride and toward a politics of self-sacrificing service on behalf of the marginalized."[24] It conceives of its vocation without, with reference to the state, as an extension of its vocation within, with reference to its existence in community and society. "[T]he church's prophetic mission", Carney continues, "entails embodying an alternative Christian politics within its own common life (. . .) In particular, the church is called to embrace the self-sacrificing politics of the cross, forming (. . .) communities of mercy, justice, righteousness, and peace who may be 'persecuted for the sake of righteousness' (Matthew 5:10)."[25] Given this lesson or agenda, we turn to a Rwandan organizer who embodies a political theology responsive to this calling, reminding the church and state of their respective, theologically-determined identities and vocations.

RUTSINDINTWARANE AS THEOLOGIAN AND COMMUNITY ORGANIZER

Rutsindintwarane was born on February 19, 1963, in Karagwe, Tanzania. Raised by his mother, Kabasinga Beltilde—his father died in 1965—he and his sister spent their early years living among an estimated 35,000 Rwandans in the Nkwenda/Kimuli Refugee Settlement in Tanzania. In 1977, when denied the government scholarship assistance he deserved while attending a secondary school in Bukoba, Rutsindintwarane first became aware of the deprivations accompanying refugee status. Excelling in school, he went on to study at Katoke Teachers Training College, also in Bukoba, and St. Paul's Theological College in Kenya, where he earned an Advanced Diploma in Theology. Returning to Tanzania after graduation, Rutsindintwarane was ordained in 1994 in the Evangelical Lutheran Church in Tanzania (ELCT), and appointed as Diocesan Assistant Coordinator of Christian Education.

23. Jennings, *The Christian Imagination*.
24. Carney, *Rwanda Before the Genocide*, 203.
25. Ibid.; Katongole, *The Sacrifice of Africa*.

Based near the Rwandan border in Ngara, he immediately faced a challenge nearly impossible to comprehend—hundreds of thousands of traumatized and desperate refugees fleeing genocide and needing support.

Rutsindintwarane worked primarily as a translator between the Tanganyika Christian Refugee Service (TCRS), associated with the Lutheran World Federation (LWF), other NGOs (e.g., Tearfund, Christian Aid), and people residing at the Benaco Refugee Camp, in addition to facilitating emergency services. With genocide threatening to undo his faith, he struggled to understand why Rwandans were killing each other and why the church was not speaking out. Recalling from degrading personal experience the loss of identity and limits on self-determination that multitudes of Rwandans faced in the past as refugees also distressed him. In September, 1994, after the massacres subsided, Rutsindintwarane accompanied a delegation sent by the Archbishop of Canterbury to assess the relief programs in Rwanda for internally-displaced persons (IDPs). Returning to the Benaco Refugee Camp in Ngara, which received one of the largest influxes of refugees from the genocide, he began transporting Rwandans, despondent about the prospect of remaining in Tanzania, across the border. One year later, Rutsindintwarane himself relocated to Rwanda, settling in Kibungo, and volunteered with the Lutheran World Federation's humanitarian work in repatriation, resettlement, reconstruction, peacebuilding, and development from 1995–1999.

Meanwhile, after living in exile for up to 35 years, Rwandan Lutherans in Tanzania returned and launched the Lutheran Church of Rwanda (LCR) on May 23, 1995. The founders include Martin Habiyakare, the head of the church and first legal representative; pastors Celeste Sarambuye, Gerard Mahirane, and Rutsindintwarane; and evangelist Faustine Muzigura. The LCR took root in the Kibungo province, with most of the Lutheran returnees settling in the Rusumo and Rukira Districts. On the challenges facing the LCR in its early years, Rutsindintwarane writes, "Thirty-two years of country divisionism, more than eight years of economic collapse, and four years of civil war and 90 days of savage genocide had left one million people dead, a collapsed nation and economy, and infrastructure destroyed. The violent legacy of genocide, civil war and of an authoritarian state has caused poverty, political instability, and social and spiritual fragility."[26] Rev. George Kalisa served as the LCR's first bishop from 2002–2011, followed by Rev. Mugabo Evalister, its current bishop. Today, comprising over 40,000 people,

---

26. Rutsindintwarane, "An Appreciative Inquiry in Rusumo and Rukira Districts, Kibungo Province of Rwanda: A Study of the Perceptions, Challenges and Needs for Empowering the Lutheran Church of Rwanda," 16.

the LCR is a member of the Lutheran World Federation (LWF) and the Lutheran Communion in Central and Eastern Africa (LUCCEA).

While serving as LCR's General Secretary from 1995–2011, Rutsindintwarane pursued further education and completed two masters degrees—the first in conflict analysis at Eastern Mennonite University in Harrisonburg, Virginia, and the second in Theology, Evangelism, and Development at Wartburg Theological Seminary in Dubuque, Iowa. At Wartburg in 2005, after conducting a needs assessment of the Rusumo and Rukira Districts in Rwanda through observation and interviews, he wrote a thesis on sustainable development, leadership empowerment, and social change to further the mission of the LCR.[27] The conclusion, connecting development to a range of political capacities, reads:

> Through practical experience with the Rwandan crisis of 1994, during repatriation, resettlement, reconstruction and reconciliation, and now with a move toward sustainable development, it is obvious that development should come from within. Development is not merely a question of economic progress, skyscrapers or material goods; it involves freedom of mind, political openness, access to education, and deconstruction of the culture of impunity and corruption that has ruined the Rwandan society over the past 45 years.[28]

Following graduate school and marriage to Robin Strickler, founder and program director of The Rwanda School Project and a missionary of the Evangelical Lutheran Church in America (ELCA), Rutsindintwarane interned with the PICO national network, a broad assembly of faith-based community organizations established in the United States in 1972 and based in Oakland, California.[29] At PICO, mentored by Father John Baumann, founder and director of special projects, and Ron Snyder, director of international organizing, among others, he learned a proven model of community organizing that immediately connected with what he believed Rwanda needed to recover and develop, especially considering the country's increasing worries about the debilitating effects of foreign aid. The Rwandan intern determined that the PICO model simply needed to be trans-

27. Ibid.

28. Ibid., 56.

29. In 2004, the Pacific Institute of Community Organizing (PICO) changed its name to PICO National Network to reflect the national scope of its work. *PICO National Network*. See Rutsindintwarane, "A Strategy for Empowering Communities," 141–44. On PICO, see Wood, *Faith in Action: Religion, Race, and Democratic Organizing in America*. On a comparable approach to community organizing in the United States, see Warren, *Dry Bones Rattling: Community Building to Revitalize Democracy*.

posed from a developed-world to a developing-world context and adapted to address Rwandans' particular experiences of dehumanization. In 2011, Rutsindintwarane was elected to the position of Lutheran Bishop of Rwanda, but declined, opting instead to expand his community organizing. His current projects include, for example, a remote rural community completing a health center; a rural community developing a roof tiling collaborative; urban women leaving prostitution for other forms of employment; youth organizing for job possibilities; a school addressing safety, discipline, and transportation issues; reforestation work; and parish development. When not in the field, the Rwandan organizer works from his office at the Jesuit Centre Christus in Kigali, where the instigators of the genocide first turned to eliminate sources of opposition to their regime.[30]

A MODEL FOR COMMUNITY ORGANIZING

Rutsindintwarane repurposes for East African use the PICO model of faith-based, non-partisan community organizing. Rooted in religious culture—the beliefs and practices of Christian communities—and leveraging established commitments to family and community, this organizing involves a set of processes by which people think, plan, and act together to build organizations, participate in public life, address the root causes of social problems, and improve their own communities and societies.[31] "In the language of democratic theory," Richard Wood explains, "each organization strives to empower its constituents to articulate their public concerns in the political arena in order to redirect governmental policy to better meet the needs of less privileged members of society. In the process, they seek to transform the relationship between citizens and public institutions."[32] Like those who recognize that individual freedom is tied to social, political, and economic realities, Rutsindintwarane recognizes that individual dignity is tied to capabilities associated with enacting one's vocations. His organizing opens spaces for vocations specifically related to one's community and country.[33] Beyond local, viable organizations, the Rwandan organizer aims

---

30. Longman, *Christianity and Genocide in Rwanda*, 322.
31. *PICO National Network*.
32. Wood, *Faith in Action*, 8.
33 Peter Uvin argues that the social and political benefits of such spaces depend more on the self-organizing of civil society organizations than on the policies or interventions of government and foreign aid agencies. "[C]ivil society is a slow historical construct that cannot be created ex nihilo from abroad. Its emergence is probably hurt, rather than helped, by excessive external intervention. Learning of the kind described above must be done by the people concerned; it cannot be imported based on outsiders' knowledge of what works (even if this knowledge were somehow objectively 'true').

for the development of the nation, region (East Africa), and continent, for Africans, as he puts it, to think for themselves, live in peace, and emerge from poverty in economically and ecologically sustainable ways.

Rutsindintwarane's community organizing consists of four sets of practices, combining religious commitment and democratic activism to create sustainable organizations for development.[34] First, local organizing committees conduct one-to-one conversations in the community to build relationships and solidarity; discern values, interests, motivations, and goals; discover common problems, how people are affected, and possible responses; and identify potential leaders, ideally reflecting the diversity of the community. Richard Wood observes, "this is social capital with a twist: these relational networks are built with an explicit moral-political content—that is, these ties are important to people because they are laden with political and ethical meaning, not seen as ends in themselves."[35] These practices contribute to the moral ecology of a community. Gary Simpson categorizes these interactions vocationally, relating them to the church's critical engagement with government, "Civil society is the location for this vocation of public moral companion, and communicative moral practice is the best model for nurturing the contemporary moral milieu and for the political accountability that political authority needs and is called for by a constitutional state of deliberative democracy."[36]

Second, local organizing committees conduct research that contributes to defining a resolvable issue, understanding the various relevant perspectives, determining what authority and/or resources are necessary to address the issue, and mobilizing communities to take action. More attention to the way dominant ideologies can determine one's self-perception and imagination of possibilities for development, or, more generally, on how to practice ideological criticism, can further strengthen these sets of practices.[37]

Any attempt to rapidly create a civil society through development aid (with the tools of the typical development project) will lead to fake, superficial results." Uvin, *Aiding Violence*, 171.

34. De Gruchy, *Christianity and Democracy: A Theology for a Just World Order*; Villa-Vicencio, *A Theology of Reconstruction: Nation-Building and Human Rights*.

35. Wood, *Faith in Action*, 35. Mobilizing the community often begins during the one-to-ones, though it's not the stated intention. Attending PICO training himself, Wood found that "leaders were encouraged to look for ways the other person was 'coping' instead of trying to change things in their community—and to invite them into a more assertive role in such change" (ibid., 36).

36. Simpson, "Toward a Lutheran 'Delight in the Law of the Lord': Church and State in the Context of Civil Society," 48.

37. See, for example, Brookfield, *The Power of Critical Theory: Liberating Adult Learning and Teaching*.

Third, local organizing committees take action that involves setting an agenda for and meeting with public officials; presenting the community's research, testimonies, and recommended actions; listening to and interacting with the officials' response; directly confronting problematic responses; determining ways to collaborate and commitments for resolving the problem; and holding officials accountable to their commitments. What Lutherans traditionally call the preaching of the law usually remains implicit in this set of practices. Interpreting Lutheran tradition, Mary Jane Haemig writes, "The church reminds the state of what its function is and encourages all citizens to be involved with their state. (. . .) By the preaching of the law, the church may admonish, proscribe, and criticize. It may challenge systems, individuals, and policies. It may even propose and give advice (. . .)"[38] Thus, vocation is at once directive and normative. "The sphere of civil government lies in keeping peace and order in a society (with force if necessary) and supporting and nourishing the lives of its citizens."[39] If the language of obedience or submission to political authorities is worth salvaging, especially in Rwanda, then it must never be understood as "an end in itself, but as a means of reaching the goal of neighbor love."[40]

Fourth, local organizing committees practice self-evaluation after every step, reviewing strategies, processes, and tactics, and critically evaluating of what happened, what was learned, and what could be done differently for better results. This built-in self-assessment, when done with explicit reference to an organization's faith-based identity and vocation in distinction from government, can also contribute to the maintenance of a critical distance to the state.

In the context of each of the four sets of practices, Rutsindintwarane uses a standard collection of eleven PICO leadership principles to mentor both people who are organizing and building local organizations, and public officials receptive to the PICO model. In meetings and training events, he often references, variously interprets, and personally illustrates the following principles.

> 1) Never do for others what they can and should do for themselves. 2) When in doubt, do a one-to-one. 3) People cannot be held responsible for what they do not understand or decisions they did not make. 4) People learn through their own experience. 5) Take people from where they are, not from where you

---

38. Haemig, "The Confessional Basis of Lutheran Thinking on Church-State Issues," 10.

39. Ibid., 7.

40. Andersen, "Lutheran Political Theology for the Twenty-First Century," 253.

want them to be. 6) The first revolution is internal. 7) There is no nice way to make change. 8) Empowerment is developmental. 9) If people cannot say no, what good is their yes. 10) Leaders have followers. 11) Organizers develop leaders, [and] leaders build organizations.[41]

Rutsindintwarane's postcolonial, appreciative, asset-based theoretical commitments further inform his leadership development work. Kofi Hadjor's book *On Transforming Africa* is an important source, contributing to his critical perspective on independence.[42] Hadjor, himself influenced by Fanon, Cabral, Lumumba, and Nkrumah, observes that "[i]ndependence has seemed to make little difference to Africa. Too often Africans have allowed others to give them independence instead of realizing it themselves."[43] Hadjor asserts that independence means no dependency without interdependency, deciding for oneself what constitutes development in addition to implementing it, and "establishing new institutions through which the sentiments of the people can be expressed."[44] The Rwandan organizer's appreciative, asset-based approach accordingly focuses on local knowledge—not ignorance, initiatives—not challenges, and resources—not scarcities, to generate further development.[45] In 2013, the Lutheran Church of Rwanda officially recognized Rutsindintwarane's practices of community development and leadership formation, and now uses similar practices in several churches across the country for parish development.

A RWANDAN POLITICAL THEOLOGY

This organizing and leadership work—the one-to-ones, research, action, and evaluation—enacts a political theology effective at critically and constructively engaging government in the context of civil society for the common good. The practices demonstrate—using faith-based, local organizing committees—the possibility of opening a gap of critical distance to the state, one of the most vital needs in Rwanda after genocide. The political capacity to hold public officials accountable to their vocation serves the maintenance of such distance. The ability to communicate one's own views regarding development and public policy is also important for cooperating with the state

---

41. These PICO leadership principles are widely available online. See, for example, *PICO Principles for Community Organizing*.

42. Hadjor, *On Transforming Africa: Discourse with Africa's Leaders*.

43. Ibid., 15.

44. Ibid., 18.

45. De Gruchy, "Of Agency, Assets and Appreciation: Seeking Some Commonalities between Theology and Development," 20–39.

in areas of mutual concern, instead of passively receiving forms of government and non-governmental intervention and aid.[46] Where reconciliation takes priority over other kinds of human development, Rutsindintwarane's community organizing conceived as political theology makes a meaningful, if indirect, contribution. "Building and sustaining peaceful transformation of deadly conflict," John Lederach explains, "is perhaps first and foremost the process of creating and keeping alive transformed spaces of interdependence and interaction between real people in real communities with histories of struggle and division."[47] How to pursue reconciliation in Rwanda continues to be a difficult question, yet through this broad-based organizing, communities can re-appropriate their situations and differences in pursuit of development, making peace along the way.[48]

Though definitions of poverty vary, a common denominator is "an insufficient command of material resources to take a part in the communications of society, so that one's social role is impeded or denied altogether."[49] By facilitating communication among people in communities and with public officials, Rutsindintwarane addresses poverty by countering social fragmentation. Citizens can now hold their government accountable to the vocation of defending and promoting the common good, on which a regime's legitimacy depends.[50] As Rwandan communities effectively organize and de-

46. In a related set of comments on ecclesiology, David Fredrickson writes, "political theology must help us imagine the church as a place of speech, where *all* voices are free to make arguments, to seek to persuade others, and to receive evaluation as whether that which is freely said promotes justice and life—all for the sake of the church's unity and mission and all without the threat of shame and exclusion." Fredrickson, "Free Speech in Pauline Political Theology," 351.

47. Lederach, "The Mystery of Transformative Times and Spaces," 258. In other words, "a geography of peace is microutopian, requiring an eschatology of 'on earth as it is in heaven'" (ibid.).

48. Cyuma, *Picking Up the Pieces: The Church and Conflict Resolution in South Africa and Rwanda.*

49. O'Donovan, *The Ways of Judgment*, 45.

50. This assessment of and recommendation for the Evangelical Lutheran Church of Tanzania (ELCT) is also applicable to the Lutheran Church of Rwanda (LCR). "Most people do not know that the general meetings of the town council are open to the public, and that everyone is free to follow the proceedings. This is where they should supervise the performance of their respective representatives and press them on the issues affecting their daily lives (. . .) Here is where we need to work more diligently as churches. We need to show our members that advocacy works, and that knowing your rights is beneficial. People need to know that a government is for the people, and that government officials should work for the people and not vice versa. They need to be convinced that it is a vocation of the church to reclaim the vocation of government, and hold their government accountable." Mwombeki, "Churches and the Vocation of Government in Africa," 231. Rev. Dr. Mwombeki is General Secretary of the Northwest

velop at local levels, like faith-based community organizations in the United States, they can scale up their work to engage issues at regional and national levels, overcoming their disadvantaged structural position in relation to global forces.[51] While organizing in communities "struggling to cope with the business of survival," Rutsindintwarane, unlike most, if not all, other faith-based NGOs working on development in Rwanda, focuses on political capacities. Martha Nussbaum's theoretical framework for social wellbeing, development, and justice expresses the importance of such capabilities. A life worthy of human dignity, Nussbaum claims, requires "control over one's environment," and "being able to participate effectively in political choices that govern one's own life (. . .)"[52] Training and empowering people to hold public officials accountable, often through role play, and accompanying them, not speaking for them, at meetings with policymakers from local to national levels, is central to Rutsindintwarane's approach to community development. Unlike trends in political theology that concentrate more on "the church as a concrete public, political space in its own right," and less on "other political formations like modern states and civil society," he assumes the need to balance attention between church, society, and state.[53] Beyond the obvious practical and strategic considerations, he holds that justice, peace, and, more specifically, poverty reduction, should be undertaken in collaboration with political institutions supposedly serving these ends.[54]

A political theology, performed across the hills of Rwanda, is embodied in Rutsindintwarane's organizing. Rwandan political theology grows out of powerful political realities—displacement, dispossession, refugee alienation, war, genocide, migration, repatriation, resettlement, reintegration, reconstruction, and reconciliation. In turn, it creates new political realities by directly engaging public officials in the context of civil society. Gary Simpson rightly recognizes that the "task and vocation of political accountability occurs most effectively in and through the public sphere of civil society in its overlapping configurations with democratically constituted states. Rather than political accountability being circumscribed solely by the office of preaching or merely by individual extraordinary heroes, now the whole public sphere of civil society exercises political accountability together with

---

Diocese of the Evangelical Lutheran Church in Tanzania.

51. Wood, *Faith in Action*.

52. Nussbaum, *Creating Capabilities: The Human Development Approach*, 34. See also, Sen, *Development as Freedom*.

53. Bell, Jr., "State and Civil Society," 433ff.

54. O'Donovan, *The Desire of the Nations*.

democratically constituted states."[55] Will these political capacities expand and effectively challenge public officials violating human rights in Rwanda today?[56] Will the church, complicit in genocide, maintain a critical distance to the state and counter ideologies, within and without, detrimental to Rwanda? There is hope.

BIBLIOGRAPHY

Andersen, Svend. "Lutheran Political Theology for the Twenty-First Century." In *Transformations in Luther's Theology: Historical and Contemporary Reflections*, edited by Christine Helmer and Bo Kristian Holm, 245–263. Leipzig: Evangelische Verlagsanstalt GmbH, 2011.

Bell, Jr., Daniel. "State and Civil Society." In *The Blackwell Companion to Political Theology*, edited by Peter Scott and William T. Cavanaugh, 423–38. Malden, MA: Blackwell, 2004.

Brookfield, Stephen D. *The Power of Critical Theory: Liberating Adult Learning and Teaching*. San Francisco, CA: Jossey-Bass, 2005.

Carney, James J. *Rwanda Before the Genocide: Catholic Politics and Ethnic Discourse in the Late Colonial Era*. Oxford: Oxford University Press, 2013.

Cyuma, Samuel. *Picking Up the Pieces: The Church and Conflict Resolution in South Africa and Rwanda*. Eugene, OR: Wipf & Stock, 2012.

De Gruchy, John W. *Christianity and Democracy: A Theology for a Just World Order*. Cambridge: Cambridge University Press, 1995.

De Gruchy, Steve. "Of Agency, Assets and Appreciation: Seeking Some Commonalities between Theology and Development." *Journal of Theology for Southern Africa* 117 (November 2003) 20–39.

Des Forges, Alison. *Leave None to Tell the Story: Genocide in Rwanda*. New York: Human Rights Watch, 1999.

Fredrickson, David. "Free Speech in Pauline Political Theology." *Word & World* 12.4 (Fall 1992) 345–51.

Gatwa, Tharcisse. *The Churches and Ethnic Ideology in the Rwandan Crises 1900–1994*. Milton Keynes: Regnum, 2005.

Hadjor, Kofi Buenor. *On Transforming Africa: Discourses with Africa's Leaders*. Trenton, NJ: Africa World Press, 1987.

Haemig, Mary Jane. "The Confessional Basis of Lutheran Thinking on Church-State Issues." In *Church and State: Lutheran Perspectives*, edited by John R. Stumme and Robert W. Tuttle, 3–19. Minneapolis, MN: Fortress, 2003.

Jennings, Willie James. *The Christian Imagination: Theology and the Origins of Race*. New Haven and London: Yale University Press, 2010.

Katongole, Emmanuel. *Mirror to the Church: Resurrecting Faith after Genocide in Rwanda*. Grand Rapids, MI: Zondervan, 2009.

———. *The Sacrifice of Africa: A Political Theology for Africa*. Grand Rapids, MI: Eerdmans, 2011.

---

55. Simpson, "Toward a Lutheran 'Delight in the Law of the Lord,'" 46.

56. Straus and Waldorf, *Remaking Rwanda: State Building and Human Rights after Mass Violence*.

Lederach, John Paul. "The Mystery of Transformative Times and Spaces." In *Artisans of Peace: Grassroots Peacemaking among Christian Communities*, edited by Mary Ann Cejka and Thomas Bamat. Maryknoll, NY: Orbis, 2003.

Linden, Ian. *Church and Revolution in Rwanda*. Manchester: Manchester University Press, 1977.

Longman, Timothy. *Christianity and Genocide in Rwanda*. Cambridge: Cambridge University Press, 2010.

Longman, Timothy and Theoneste Rutagengwa. "Religion, Memory, and Violence in Rwanda." In *Religion, Violence, Memory, and Place*, edited by Oren Baruch Stier and J. Shawn Landres, 132–49. Bloomington, IN: Indiana University Press, 2006.

Mamdani, Mahmood. *When Victims Become Killers: Colonialism, Nativism, and the Genocide in Rwanda*. Princeton, NJ: Princeton University Press, 2001.

Mwombeki, Fidon R. "Churches and the Vocation of Government in Africa." In *Communion, Responsibility, Accountability: Responding as a Lutheran Communion to Neoliberal Globalization* (LWF Documentation Series 50), edited by Karen L. Bloomquist, 223–32. Geneva: Lutheran World Federation, 2004.

Nussbaum, Martha. *Creating Capabilities: The Human Development Approach*. Cambridge, MA: The Belknap Press of Harvard University Press, 2011.

O'Donovan, Oliver. *The Desire of the Nations: Rediscovering the Roots of Political Theology*. Cambridge: Cambridge University Press, 1996.

———. *The Ways of Judgment*. Grand Rapids, MI: Eerdmans, 2005.

PICO National Network. Pico National Network. Online: http://www.piconetwork.org/about/history (accessed 10/02/2014).

PICO Principles for Community Organizing. The Micah Project. Online: http://www.micahpico.org/resources?id=0002 (accessed 10/02/2014).

Prunier, Gerard. *The Rwanda Crisis: History of a Genocide*. NY: Columbia University Press, 1995.

Rittner, Carol, John K. Roth, and Wendy Whitworth, editors. *Genocide in Rwanda: Complicity of the Churches*. Saint Paul, MI: Paragon House, 2004.

Rutsindintwarane, John. "An Appreciative Inquiry in Rusumo and Rukira Districts, Kibungo Province of Rwanda: A Study of the Perceptions, Challenges and Needs for Empowering the Lutheran Church of Rwanda." Master's thesis, Wartburg Theological Seminary, 2005.

———. "A Strategy for Empowering Communities." In *So the poor have hope, and injustice shuts its mouth": Poverty and the Mission of the Church in Africa*, edited by Karen L. Bloomquist and Musa Panti Filibus, 141–44. Geneva: Lutheran World Federation Studies, 2007.

Sen, Amartya. *Development as Freedom*. New York: Anchor, 1999.

Simpson, Gary M. "Toward a Lutheran 'Delight in the Law of the Lord': Church and State in the Context of Civil Society." In *Church and State: Lutheran Perspectives*, edited by John R. Stumme and Robert W. Tuttle, 20–50. Minneapolis, MN: Fortress, 2003.

Straus, Scott and Lars Waldorf, editors. *Remaking Rwanda: State Building and Human Rights after Mass Violence*. Madison, WI: The University of Wisconsin Press, 2011.

Uvin, Peter. *Aiding Violence: The Development Enterprise in Rwanda*. West Hartford, CT: Kumarian, 1998.

Vansina, Jan. *Antecedents to Modern Rwanda: The Nyiginya Kingdom*. Madison, WI: The University of Wisconsin Press, 2004.

Villa-Vicencio, Charles. *A Theology of Reconstruction: Nation-Building and Human Rights*. Cambridge: Cambridge University Press, 1992.

Warren, Mark R. *Dry Bones Rattling: Community Building to Revitalize American Democracy*. Princeton, NJ: Princeton University Press, 2001.

Wood, Richard L. *Faith in Action: Religion, Race, and Democratic Organizing in America*. Chicago, IL: University of Chicago Press, 2002.

13

Transforming Domination Then and Now

KAREN L. BLOOMQUIST

Why are churches not more forthrightly speaking out and acting to transform today's realities of domination—the injustices, illusions, and empire—that fly in the face of the faith Christians confess? How might churches become places where "subversions" of reality can be nurtured and alternative public visions held forth and pursued, for the sake of the world? These questions lie behind the focus of this chapter.

I propose that ecclesia be considered an "event" of seeing, remembering, and connecting, of putting together what is fragmentary, pointing to what is true, enabling us to see and act, including in organized actions with others. This implies the long-term challenge of nurturing and organizing communities of resistance against the dominant scripts and the systemic injustices they entail today, communities that are intentionally collaborative across boundaries of religion, geography and self-interest.

How then might "seeing, remembering, and connecting" be developed theologically as a dynamic set of practices for transfiguring what Luther was uncovering/ re-discovering in the sixteenth century, for connecting us today across contexts, and for the transformation, through the power of the Spirit, of the bondages and dominations that hold people and creation captive today?

THE THEOLOGICAL CRISIS IN THE SIXTEENTH CENTURY REFORMATION AND TODAY

In the sixteenth century, the crisis was over the gospel that frees people from the fear and bondage of sin, which became embedded in systems needing to be challenged. Today, people also are in fear and bondage—over the sin of greed, as embedded in the economic system. They fear what the future will hold, unless dramatic changes are made for the sake of global economic and environmental justice. (. . .) Systemic greed becomes like the domination or bondage of sin that is expressed through the theology of Paul (e.g., Romans 6) and Luther.[1]

New awareness of this state of bondage has continued to grow and become more obvious, but usually in ways that churches have not dealt with on explicitly theological grounds. People today are feeling acutely betrayed by the promises they have bought into, often with blind faith that now is increasingly feeling betrayed, e.g., by large corporate interests determined to keep the market as "free" as possible. Matters of basic meaning, hope and values were at stake at the time of the Reformation, as well as today. But there have been significant shifts in where that salvific hope is lodged.

In Luther's time, the Papacy had become the most powerful institution ruling over people's lives, with closely intertwined religious, social, cultural, and political aspects. Under this system, no one could do enough so as to be certain of his/her salvation. Luther came to view this institutional power of domination as a theological matter which threatened salvation itself.[2] His theological critique of this domination, which he raised out a pastoral concern for people's salvation, became the means through which Luther began to break through the whole Roman system of domination.

THE EUCHARIST

One focus in Luther's protest against this domination, was how the sacraments (especially Holy Communion) were being used by the Roman church for power and control over the people, and thus distorted as God's gift of grace and freedom "The Eucharist became a locus where the Church could exercise its control over the sacred (. . .) the mystery itself (. . .) instrumentalized."[3]

1. Lutheran World Federation, *Daily Bread Instead of Greed*.
2. Hendrix, *Luther and the Papacy*, xii.
3. Schwartz, *Sacramental Poetics at the Dawn of Secularism: When God Left the World*, 20.

By the middle of the twelfth century, the church, eager to assert the real presence of the human and the divine Christ against various spiritualizing challenges, began to refer to the host as the *corpus Christi*, the body of Christ, such that the term for the host, *corpus mysticum*, was gradually transferred to the Church. Rather than the church referred to as the body of Christ (*corpus Christi*), the host in the Eucharist was referred to as such.

In this climate, the Eucharist was given a strategic function: to consolidate the Church, by positing not just the equivalence but the identity between mystical reality and the visible, and by making that depend upon hierarchical authority. Hence, the Eucharist became a miracle made possible through the power of the Church—a power seemingly prior to the miracle. In this way, the Eucharist became a locus where the Church could exercise its control over the sacred. This co-optation of the Eucharist also vastly accentuated the institution's hierarchy, formalism, and legalism.

> (. . .)[Thus] the profound difference between a hierarchical institution appropriating the right to dispense the medicine of the Eucharist versus the belief that the Eucharist itself has the sacramental power to create a healthy social body. Mystery is the domain beyond human control but here *sacramentality* is no longer contrasted to *instrumentality* for the mystery itself has been instrumentalized.[4]

There is a profound difference between a hierarchical institution appropriating exclusive salvific power, and the much earlier Christian belief that the Eucharist itself has the sacramental power to create a healthy social body. Schwartz views the Reformation as an assault on pre-modern understandings of sacramentality,[5] with a version of transubstantiation then migrating into poetry, particularly in England, as well as being appropriated by the state (Christ embodied not in the host but in the social body of the nation).

Luther broke open this system of domination, by proposing a much different relationship with God. He responded both to people's fears/captivity connected with their social longings (desires) *and* touched the ecclesial nerve center: its financial support and its divine legitimacy.[6] Luther wanted to find a crack/crisis in the reigning consensus of *ecclesia, oeconomia, politia* (church, economy, and politics), by cracking the surface; the justice of God breaks in and fragments the systems of the world.[7] The theology of the cross frees theology from captivity to the dominant modes of rationality

---

4. Ibid.
5. Ibid., 11.
6. Altmann, "Justification in the context of exclusion—Latin America," 121.
7. Westhelle, *The Scandalous God*, 41.

operating in theology and economy, which is why Luther attacked both indulgences and usury.[8]

Justification by grace overcomes in principle and in practice the division between religious and secular aspects of life in the medieval world. God's justification causes us to see ourselves, our neighbor and the world differently, not based on inherent acceptability or net worth, but in ways that are countercultural, even subversive of the reigning ideologies. "Justification is prophetic speech from the heart of the divine pathos (. . .) a call to remembrance that is deeper than morality or civility."[9] It is transcendent beyond any promise of the reigning structural or ideological bondage. "Justification is God's mission of love for the world."[10]

A pervasive thread running throughout Luther's writings was his intent to make this breakthrough practical, experiential, accessible to common ordinary folk in the struggles they face. So what kinds of practices can break open insights into systems and spaces today, not only with those in churches, but also the public as a whole?

The signing in 1999 of the Joint Declaration on the Doctrine of Justification by the Catholic and Lutheran churches was celebrated as an ecumenical milestone, and indeed it was, however, *oecumene* has to do not only with the church, but with the whole world. Here, where people's many kinds of bondage, fears and hopes are focused today is where these central theological insights of the Reformation have hardly begun to penetrate.

FOR THE SAKE OF THE WORLD

I propose to begin with the world—what is going on there becomes a "wake up" call to the church. The world is "in our face" as a church, because the world is very much "in" us. The real faith struggles of our day are not necessarily with other recognizable faiths (Islam, etc.), but with the unquestioned ideologies that reign over and distort our lives. Churches that assume they are set apart from the world often operate with assumptions and practices that actually are more affected or shaped by the ideologies and practices reigning in their world or culture than they are by biblical/theological perspectives—particularly in their quest to be "successful." It is not that the world tells the church how to be the church, but the world opens up challenges that the church must engage if it is to be faithful—bearer of news that actually is "good" today—i.e., liberating, healing, transformative of what holds us and all of creation in bondage.

8. Ibid., 47.
9. Tiede, "Justifying faith and the net worth of productivity—USA," 113.
10. Ibid., 114.

"For the sake of the world" may seem like a significant shift from how sixteenth century reforming movements tended to be preoccupied with the church and salvation, rather than with what was going on in the world. Yet if Reformation insights are to have an enduring, living significance in the world today—a world of massive injustice, illusions, and bankrupt hopes—then its insights must be able to communicate not only with those who bear the name "Lutheran" but more importantly, for the sake of *this world* that God so loves. What new possibilities might this open up for how the faith can be embodied and conveyed, especially among those who are skeptical as to whether the church has anything worthwhile to offer the world today?

For North Americans, beginning with the world is also strategic because of how this "subverts" our usual tendency to focus on ourselves, on a private, spiritual realm as a refuge (or fortress) from "all the bad stuff out there." The usual sequence is that we are fed, inspired, get ourselves together and then go out—sharing what we have for the sake of others. But the shortfall of this is that we often don't seem to get it together enough (our internal church activities) to get around to the missional "going out" dimensions. We stay focused on ourselves (those in church), rather than on an enlarged sense of "us" that a focus on *the world* in all its diversity brings in from the beginning.

HOW CAN REALITIES OF DOMINATION BE TRANSFORMED?

Luther seemed aware of the need to deal with both the objective and subjective realities of what was holding people in bondage in his time. Rather than primarily mounting a frontal attack on the institution holding people captive then, he attacked the actual practices that played into and supported the reigning system of domination. He did so on deeply theological grounds. Luther boldly declared that through the preaching of faith, centered especially in the doctrine of justification, practices such "indulgences, purgatory, vows, Masses, and similar abominations come tumbling down, taking with them the ruin of the entire papacy (. . .) solely by the Spirit."[11]

The subjective/internal reality of God's justification/salvation has external/objective consequences. If justification remains confined to a spiritual realm apart from societal implications, or in distinction from the critical relational dimensions of *communio* that flow from it, then injustices will continue to have free reign, distorting our most basic relationship, to God, ourselves, and one another. This is not to imply that the world can be governed by the gospel—we need to resist any theocracy tendencies. But

---

11. Luther, *Lectures on Galatians*, LW 26, 221, 223.

what is unleashed is a power that cannot remain quiet or passive in the face of unjust systems—because of how they themselves distort theological anthropology and hold people in captivity both spiritually and materially. In this sense, justification and justice are intimately connected. [12] Exposing what is operating today is not simply a matter of denouncing and extricating ourselves from it. This must not lapse into an otherworldly escapism, and with it, an increasing privatization of the faith disengaged from the reigning material realities.

Yet we are too enmeshed in their complexities for a straightforward denunciation of this idolatry to be persuasive, especially by those who benefit from the compensations. Thus, there needs to be long-term nurturing of resistance practices, grounded in the Bible and in our faith perspectives that go beyond what is. Walter Brueggemann refers to Scripture as a "subversion"—a rendering of reality that lives under the dominant version,[13] a dominant imagination that screens out all other neighbors, who can be screened out if the God of all Neighborliness is fashioned instead as a God who celebrates individual achievement.

Regina Schwartz, along with others, proposes that the Reformation inaugurated the beginning of modernism and the birth of the modern Self, and the subsequent dominations to which this led: "the figure of the Other is gradually replaced by the Self who defines and controls all he [sic] sways."[14] Instead, the intention of the Eucharist is "to create a community that coheres not through particular identities" but through "the potential of reconciliation harbored by communion to inspire a world of community,"[15] based on God's justice and compassion for all.

TOWARD A SUBVERSIVE *ECCLESIA CRUCIS*

Guillermo Hansen provocatively suggests how the "Lutheran theological code" might become transformative of the challenges we face in today's world. This code includes how the cross (dis)locates the sacred into the realm of the profane—into the world. The cross is a subversive code that

---

12. I recall how the Reformed churches (WARC) refrained from sign onto the Joint Declaration on the Doctrine of Justification until the connections between justification and justice were made more explicit. Although Lutherans had pursued that earlier, especially in relation to Latin American realities of injustice, this was not further pursued in theological work underlying the official Lutheran/Catholic dialogues on justification.

13. Brueggemann, *The Word Militant: Preaching a Decentering Word*, 152.

14. Schwartz, *Sacramental Poetics at the Dawn of Secularism: When God Left the World*, 139.

15. Ibid., 141.

challenges all cultural and religious notions of what is considering transcendent or successful in life.[16] It is where our current ways of knowing are questioned and destabilized, making room for what is truly new and different. It is a verdict that something is fundamentally wrong with how the world is structured.[17] The cross interrogates and destabilizes what is generally known, thus opening up space for what is truly new and different. The cross appears as the center of a new gospel, as a sociopolitical event. Furthermore, the God who transcends ("falls") into our world, justifies the victims of imperial power,[18] radically redrawing the boundaries of God's domain to include those considered outcasts. "God's twofold rule is for the sake of a public theology, to bring forth worlds in which people can live, through radical democracy as a living alternative through the networks spawned by empire."[19]

The church living by a theology of the cross is taken more fully and deeply into the world. This key emphasis in Luther's theology needs to be pursued further, for the sake of forming an *ecclesia* that is transformative, even subversive, of the injustice, empire, and domination of many kinds that hold the world captive today.

The vantage point of the cross, along with a collective sense of the structural sin in which we are complicit, is a critique that should be undergone, rather than adopted and employed, thereby exposing vulnerability and fallibility. Thus, we must engage in practices to "see in truthful ways," so that the knowing might become "compelling," so that we might "glimpse the presence of God and the holiness of the church in unlikely places."[20] In the "privileging" of sites of vulnerability, God and we ourselves can be seen more truly.

An epistemology of the cross becomes especially crucial when illusions fall apart, when they no longer hold. We begin to see what really is going on, understand our implications in it, and accept our accountability to act accordingly. The cross is the fulcrum for knowing—the hinge point of true reality and the gift to see it.[21] To know truly is to know from the margins (. . .) of life, sanity, dignity, power. Friends of the cross are those

---

16. Hansen, "Resistance, Adaptation or Challenge: The Versatility of the Lutheran Code," 30.

17. Ibid., 31.

18. Ibid., 32.

19. Ibid., 35.

20. Mahn, "What are Churches *For*? Toward an Ecclesiology of the Cross after Christendom," 18–19.

21. Solberg, *Compelling Knowledge: A Feminist Proposal for an Epistemology of the Cross*, 90.

who "live in the world as it is, without illusions."[22] "The church of the cross becomes a visible alternative to the ways of the world *in and through* its immersion in it."[23]

In deeply encountering persons and realities far different from their own—in "relocating" ourselves—our complicity with injustice is exposed. Building on these understandings and practices distinctive to a church that is porously and intentionally open to the world, how can this nurture and lead toward transformation of what is holding people in bondage today, ideologically and practically?

SEEING, REMEMBERING, AND CONNECTING AS SUBVERSIVE ECCLESIAL PRACTICES

Through the power of the indwelling and connecting Spirit, active in and through our interconnections with those who are most different or "other" from us, through *their* realities and perspectives, we are transformed. This transformative power becomes "subversive" of what we take for granted as inevitable certainties. This transforms what we are able to *see, remember, and connect*, which I suggest are key verbs, practices or theological movements by which *ecclesia crucis* for the sake of the world emerges.

People regularly see, remember, and connect; there is nothing esoteric or "churchy" about these verbs. These are practices basic to what it means to be human, accessible to those who do not identify with the institutional church. But these practices also have theological underpinnings that can be formative over the long haul, forming inclusive communities that can resist ideological captivity, opening transcendent space for the redeeming, liberating, transforming power of God—in ways that cut across boundaries.

Most pivotally this occurs through practices of proclaiming the Word and celebrating the Sacraments. The Word provokes and unsettles, it is a foretaste of this subversive reality that God is bringing into our midst. In the Eucharist, "the Kingdom irrupts into time and 'confuses' the spiritual and the temporal. (. . .) calls the church to be what eschatologically it is (. . .) living out a vision of what really is real (. . .) the reign of God disrupting dominating reigns of injustice".[24]

---

22. Ibid., 83.

23. Mahn, "What are Churches *For?* Toward an Ecclesiology of the Cross after Christendom," 21.

24. Cavanaugh, *Torture and Eucharist: Theology, Politics, and the Body of Christ*, 206.

One key practice is cited by Mahn: "The holiness of the church is made visible—obscurely and compellingly—in its very repentance for sin."[25] The gathered worshipping community, through the opening liturgy of confession and forgiveness, "comes to see itself truly." This is a kind of re-locating, turning outside-in, and a re-envisioning. It is a sight check, both internally and externally. We "become aligned with God's knowing," seeing ourselves as *simil justus et peccator*. Because of how deeply we are implicated in and complicit in the social nature of sin, we need one another to know truthfully. This beginning of the liturgy corresponds with the final sending, when again we are turned out to remember the poor, in other words, to be where a cross theology calls us to be.

Truth telling emerges through remembering (a) who/whose we are in relation to God, (b) what has come before us, and (c) the realities of our neighbors globally as well as locally. Empowered through the Holy Spirit, this has the potential to transform what is occurring in light of God's in-breaking new reality. Subversive remembering is a theologically-empowered social practice of expressing "when/who/what" has been forgotten or overlooked. It exposes our illusions, false gods and the domination (empire) and injustices they perpetuate, and impels truth-telling and organized action (resistance) for the sake of God's world.

The challenge is to be able to discern (to *see*) the places and times in which broken and damaging crises are "receiving a facelift from the high priests of the new global gospel."[26] In short, we begin to actually *see* more deeply with new vision rather than captive to illusions that block our vision of what really is happening in our lives and world. This becomes possible as we *remember* a God who became radically incarnate and vulnerable in this world. This God frees and empowers us to engage with these realities today, remembering what has been forgotten in our past *and* remembering those who are forgotten around us and throughout the world today. We *connect* in ways that heighten the contradictions between the ideologies and the actual realities, we connect with those who are other from us, and we connect in collaborative actions with others for the sake of the world—connections made possible through the power of the Spirit, and that *do* make a difference in the world.

This connecting is itself *ecclesia*, formed in ways that can challenge or at least go beyond the confines of the institutional church. These practices come together in overlapping ways, leading us into alternative worldviews,

---

25. Mahn, "What are Churches *For?* Toward an Ecclesiology of the Cross after Christendom," 21, 22.

26. Westhelle, *The Scandalous God*, 59.

interpretations, praxis, ways of being in this world, empowering us to engage with the realities out there. Indeed, faith communities—of various kinds—may be among the last places around where a subversion of reality can be articulated and an alternative vision held forth.

Today, much of seeing is socially conditioned to become a distraction or diversion from what really matters—seeing that entertains rather than leading toward greater understanding, and allows the domination to continue. Thus, attention must be given to seeing that exposes "the big picture" of what is actually occurring—through wider social-economic-political analyses—instead of what is assumed in customary, popularized or officially authorized interpretations that portend to be true or authoritative. This calls for seeing through the pretenses, honestly and authentically, seeing beneath the surface of what is assumed to be the case. Helping people to see in such ways, especially by delving deeper into what is going on, is a crucial practice that is at the same time both pastoral and prophetic. It is a practice that takes seriously what people are experiencing in their everyday lives but sets it within a wider framework of what needs to change.

How might this be pursued today in ways that lead toward the transformation rather than legitimation of the spirit and practices of domination that hold people captive and generate injustices in our day? To do so we must first interpret this many-faceted domination—as it is actually impacting people on the ground—in order to better grasp the deeper theological matter that needs to be addressed today.

Here we might learn, for example, from indigenous communities. On the Pacific Northwest rim of the U.S. "seeing, remembering, connecting" is empowering Native-led resistance to the proposed development of what would become the largest coal terminal in North America, projected to ship up to 50 million tons of coal each year from Cherry Point in Washington state to China.

In September 2012 the Lummi people invited many of us in the wider community, to "come and *see* Cherry Point"—a rocky undeveloped shoreline and deep water bay of the Salish Sea (north Puget Sound) that has long been their fishing grounds, on a beautiful land, overlooking Bellingham Bay, sacred land of the Lummis for thousands of year.

There the Lummis *remember* the stories of suffering, both before and after contact with European settlers. They remember their countless ancestors whose bones are still buried in this land or at the bottom of the sea. These are sacred memories that sustain their identity and sense of being a people today. They remember when fish were more plentiful in these waters, before oil tankers began transiting these waters, catching up fish traps in their wake. And, they remember the Great Spirit who opposes this!

Emboldened by this remembering, they make public their refusal to be bought off, which was vividly symbolized in the burning of a huge facsimile of a multi-million dollar check marked "non-negotiable."

Further, the Lummi people *connect* the exploitation of the land and water that has long been a part of their narrative, with the profit-driven corporate interests who now want to build a coal terminal here, occupying and destroying land and water further. They connect what is proposed here, not only with the exploitation they have long experienced, but also with what this will do to the air globally, if this area were to become complicit in the shipping of such massive amount of coal that, when burned, would contribute significantly to climate change. The whole of the earth, water, air, in their fragile inter-related global web would be further destroyed.

Further, they *connect* with non-Native people who share and fish these waters, and who join them in organized resistance to this development. The spirituality, values and resistance of the Lummis have become the heart of the widespread resistance to this controversial project across the Northwest, including in states such as Montana from which much of the coal would be extracted. This has led a candidate there for the US Senate to declare,

> Coal is dead. I will not be dishonest about this for political gain. Lying isn't going to help those [coal industry] workers. (. . .) I'm going to serve the impacted citizens by dealing with reality, rather than serving myself by hustling concerned workers for votes with promises no candidate will keep.[27]

This is a connecting that exposes illusions by engaging in truth-telling. Such truth-telling is a political practice but also an implicitly theological practice that is empowered by remembering who and whose we are. Seeing, remembering and connecting—as subversive Christian practices—have the potential to lead into many similar examples of organized resistance over the long haul.

An objective naming or lashing out at what is holding us in bondage, without engaging and subsequently transforming both the subjective and objective aspects of this domination, is not likely to lead to change, as Luther himself realized. How can we disassociate from these powers on which we depend for our sense of worth and future? What is needed is a critically engaged relationship with this illusive idolatry. Only by seeing, remembering, making connections and thus resisting for the sake of a more just and humane reality can the existing system's idolatry be exposed. This occurs through a process of immanent critique that exposes the gap between the

---

27. Adams quoted in "Montana Senate Candidate Bucks the Trend, Declares 'Coal Is Dead.'"

illusive promises and the actual realities in people's lives, through a process of seeing, remembering and connecting, which counters the prevailing Individualism, Victimization and Privatization.

As I wrote some years ago with regard to U.S. American working-class reality, "freedom" from domination is typically sought through the vicious cycle of individualism, victimization, and privatization, which functions as an idolatrous "trinity," holding the reigning reality of domination in place.

> Individualism puts the burden on the individual to (. . .) succeed (. . .) Yet the pervasive experience of working people is that despite their works and hopes, they have not acquired the fruits of this individualism. Consequently, there is a shift (. . .) to a worldview of victimization: 'it was done to me.' The active idealism as the core of American individualism is transfigured into a stance of passivity, resignation or inevitability: 'there's nothing that I as an individual can do about the forces out there.'[28]

This results in an intensified privatization of life, aided by an increasingly individualized, spiritualized a-historical theology, cut off from the public and economic realities that do shape, dominate and violate people's lives. The illusion is perpetuated that the loss of being active subjects, under victimization, results in a regaining of subjectivity through privatization, but this is cut off from and compounds rather than transforming what holds people captive.

Here I have begun to suggest some theological sensitivities for how practices central to the church might lead toward transformation not only of us, not only of church, but also of the world and the various "isms" prevalent there.

Admittedly in his day Luther focused more on "hearing" than on "seeing." Yet "seeing" is implicit in the illusion-exposing dynamic of Luther's theology of the cross. These ordinary practices become extraordinary when viewed through theological lenses: *God is revealing, remembering, and connecting*, becoming manifest in and through what these verbs imply, but always as far more than what we can grasp, comprehend or realize—as transcendently immanent. *That is, we glimpse a sense of what God is about in our lives and world through seeing, remembering, connecting.* We begin to see, remember, connect what we would not otherwise, and to do so collaboratively, for the sake of the world. Through its distinct practices, the church as *ecclesia*—in collaborative action with those far beyond the organized church—begins to counter the illusion, amnesia, and disconnectedness, i.e.,

---

28. Bloomquist, *The Dream Betrayed: Religious Challenge of the Working Class*, 52.

the sin, bondage, blindness, ahistoricity, and privatization that enable the domination of empire to prevail.

The church is "one holy apostolic and catholic," a gift of God that comes from beyond current realities, thus transforming all that is in light of what has been (the past) and what will be (the future). We see, remember, and connect with another reality that is becoming manifest here and now. Through practices such as preaching, teaching, celebrating, caring, community-formation, and organizing, the church as *ecclesia* begins to counter the illusion, amnesia, and disconnectedness, i.e., the sin, bondage, blindness, ahistoricity, and privatization that enable the domination of the many facets of empire to prevail.

Practices such as these need to be more intentionally nurtured, developed, embodied in and through local faith communities—through recognizable practices, but in ways that are more porous, publically accessible to others. This involves crossing some of the usual boundaries between sacred and secular, between "us" and "them," between local and global realities, between Christians and those of other faiths, between humans and the rest of nature. This means cutting across contexts and thereby is "trans-contextual," in ways such that symbols acquire new meanings in new contexts, and thereby are transfigured, and in ways that are transformative of the prevailing dominations and injustices[29]—for the sake of the world that God creates, loves, redeems and continually transforms.

BIBLIOGRAPHY

Adams, Dirk quoted in "Montana Senate Candidate Bucks the Trend, Declares 'Coal Is Dead'" by Tom Kenworthy, *ThinkProgress* Online: http://thinkprogress.org/climate/2014/02/28/3333501/montana-senate-coal-dead/ (accessed 28/02/2014).

Altmann, Walter. "Justification in the context of exclusion—Latin America." In *Justification in the World's Context*, edited by Wolfgang Greive. Geneva: Lutheran World Federation, 2000.

Bloomquist, Karen L. *The Dream Betrayed: Religious Challenge of the Working Class*. Minneapolis: Fortress, 1990.

———. "Lutheran Theology in the Future?" In *Transformative Theological Perspectives*, edited by Karen L. Bloomquist, 193–204. Theology in the Life of the Church 6. Geneva: Lutheran World Federation/Minneapolis: Lutheran University Press, 2009.

Brueggemann, Walter. *The Word Militant: Preaching a Decentering Word*. Minneapolis: Fortress, 2010.

---

29. In the concluding volume of the LWF "Theology in the Life of the Church" program (2005–2009), I proposed that the future of Lutheran theology in a global communion needs to be "trans-contextual, trans-figuration, and transformative," Bloomquist, "Lutheran Theology in the Future," 199ff.

Cavanaugh, William T. *Torture and Eucharist: Theology, Politics, and the Body of Christ.* Oxford: Blackwell, 2008.
Hansen, Guillermo. "Resistance, Adaptation or Challenge: The Versatility of the Lutheran Code." In *Transformative Theological Perspectives,* edited by Karen L. Bloomquist, 23–38. Theology in the Life of the Church 6. Geneva: Lutheran World Federation/Minneapolis: Lutheran University Press, 2009.
Hendrix, Scott H. *Luther and the Papacy: Stages in a Reformation Conflict.* Minneapolis: Fortress, 1981.
Luther, Martin. *Lectures on Galatians* (1535). LW 26. St. Louis: Concordia, 1963.
Lutheran World Federation. *Daily Bread Instead of Greed,* public statement of the 2010 Assembly. Online: www.lwf-assembly.org/assembly-documents/ (accessed 30/10/2013).
Mahn, Jason A. "What are Churches *For?* Toward an Ecclesiology of the Cross after Christendom." *Dialog* 51:1 (Spring 2012) 14–23.
Schwartz, Regina M. *Sacramental Poetics at the Dawn of Secularism: When God Left the World.* Stanford, CA: Stanford University Press, 2008.
Solberg, Mary. *Compelling Knowledge: A Feminist Proposal for an Epistemology of the Cross.* Albany: State University of New York, 1997.
Tiede, David. "Justifying faith and the net worth of productivity—USA." In *Justification in the World's Context,* edited by Wolfgang Greive, 103–5. Geneva: Lutheran World Federation, 2000.
Westhelle, Vítor. *The Scandalous God: The Use and Abuse of the Cross.* Minneapolis: Fortress, 2006.

14

Eros, Ethics, and Politics

Nuptial Imagery in Luther Read as a Challenge to Traditional Power Structures

ELISABETH GERLE

Body, sexuality, and the erotic are close, divine and vulnerable. In a Lutheran tradition they are seen as part of the good creation, interpreted as God's continuous creation. Pleasure, pain, and passion are intertwined in human experience. The incarnate God is a passionate God. Hence, the erotic has in Christian history also been seen as a path to God. A well known reading of Martin Luther is, however, that he and other Reformers challenged the Eros tradition where Mystics, since the early centuries of Christianity, had tried to be unified with the divine through body and erotic ascetics where pain, pleasure, and passion were interwoven in intricate patterns of desire. In this Mystical tradition the biblical poem the *Song of Songs* was central.

In this chapter I will show that Luther drew on this tradition but in new ways. He gave another direction and interpretation of Eros and passion that was more reflexive and mutual. The actual union was highlighted rather than longing, i.e. desire for the bittersweet, non attainable. His emphasis was further less individualistic than modern readings of Luther claim and more directed towards the community. Desire and the love language of the *Song of Songs* became reflexive and mutual, expected to be present in ordinary life, within the family, in economy and in politics. Thus the erotic imagery for Luther was a resource for ethics and politics and hence, for society, a resource with contemporary implications.

As the erotic language in Luther's writing has been a resource used in ethics and politics I will continue in this tradition of reinterpretations. Based on a historical account I will suggest a constructive contemporary use where erotic language can be an inspiration for expanded neighborly love.

NUPTIAL IMAGERY OPEN FOR DIFFERENT INTERPRETATIONS

This chapter takes as its point of departure an analysis of the nuptial imagery in Luther's treatise *The Freedom of a Christian* written in 1525. Here, Luther draws on the erotic language from the tradition of *Song of Songs*, playing with exchange of roles and queer imagery.

First, I give a brief background to the use of this theme in the mystical tradition. Then, I will show that Martin Luther gives another, quite unusual, peculiar interpretation related to politics, based on a new understanding of justification. He claims that the *Song of Songs* is a political text.[1]

However, I will show that Luther also uses bridal language in his wedding sermon from 1531. In this sermon he uses almost identical formulations as those used by Bernard de Clairvaux 400 years earlier when he describes the relationship between God and the soul.

Based on an analysis of the human being *coram Deo* and *coram hominibus*, i.e. in relation to God and in relation to one's fellow human beings, I will then argue for a constructive use of nuptial imagery today. Luther's theology had a soteriological focus, i.e. on the relationship *coram Deo*. This did not mean that he was apolitical. It is more that he did not want to see ethics as merit *coram Deo*. Ethics had to do with love towards one's neighbor, *coram hominibus*.

My argument is that the politics of neighborly love today needs to transform structures. The boundary between private and public is being undermined in contemporary society despite a liberal insistence to the contrary. Like the notion of "creation," the Aristotelian language of spheres or estates *politia, familia/oeconomia* and *ecclesia* that Luther used, can be interpreted in two different ways, as preserving and upholding static orders

---

1. Bo Kristian Holm maintains that for Luther the *Song of Songs* is not about either heterosexual love or God's relationship with either the Church or the human soul. It is about politics. See Holm, "Luther's theological and political use of the nuptial metaphor." This lecture of Holm builds on studies presented in Holm, *Gabe und Geben bei Luther. Das Verhältnis zwischen Reziprozität und reformatorischer Rechtfertigungslehre*; Holm, "Justification and Reciprodity. Purification of 'Gift-Exchange' in Martin Luther and John Milbank," 87–116; Holm, "Rechtfertigung als gegenseitige Anerkennung," 23–42; Holm, "Der fröhliche Verkehr. Rechtfertigungslehre als 'Gabe-Theologie,'" 33–54.

(as in the theology of orders) and as daily new creation and transformation.[2] Today the "spheres of promises," need to be reinterpreted in ways that see them as spheres of solidarity involving passion and curiosity.[3]

Jewish mysticism saw the *Song of Songs* as a love poem describing the relationship between God and his people. Origen (185–254) read the Bible allegorically and is often said to have established the allegorical tradition. He is also the portal figure for the mystical tradition and had an enormous influence on Gregory the Great, Maximus the Confessor, and Bernard de Clairvaux. It is hard to find interpretations in the history of commentary that do not have their basis in Origen.[4] The mystical tradition from Origen onwards read the erotic imagery in the *Song of Songs* as a poem about the love of God and the soul or between God and the Church.

A dualism between soul and body, mind and sensuality, and higher or lower spiritual forces often became part of the mental state. While Plato was a monist thinker in terms of hierarchies and different distances in relation to the divine, the Neo-Platonists saw a contrast between the material and the spiritual. For instance, Origen wrote, in his *Prologue to the Commentary on the Song of Songs*, about the necessary choice of sowing either in the flesh or in the soul. Those who carry the face of earth are driven by earthly desire and love while those who have a heavenly face are led by heavenly desire and love.[5] Origen claimed that the love of God cannot love anything material, or anything that can be corrupted, as the love of God is the source of incorruptibility.[6] Origen, therefore, formulates an explicit warning that everyone "who has not yet withdrawn from the desires of corporeal nature should completely refrain from reading this book."[7]

---

2. For the latter position see Wingren, *Creation and Gospel. The New Situation on European Theology*; Wingren, *Man and the Incarnation. A Study in the Biblical Theology of Irenaeus*; Wingren, *Creation and Law*; For a theology of orders see e.g. Brunner, *Das Gebot und die Ordnungen. Entwurf einer protestantisch-theologischen Ethik*.

3. I have used the expression "spheres of promise" elsewhere e.g. in Gerle, "Var dags och varje människas upprättelse"; Gerle, *Mänskliga rättigheter för Guds skull. Tolka text, tro och tradition*. The estates have their background in Aristotelian ethics and is not an invention of Luther. Yet they are especially connected with his social teaching. See Brock, "Why the Estates? Hans Ulrich's Recovery of an Unpopular Notion," 179. Brock claims that "the orders indicate the steady states set up by the divine promises and in which truly human life can exist. In these terms, to act or think as if we are gods is to obscure the divine address, and so to introduce a decaying interference into the states of activity in which human fullness of life exists."

4. Rubenson, "Himmelsk åtrå. Höga Visan i tidigkristen tolkning," 113.

5. Origen, *Prologue to the Commentary on the Song of Songs*, 223.

6. Ibid., 226.

7. Ibid., 91.

The spiritual senses were seen as parallel to the physical senses.[8] Jesus' parable of the sowing man gave the background to an allegorical interpretation, where the human being, i.e. the man, had to choose between nurturing his flesh and bodily senses or his soul. The physical body and its senses were, according to Origen, numbing the spiritual senses and making them insusceptible to the spiritual. Hence, the path to purification was to develop a strict discipline over the physical senses so as not to numb the spiritual ones.[9]

Grace M. Janzten, feminist philosopher and theologian, has criticized this mystical tradition for being dualistic and more or less excluding women. From a Neo-Platonic perspective, women were seen as closer to the material, while men were connected with the mind, the soul, and God. Jantzen claimed that this had consequences for human love.[10] The love of the heavenly bridegroom led to suspicion in relation to all other love, especially every other sexual love.

In this tradition which gained an enormous influence within Christianity, erotic imagery was used at the expense of human sexual relations, according to Jantzen. Using the language of passion, physical, sexual passion was denounced in an attempt to channel all desire towards God. Human sexuality was seen as distraction and corruption, "distasteful and gross."[11]

Luther introduced a new anthropology that saw body and soul as one unity. He praised the mind and affirmed the Aristotelian description of the human being as *"animal rationale."* He even described the mind as "divine."[12] In line with earlier tradition, he also thought that men were more rational than women.[13] However, he perceived the human being as *totus homo*. The fight between good and evil does not thus refer to parts of the human being or to different life principles, but to the total human being.[14] He describes the human with the metaphor of daybreak, or dawn, which is neither night nor day, but both, yet a bit more day, as it is drawn towards day. Luther does not accept Jerome's interpretation that is built on

---

8. Ibid., 222–23; Cf. Louth, *The Origins of the Christian Mystical Tradition. From Plato to Denys*, 66.
9. Jantzen, *Power, Gender, and Christian Mysticism*, 90.
10. Ibid., 91.
11. Ibid., 91.
12. Hägglund, *Arvet från Reformationen*, 74.
13. Luther, *Reihenpredigten über 2. Petrus, Judas und 1. Mose*, WA 14, 129–30.
14. Hägglund, *Arvet från Reformationen*, 80.

Origen, about the Holy Spirit being confined to the mind. Neither does he accept that flesh is something constrained in the body.[15]

When he argued against the scholastics he claimed that they only made the soul or its finer parts the subject of grace while Luther held that it is the whole human being that is flesh and the whole human being that is spirit, flesh when she hates, and spirit when she loves the law of God.[16]

Luther interpreted the *Song of Songs* in a quite unusual, even peculiar way. Instead of reading it literally, as a poem about conjugal love between two lovers, he read the poem metaphorically as the love song of King Solomon and his people.[17]

For Luther the erotic language became political. Following Bo Kristian Holm and Hans-Martin Gutman one could say that "the political sphere becomes eroticized."[18] Hence, nuptial imagery seems to be open to different interpretations. Despite Luther's critique of the tradition of allegorical interpretation, he himself used metaphors. He also reformulated the three estates using the Song in defense of political authority:

> The consequence of Luther's reading is that the political realm with the help of the nuptial imagery is interpreted under the headline of the utopia of the harmonized public domain, marked by tranquility, harmony and peace.[19]

This understanding of the harmonious state meant that anything that ruins this harmony had to be silenced, i.e. the schwärmer, the peasants, and the nobility.[20]

Having left a monolithic Lutheran society behind, we are aware of the danger of idealizing and expecting harmony in the political realm just as in the realm of *oeconomia* that in Luther's days meant the great family. As all history and tradition are ambivalent I will, however, also emphasize that Luther's interpretation makes the boundary between *oeconomia* and *politia* less clear. *Politia* is namely for Luther also a matter of mutual care.[21] Further,

---

15. Ibid., 79–80.

16. Luther, *Resolutiones Lutherianae super propositionibus suis Lipsiae disputatis*. WA 2, 415; cf. Hägglund, *Arvet från Reformationen*, 80.

17. Luther, *Vorlesungen über Jesaja und Hoheslied*, WA 31. II, 585–769.

18. Gutmann, *Über Liebe und Herrschaft. Luthers Verständnin von Intimität und Autorität im Kontext des Zivilisationsprozesses*, 211; Holm, "Luther's theological and political use of the nuptial metaphor."

19. Holm, "Luther's theological and political use of the nuptial metaphor."

20. Ibid.

21. Ibid.

Holm claims that the background for Luther's political use of nuptial imagery is his understanding of justification.

THE NUPTIAL METAPHOR—CRUCIAL TO LUTHER'S THEOLOGY

According to Holm, the nuptial metaphor emerges at "crucial places in Luther's theology." It "helps him to develop his doctrine of justification at a very crucial point."[22] In 1517 Luther states that every true Christian participates in all the blessings of Christ and the Church, even without indulgence letters.[23]

In his *Resolutiones* from 1518, Luther "now brings quotations from the *Song of Songs* into his argument, thereby giving thesis 37 a meaning that points towards its further development in *De duplici iustitia* and *De libertate Christiana*."[24]

Luther claims that it is impossible to be Christian without possessing Christ and all his gifts. Here, Luther quotes the Song of Songs 2:16 "My beloved is mine and I am his." In this context he argues that by "faith in Christ, a Christian is made one spirit and one body with Christ. For the two shall be one flesh (Gen 2:14). This is a great mystery, and I take it to mean Christ and the Church (Eph 5:31–32).[25]

22. Bo Kristian Holm traces Luther's new definition of justice to the time between 1516 and 1522, more specifically in Luther's commentary to the 37th of the 95 theses. See Holm, "Justification and Reciprocity," 101.

23. Luther, *Predigten, Disputationen*, WA 1, 235:9-11: "Quilibet verus christianus, sive vivus sive mortuus, habe participationem omnium bonorum Christi et Ecclesiae etiam sine literis veniarum a deo sibi datam."

24. Holm, "Luther's theological and political use of the nuptial metaphor."

25. Luther, *Predigten, Disputationen*, WA 1, 593:7-24: "Impossibile est esse Christianum, quin Christum habeat, Quod si Christum, et omnia simul quae Christi. Dicit enim B. Apostolus Ro: xiij. Induimini dominum Ihesum Christum. Et Ro: viij. Quomodo non omnia nobis cum illo donavit? Et i. Corin. iij. Omnia vestra, sive Cephas sive Paulus, sive vita sive mors. Et i. Cor: xij. Non estis vestri, sed membra de membro. Et aliis locis, ubi describit, unum corpus, unum panem, nos omnes esse in Christo singulos, alterum alterius membra. Et in Can: Dilectus meus mihi et ego illi. Quia per fidem Christi efficitur Christianus unus spiritus et unum cum Christo. Erunt enim duo in carne una, Quod sacramentum magnum est in Christo et Ecclesia. Cum ergo spiritus Christi sit in Christianis, per quem fratres cohaeredes, concorporales et cives fiunt Christi, quomodo ibi possit non esse participatio omnium bonorum Christi? nam et Christus ex eodem spiritu habet omnia sua. Ita fit per inaestimabiles divitias misericordiarum dei patris, ut Christianus possit gloriari et cum fiducia presumere in Christo omnia, scilicet quod iusticia, virtus, pacientia, humilitas, omnia merita Christi sint etiam sua per unitatem spiritus ex fide in illum, Rursum omnia peccata sua iam non sint sua sed Christi per eandem unitatem, in quo et absorbentur omnia." See also LW 31, 189–90.

Holm sees this as connected to "the centrality of economic considerations in Luther's theological development, especially concerning the inherent economy, i.e. the financial aspect in the theology of indulgencies."[26] Medieval theology is read as "focusing on the reciprocity of the cross of Christ and the 'self-crucifixion' of man, or its monetary equivalent."[27] For Luther the way to solve the absence of man to give anything back "was to focus on the plenitude only Christ could offer, because He makes it possible for human nature to participate in the divine. Human gifts are only possible as partaking in divine giving."[28] Here, according to Holm, Luther needs a strong metaphor for unification,[29] hence the use of nuptial imagery and the reference to Gen 2:14 where the two are said to become one flesh.[30] The first "righteousness follows the example of Christ (. . .) and is transformed into His likeness. (. . .) Not seeking His own good but ours only."[31] This is possible through the union between Christ and the Christian, which is like a marriage. Luther argues:

> Therefore through the first righteousness arises the voice of the bridegroom who says to the soul, "I am yours," but through the second comes the voice of the bride who answers, "I am yours." Then the marriage is consummated; it becomes strong and complete in accordance with the Song of Songs 2:16, "My beloved is mine and I am his." Then the soul no longer seeks to be righteous in and for itself, but it has Christ as its righteousness and therefore seeks only the welfare of others.[32]

26. Holm, "Luther's theological and political use of the nuptial metaphor." See also Holm "Der fröhliche Verkehr. Rechtfertigungslehre als 'Gabe-Theologie,'" 102.

27. Holm, "Luther's theological and political use of the nuptial metaphor."

28. Luther, *Predigten, Disputationen*, WA 1, 593:7-24; cf Holm, "Luther's theological and political use of the nuptial metaphor." See also Holm, "Der fröhliche Verkehr. Rechtfertigungslehre als 'Gabe-Theologie,'" 100.

29. Holm, "Der fröhliche Verkehr. Rechtfertigungslehre als 'Gabe-Theologie,'" 102-3.

30. Luther, *Sermo de duplici iustitia*, WA 2, 147:19-29. The first kind of righteousness is from God. It is alien to the human being. The second kind of righteousness, however, belongs to the human being. LW 31, 297.

31. Luther, *Sermo de duplici iustitia*, WA 2, 147:19-29; LW 31, 300.

32. Luther, *Sermo de duplici iustitia*, WA 2, 147:26-29: "Igitur per [27] iusticiam priorem oritur vox sponsi qui dicit ad animam 'tuus ego', per [28] posteriorem vero vox sponsae quae dicit 'tua ego': tunc factum est firmum, [29] [Hohel. 2, 16.] perfectum atque consummatum matrimonium, ut in Canticis: Dilectus meus [30] mihi et ego illi, q. d. 'dilectus meus est meus et ego sum sua'. Tunc anima [31] non querit amplius esse sibi iusta, sed habet suam iusticiam Christum, [32] quaerit ergo aliorum salutem tantummodo. Unde per Prophetam minatur [33] [Jer. 7, 34.] dominus Synagogae, quod auferetur ab ea vox leticiae, vox sponsi et vox sponse."

This is a way for Luther to create an opening for mutuality despite his early insistence on unilaterality:

> With the help of the Song of Songs 2:16 a certain mutuality is incorporated in the quite unilateral process of justification. The consummation of the marriage is constituted through the mutual self-giving expressed by the help of a quotation from the Song of Songs.[33]

DIVINE EMBRACE WITH ETHICAL IMPLICATIONS

For Martin Luther the heavenly embrace had ethical and political implications on earthly matters. As Bo Kristian Holm has shown Luther developed his sense of the gift in a direction that opened up for simultaneous giving between God and the human. This economy of the gift was thus opening up for mutuality and shared life, also in this world.

However, in this context I think it is important to stress that this is a mutuality with two distinct partners, yet together. Not even the consummation of the marriage is described as one partner disappearing or being dissolved into the other. Mutuality and union are not to be the same. Rather it has to do with sharing and with common ownership. It is not an attempt to *be* the other, but to be *with* the other. Yet, in a relationship I am changed as an individual. Kathryn A. Kleinhans suggests that "I am who I am in a relationship with others."[34] Christ is also changed. The word that became flesh is different after incarnation. While the Nicaean expression *homoousious* expressed Christ's unity with God, Calcedon 451 took a further step and emphasized that Christ is fully divine and fully human, with the Father and with us.[35] Such convivilatiy also has political implications.

The insight that "a single being is a contradiction in terms" is acquiring growing strength among philosophers, something that is opening up new understandings also of symbiosis. Catherine Keller claims that the existence of "*togetherness of life*, the *bios* of co-existence" is a form of symbiosis. She draws on Deleuze and Guattari who suggest that "each mulitiplicity is symbiotic" and argue that there are ties between "animals, plants and microorganisms, mad particles, a whole galaxy."[36] Keller therefore holds

33. Holm, "Luther's theological and political use of the nuptial metaphor."
34. Kleinhans, "Christ as Bride/groom: A Lutheran Feminist Relational Christology," 129.
35. Ibid., 130.
36. Keller, "Be a multiplicity. Ancestral anticipations," 83; See also Nancy, *Being Singular Plural*, 12; Deleuze and Guattari, *A Thousand Plateaus: Capitalism and Schizofrenia*, 250.

that a polydoxical theology ought to register a "creaturely multiplicity of us all, now, becoming." She suggests that we call this the *conviviality of the creation*.³⁷ Such a living together could take on an "atmosphere of gracious commensality, of unsentimental care and celebration."³⁸

Martin Luther drew on the symbol of marriage for the whole creation and used nuptial imagery to argue in favor of unsentimental care combined with desire and celebration in our shared life. In one of the table talks he lyrically speaks about how animals, trees, and plants are created for each other and lean towards each other in desire. In a sensuous language he argues that just as God has created man and woman for each other, all of creation is gendered, sexual and erotic. This pattern of marriage is something that is inscribed even in stones and corals. He exclaims: "This magnification of marriage is beautiful." ³⁹

Despite all the years in between and a different vocabulary I think that a focus on unsentimental care combined with celebration in our shared life is not a bad summary of some of Martin Luther's thoughts, especially when he draws on nuptial imagery. He would definitely argue that we all belong to the web of life and that our response to the divine gift ought to be celebration, or praise, and unsentimental care for the neighbor.

Unification leading to the sharing of everything is crucial in the treatise of *The Freedom of a Christian*, where nuptial imagery is used to describe what is referred to as the "happy exchange." The union between Christ and the soul is compared with the union between wife and husband.⁴⁰

GENDERED CONTRAST OR GENDER TRANSGRESSING?

If we are to think politically about mutuality and sharing in contemporary politics, it is important to discern constructive and oppressive elements in the imagery. As we know, the "happy exchange" is not described as

---

37. Keller, "Be a multiplicity. Ancestral anticipations," 83.

38. Ibid., 83.

39. Luther, Tischreden, WA TR 1, 560:12-24. See also Karant-Nunn, "The Masculinity of Martin Luther. Theory, Practicality, and Humor," 169.

40. "The third incomparable grace of faith is this, that it unites the soul to Christ, as the wife to the husband; by which mystery, as the Apostle teaches, Christ and the soul are made one flesh. Now if they are one flesh, and if a true marriage—[112] nay, by far the most perfect of all marriages—is accomplished between them (for human marriages are but feeble types of this one great marriage), then it follows that all they have becomes theirs in common, as well good things as evil things; so that whatsoever Christ possesses, that the believing soul may take to itself and boast of as its own, and whatever belongs to the soul, that Christ claims as his. Luther, *De libertate christiana*, WA 7, 110-12.

an exchange between equals. It is, furthermore, a gendered contrast: "If we compare these possessions, we shall see how inestimable is the gain. Christ is full of grace, life, and salvation; the soul is full of sin, death, and condemnation."[41] Hence, what is known as the happy exchange can be read through a heteropatriarchal, even misogynicistic, prism. The husband, Christ, has everything that is good, while the bride brings everything that is bad. This gendered contrast easily lends itself to a support for the subordination and disregard of women.

However, Luther "explicitly rejects androcentric generalizations."[42] A literal reading of gender in these texts, as performed by some early feminists, is not really relevant.[43] As Else Marie Wiberg Pederson points out, Luther's language explicitly rejects literalizing gender when talking about Christ. Furthermore, neither the New Testament nor Confessio Augustana describes Christ as a man, i.e. as *aner*, *vir*, or *Mann* in German. The emphasis is on the relationship between God and the human being that is called *antropos/sarx*, *homo* or *Mensch*. This is less visible in English, where a human being is called "man."[44] Wiberg Pedersen claims that for Luther the passion had to do with salvation and thus with the relationship between God and human beings, not between man and woman.[45]

An intertextual reading of Luther shows even more flexibility and reveals that the nuptial imagery also has gender transgression, i.e. queer qualities. Christ is not only the pursuer but also the pursued. He awaits the response from the bride. In a series of lectures on Isaiah Luther also describes the Christian as bridegroom and Christ as bride.[46]

---

41. Ibid., WA 7, 110–112.

42. Kleinhans, "Christ as Bride/groom," 130.

43. See e.g., Ruether, *Sexism and God-Talk: Towards a Feminist Theology*. Such a use of gender had been criticized among others by Eriksson, *The Meaning of Gender in Theology. Problems and Possibilities*.

44. Wiberg Pedersen, "One body in Christ? Ecclesiology and Ministry between Good Theology and Bad Anthropology," 59–82.

45. Wiberg Pedersen, "A Man Caught Between Bad Anthropology and Good Theology? Martin Luther's view of women generally and of Mary specifically," 191–201.

46. Luther, *Vorlesungen über Jesaja und Hoheslied*, WA 31, 2:261–585. "Thus all of us who believe are by faith bridegrooms and priest, something the world does not see but what faith accepts." When he ponders the mother image in Isaiah 66:9, he ascribes a double identity to Christ as bride and bridegroom who is able to conceive and give birth as well as give others the power to conceive. Else Marie Wiberg Pedersen has shown in Wiberg Pedersen, *Bernhard af Clairvaux. Teolog eller mystiker?*, 90, that Luther is influenced by Bernard who lived more than 400 years earlier when he uses erotic imagery and gender transgressing.

These applications may be a resource for politics, including a more reflexive, or oscillating, understanding of love beyond polarizations between *eros* and *agape*. Queer language opens up for a variation of relationships, intimate as well as political.

INTIMATE APPLICATIONS BECOME POLITICAL

In Luther's wedding sermon from 1531, after Luther had married Katharina von Bora, June 13, 1525, he uses almost identical formulations as Bernard of Clairvaux. Luther now applies nuptial language—or rather reapplies erotic language—on a love relationship between man and woman. Luther writes:

> The ancient doctors have rightly preached that marriage is praiseworthy because of children, loyalty and love. But the physical benefits are also a precious thing and justly extolled as the chief virtue of marriage, namely that spouses can rely upon each other and with confidence entrust all they have on this earth to each other, so that it is as safe with one's spouse as with oneself.[47]

If the physical benefits should be read as a physical closeness of their bodies, or rather as sharing a household, is not quite clear. It is not necessarily a contradiction. What is obvious is that Luther applies the metaphorical erotic language from the tradition to quite concrete conviviality in ordinary life as love between husband and wife and their household. It may actually be read as confirming love in this life, a consummation of the marriage rather than as erotic desire for the bittersweet, never fully available love in

---

47. Luther, Martin, *Eine hochzeit predigt uber den spruch zun Hebreern am Dreyzehenden Capitel*, WA 34, 52:5–9. "[5] Wol haben die alten Doctores geprediget, das der ehestand der frucht, [6] trew und lieb halben zuloben sey, Jst aber nicht auch die leibliche nuetzung [7] ein koestlich ding, das die erste tugent des ehestands geruemet ist, das sich ein [8] man auff sein weib verlassen darff, sein leib und gut auff dieser erden dem [9] weib troestlich befehlen, das es bey jhr als wol bewaret sey als bey jhm, Diese [10] frucht were auch wol eine, Aber wir wollen die selbigen nicht erzelen, befehlen [11] solchs den Rhetoren. Christlich und gottlich davon zu reden, ist das das [12] hochste, das Gottes wort an deinem weibe und an deinem man geschrieben ist, [13] wenn du dein weib also ansihest, als were nur eins und keins mehr auff [14] dieser welt, und wenn du deinen man also ansihest, als were nur einer und [15] sonst keiner mehr jnn der welt, das kein koenig, ja auch die Sonne nicht [16] schoener scheinen und jnn deinen augen leuchten sol als eben dein fraw odder [17] dein man, Denn alhie hastu Gottes wort, welchs dir die fraw odder den man [18] zuspricht, schenckt dir die [Bl. a iij] fraw oder den man, Spricht: der man sol dein [19] sein, die fraw sol dein, das gefelt mir so wol, alle Engel und Creaturn haben [20] lust und freud darob, Denn es ist jhe kein schmuck uber Gottes wort, damit du [21] dein weib ansihest als ein Gottes geschenck, Also kanstu kein bloedes gewissen haben."

the *eros* tradition.⁴⁸ Luther's use of nuptial imagery in his wedding sermon is yet another sign of his independent—and political—use of this metaphor.

If the erotic is understood as bittersweet and not fully available, one could say that Luther's "realm of intimacy" becomes "de-eroticised." Love as embrace and consummation is related to the present. Love between bride and bridegroom is physical and concrete and so is the divine embrace given in bread and wine.⁴⁹ Luther uses nuptial imagery both to describe the relationship between Christ and the soul, between husband and wife and, as Luther explicitly argues, between the King and his people. For Luther, the nuptial imagery can be read in various metaphorical ways; as a worldly application of divine love, in intimate relations, in the household and in society. I will argue that this way of reading Luther can make a constructive contribution to politics today, as "the political sphere becomes eroticised."⁵⁰

CONTEMPORARY POLITICAL CONTEXTS

Our time has witnessed a privatization of the public domain that includes sexualization. Concurrently politics is, however, often seen in technical terms as a game or as a technique for rational deliberation, without passion being involved. Such a perception of politics has been criticized by political scientist Chantal Mouffe, among others, who argues against what she labels the post-political rhetoric, where political disagreements are supposed to have ended.⁵¹ Instead she holds that group-based and more passionate politics also need to be part of the political discourse.⁵² She claims that a precondition for democracy is a "conflictual consensus" where you agree on basic values of freedom and egalitarianism but accept disagreements on how these values ought to be implemented. A distinction needs to be made between those accepting these basic values but fighting for another interpretation and those who do not accept them at all. While *antagonism* emerges between real enemies, between us/them who do not share any common ground and hence threatens to destroy the political community, *agonism*,

---

48. See Carson, *Eros the bittersweet: an essay*.

49. Martin Wendte claims that Luther argues "that the words of institution ("This is my body") are to be taken literally: Christ is present." Wendte, "This is my body, which is for You. Exploring the Significance of Luther's Theology of the Eucharist in a Technological Age," 99.

50. Holm, "Luther's theological and political use of the nuptial"; Gutmann, *Über Liebe und Herrschaft*, 211.

51. Mouffe, *On the Political*, 8, 20–21, 120–30.

52. Ibid.

according to Mouffe, is an alternative where the parties acknowledge their opponents as adversaries, but not as enemies.[53]

With this type of understanding, fighting over different interpretations, without violence and with respect for the other, is a basis for democracy. In many parts of the world this seems to be absent. Rather than *agonism* we witness *antagonism*. When Luther advised the princes to meet the peasant revolt with violence and repression, he did not respect the peasants or their human needs. The world Luther lived in was organized in authoritarian ways. His struggle for the freedom of a Christian implied liberation from papal authority but not from unjust worldly relationships.

Luther used the *Song of Songs* to argue in favor of political authority. The harmonic community where local princes or kings were seen as new King Solomons with a deep love of God seems to be an idealization with the practical purpose of distancing himself both from the Pope and from the Schwärmer.

With a historic distance it is easy to see that such an idealization of political authority and of the princes is dangerous and easily leads to complacency in relation to dominant structures of power. This is what happened in the Nordic countries during many centuries after Reformation. In contemporary politics we need to question an overemphasis on technological rationality and of politics as pure technique for rational deliberation. Today we may need more passion in politics. We also, however, need a passion for human rights that is able to discern. To be equal is not to be similar or the same. We need a passion that is realizing issues of power and asymmetries and tries to prevent healthy differences to be an excuse for or a disguise for injustice.

Moreover, Luther's understanding of marriage was developed at a time when gender hierarchy was seen as natural. As many feminists have pointed out, an emphasis on agape, and an idealization of marriage, can be exploitative and may neglect mutuality, not to mention the fact that love thrives in many contexts and forms, hetero, homo, and queer.

We therefore need to be sceptical of idealizations of the political as well as of the intimate. Neither the spheres of *oeconomia* or of *politia* are necessarily harmonious and fair. Having said that, I would nonetheless argue that Luther's use of nuptial imagery, with gender transgression and an emphasis on shared responsibility, is an important contribution in a globalised world, struggling with poverty and climate change.

53. Ibid.

RE-EROTICISING ETHICS AND POLITICS

If Luther "de-eroticised the realm of intimacy and eroticised the political realm," today we need both the desire of *eros* and the inspiration of mutual sharing to expand our sense of politics and responsibility.

As we know, Martin Luther was passionate in his insistence on the freedom of a Christian. Paradoxically, he argued that the Christian was the freest of all in relation to God. At the same time, the very same human being was a slave in relation to other humans who needed care. In relation to God, *coram Deo*, the Christian is free. No deeds are needed as the love of God is a gift, an embrace. In relation to the neighbor, *coram hominibus*, however, the Christian is not free at all. Your neighbor needs your care and tenderness. The ethical demand is thus part of ordinary life.[54] A need for forgiveness, solace and new start is therefore part of Christian life. For Luther this is to die and to be resurrected every day in Baptism.[55]

In my reading of Luther there is a relation between various forms of love. Divine love creates abundance, an overflow that is directed towards other fellow human beings. Responding to the need of the neighbor is therefore not only a response to claims, to the law, ethics, but also a response out of love, both understood as self-giving, agape, and as desire, *eros*.

Ethics without *eros* will namely wither. It dries out if law is all that remains. Yet, there is no escape from the tension of ethics and *eros*. As Catherine Keller reminds us, "*eros* severed from ethics will stimulate the ravishing violations that belong to a social structure of dominance and submission, which will strangle *eros* itself. Yet, an anti-erotic ethos ironically yields the same result."[56]

Eros theology has emphasized incarnation and *eros* and desire as a mutual process between God and humans. Carter Heyward's theology of mutuality led to the consecration of same-sex love and to developing the relationship between desire and justice.[57] Rita Nakashima Brock moves beyond the apathetic God to Eros as "the energy of incarnate love."[58] Furthermore, Catherine Keller claims that this is a challenge to traditional

---

54. Løgstrup, *The Ethical Demand*.

55. Luther, *Ein Sermon von dem heyligen hochwirdigen Sacrament der Tauffe*, WA 2, 724–37. Luther argues that Christian life is nothing else than the commencement of dying, from the time of baptism until the grave; for God wants to create men anew at the last day.

56. Keller, "Afterword: A Theology of Eros, After Transfiguring Passion," 372.

57. Heyward, *Touching our Strength: The Erotic as Power and the Love of God*.

58. Brock, *Journeys by Heart: A Christology of Erotic Power*, 49.

Aristotelian theology, which has portrayed God as perfect, without feelings and as the unmoved mover:

> The Christian Father's passionate love of the Son at least, and by implication the rest of us, found rich symbolization. But the metaphor of divine Eros, as the very God of monoteheism rather than a cute iconic residue of polytheism, remained until the twentieth century virtually unspeakable in theology. For the metaphysics cut into the opposite direction: Whether eros signifies too much sex or too little, mere lack seeking fullness, or an interplay of want and plenitude, it could not stand for the (differently classisized) God of closed perfection, the *actus purus* incapable of reception, of feeling, of so of change. The Aristotelinized deity could not by definition desire; desire had come to signify lack—and isn't He already perfect and self-sufficient?—The God of ontotheology can only "love" us in the sense of "doing what is good for us, for our sake, and never also for God's own."[59]

Keller and other Eros theologians have challenged the notion of the dispassionate Father and instead advocated an understanding of love as mutual between the divine and human. Keller is also arguing in favor of oscillating between love described as *eros* and *agape*. Such a "feminist Eros desires a world whose beauty is steeped in justice."[60] In my attempt to draw on nuptial imagery for politics, as Luther himself did, I think that this is an important challenge and an inspiration to rethink ethics in ways that bring the revolutionary embrace of love to bear on politics.

FROM CLOSE(D) COMMUNITIES TO A GLOBAL SOLIDARITY

Mutuality between Christ and the soul is described as an embrace between bride and bridegroom where the gift of love is given at the same moment.[61] Both exchange roles and both are being changed. Such an embrace could have radical political implications.

Desire and longing for the other and the gift of love give inspiration not only for intimate love between lovers, partners and spouses but within all spheres of society. Eros theology has challenged one-sided notions of love in favor of more oscillating versions of love where curiosity, longing,

---

59. Keller, "Afterword: A Theology of Eros, After Transfiguring Passion," 368–69.
60. Ibid., 372.
61. Holm, "Luther's theological and political use of the nuptial metaphor."

and desire for the unknown are resources to be tapped. If Martin Luther affirmed sexuality and ordinary life in the sixteenth century, today we need to eroticise politics in new ways. Again, to perceive love as more complex than traditional Lutheran ethics used to may emphasize exchange and oscillation. Keller holds that theology may help to heal the schism between the two forms of love as we do not wish to collapse the eros into agape, or vice versa.

> The dualism may better be healed by transmuting it into a figure of amatory oscillation. Eros irreducibly encodes desire for something more, for an other in excess of the self. Agape just as stubbornly signifies the gift of that excess. Eros may drive either greed or invitation; agape may express either domination or welcome. If, however, they oscillate as complementary flows or gestures of love, the desire grows in generosity, even as the gift becomes ever more inviting.[62]

If Luther idealized the relationship between King, the people and God to defend political authority, today we need passionate politics for mutuality and shared responsibility on a global basis. Where Luther saw *politia* as a sphere of promise in a relationship between God, the King and the people, we today need to go beyond imagined communities be they national or ethnic.

Living in a global world, where borders between the religious and the secular as well as between nations and states are becoming blurred, is a challenge to rethink what it means to be Christian. Many cultural traditions and varying modes of reasoning are already embedded within Christianity. It is plural, "polydox," claims Laurel Schneider.[63] She holds, in line with Thomas Reynolds, that to be a Christian already entails "being 'beyond' one's own local faith perspective."[64]

Hence, if a Lutheran confession once went hand in hand with national citizenship, we today need to rethink how the stands that Luther used in the tradition from Aristotle can be interpreted as spheres of solidarity. In such an ongoing interpretation of what I call the "spheres of promise" every human being is seen as created in the image of God, in need of solidarity and care within all spheres of society, within *Oeconomia*, *Politia*, and *Ecclesia*.

Solidarity, rather than charity, grows out of an insight that next time I could be the one in need. Its fertile soil is interdependence and relationality, between humans all over the world and between multiple ways of being Christian, Jewish, Muslim, Buddhist, and secular. It is in the in-betweens, in

62. Keller, "Afterword: A Theology of Eros, After Transfiguring Passion," 373.
63. Schneider, "Crib notes from Bethlehem," 21.
64. Ibid., 21.

the blurred borders between different spheres of life but also between God and humans, that we may facilitate and celebrate new creations.

For the sensual Martin Luther *eros*, sensuality and other blessings in life such as food, wine, community, and shelter were seen as gifts. To eat, drink, sing, and enjoy the company of friends is something that Luther recommended as a way of keeping doubts and distrust at bay, i.e. for Luther, the devil. If you find joy by thinking of a girl, please do so, he says.[65]

In this chapter I have been connecting earthly care and concern with divine *eros* and with the gift of love, *agape*, which Luther described as an unconditional gift. If *eros* nurtures an inspiration to search for a world of beauty and justice, *agape* is reminding us of the unconditional divine gift. Hence, where contemporary politics emphasize ambition and success as a condition for shelter, housing and community, drawing on the gift of love that Luther emphasizes in his nuptial imagery, i.e. both *eros* and *agape* could be an inspiration to a politics of solidarity, affluence, and generosity, in local as well as global relations.

However, just as *eros* without *agape* could become a "greedy grasp," so "agape without eros is immediately transformed into moralism."[66] According to Keller we are currently witnessing "the marriage of predatory transnational corporate power with that of a theocratically inclined state."[67] Rather than such a marriage I am arguing in favor of allowing the inspiration of the divine embrace, as expressed in nuptial imagery, to be an inspiration for justice and solidarity. At times we need a deep awareness that politics as technical dialogue could become a veil for dominance and hegemonic power and unfair structures. Just as feminist theologians have reminded us that one sided emphasis on *agape* is at risk of supporting the strong at the expense of the weak we today need to reveal global power structures centered on greed not on mutuality or shared responsibility.

As Luther had the courage to challenge an authority where only the wealthy could be saved, we today need to challenge power structures that claim that everything can be bought and sold. Structures need to be rethought in relation to an eschatological vision desiring a world steeped in justice and beauty. Luther dared to rethink the estates of Aristotle and to see them as spheres of promise for the good life. Today we need to expand the structures, the spheres of promise beyond national borders. In such a process we also need to challenge our own traditions and go from hierarchical

---

65. Luther, *Tischreden*, WA TR 1, 490 (nr 968). Cf. Stolt, *Luther själv, Hjärtats och glädjens teolog*, 18, 45.

66. Keller, "Afterword: A Theology of Eros, After Transfiguring Passion," 373.

67. Ibid., 373.

to democratic communities based on equality and respect of all individuals. We need to challenge closed spheres kept separate and realize that we live with porous boundaries between the individual and the communal, between the spheres of *oeconomia* and *politia* that both have to do with mutual care. If *eros* could be perceived as bitter sweet, not fully available, we may be inspired by the fact that Luther emphasized presence and materiality. The mutual gift transformed both bride and bridegroom and gave inspiration to an unsentimental care. To take the gift and the embrace as a point of departure is a way to allow the *eros* in nuptial imagery and in our lives to nurture passion for politics as care and mutuality. A divine embrace, as expressed in nuptial imagery, could thus become an inspiration for justice and solidarity.

BIBLIOGRAPHY

Brock Brian. "Why the Estates? Hans Ulrich's Recovery of an Unpopular Notion." *Studies in Christian Ethics* (2007) 20.

Brock, Rita Nakashima. *Journeys by Heart: A Christology of Erotic Power*. New York: Crossroads, 1994.

Brunner, Emil. *Das Gebot und die Ordnungen: Entwurf einer protestantisch-theologischen Ethik*. Tübingen: Mohr, 1939.

Deleuze, Gilles and Félix Guattari. *A Thousand Plateaus: Capitalism and Schizofrenia*. Minneapolis: University of Minnesota Press, 1987.

Carson, Anne. *Eros the Bittersweet: An Essay*. Center for Hellenic Studies. Princeton: Princeton University, 1998.

Eriksson, Anne Louise. *The Meaning of Gender in Theology: Problems and Possibilities*. Uppsala: Acta Universitatis Upsaliensis, 1995.

Gerle, Elisabeth. *Mänskliga rättigheter för Guds skull. Tolka text, tro och tradition*. Nora: Nya Doxa, 2006.

———. "Var dags och varje människas upprättelse." In *Luther som utmaning, Om frihet och ansvar*, edited by Elisabeth Gerle. Stockholm: Verbum, 2008.

Gutmann, Hans-Martin. *Über Liebe und Herrschaft. Luthers Verständnin von Intimität und Autorität im Kontext des Zivilisationsprozesses*. Göttingen: Vandenhoech & Ruprecht, 1991.

Heyward, Carter. *Touching our Strength: The Erotic as Power and the Love of God*. San Francisco: Harper & Row, 1989.

Holm, Bo Kristian. *Gabe und Geben bei Luther. Das Verhältnis zwischen Reziprozität und reformatorischer Rechtfertigungslehre*. TBT 134. Berlin, New York: Walter de Gruyter, 2006.

———. "Der fröhliche Verkehr. Rechtfertigungslehre als 'Gabe-Theologie.'" In *Die Gabe. Ein "Urwort" der Theologie?*, edited by Veronika Hoffmann, 33–54. Frankfurt am Main: Verlag Otto Lembeck, 2009.

———. "Justification and Reciprocity. Purification of 'Gift-Exchange' in Martin Luther and John Milbank." In *Word—Gift—Being*, edited by Bo Kristian Holm and Peter Widmann, 87–116. RPT 37. Tübingen: Mohr Siebeck, 2008.

———. "Luther's theological and political use of the nuptial metaphor," forthcoming.

———. "Rechtfertigung als gegenseitige Anerkennung." In *Angeklagt und Anerkannt. Luthers Rechtfertigungslehre in gegenwärtiger Verantwortung*, edited by Hans-Christian Knuth, 23–42. VLASR 6. Erlangen: Martin-Luther-Verlag, 2009.
Hägglund, Bengt. *Arvet från Reformationen, Teologihistoriska studier*. Göteborg: Församlingsförlaget, 2002.
Jantzen, Grace M. *Power, Gender, and Christian Mysticism*. Cambridge: Cambridge University Press, 1995.
Karant-Nunn, Susan C. "The Masculinity of Martin Luther. Theory, Practicality, and Humor." In *Masculinity in the Reformation Era*, edited by Scott E. Hendrix and Susan C. Karant-Nunn, 167–89. Kirksville, MI.: Truman Sate University Press, 2008.
Keller, Catherine. "Afterword: A Theology of Eros, After Transfiguring Passion." In *Toward a Theology of Eros: Transforming Passion at the Limits of Discipline*, edited by Virginia Burrus and Catherine Keller, 366–74. New York: Fordham University Press, 2006.
———. "Be a multiplicity. Ancestral anticipations." In *Polydoxy: Theology of Multiplicity and Relation*, edited by Catherine Keller and Laurel C. Schneider, 81–102. New York: Routledge, 2011.
Kleinhans, Kathryn A."Christ as Bride/groom: A Lutheran Feminist Relational Christology." In *Transformative Lutheran Theologies: Feminist, Womanist, and Mujerista Perspectives*, edited by Mary J. Streufert, 123–34. Minneapolis: Fortress, 2010.
Lögstrup, Knud Eiler. *The Ethical Demand*. Notre Dame: University of Notre Dame Press, 1997.
Louth, Andrew. *The Origins of the Christian Mystical Tradition: From Plato to Denys*, Oxford: Oxford University Press, 2009.
Luther, Martin. *De captivate Babylonica ecclesiae praeludium* (1520). In Martin Luther, Studienausgabe, Band 2, edited by Hans-Ulrich Delius et al., Berlin, Evangelische Verlagsanstalt, 1992 (see also WA 6: 497–573).
———. *De libertate christiana* (1520). WA 7. Weimar: Hermann Böhlaus Nachfolger, 1897.
———. *Eine hochzeit predigt uber den spruch zun Hebreern am Dreyzehenden Capitel* (1531). WA 34, Erste Abteilung. Weimar: Hermann Böhlaus Nachfolger, 1908.
———. *Ein Sermon von dem heyligen hochwirdigen Sacrament der Tauffe* (1519). WA 2. Weimar: Hermann Böhlau, 1884.
———. *Epistel S. Johannis von der Liebe. 1. Johannis. 4* (1532). WA 36. Weimar: Hermann Böhlaus Nachfolger, 1909.
———. *Predigten, Disputationen* (1512–1518). WA 1. Weimar: Hermann Böhlau, 1883.
———. *Reihenpredigten über 2. Petrus, Judas und 1. Mose* (1523–1524). WA 14. Weimar: Hermann Böhlaus Nachfolger, 1895.
———. *Resolutiones Lutherianae super propositionibus suis Lipsiae disputatis* (1519). WA 2. Weimar: Hermann Böhlau, 1884.
———. *Sermo de duplici iustitia* (1519). WA 2. Weimar: Hermann Böhlau, 1884.
———. *Tischreden* (1531–1535). WA TR 1. Weimar: Hermann Böhlaus Nachfolger, 1912.
———. *Vorlesungen über Jesaja und Hoheslied* (1530). WA 31, Zweite Abteilung. Weimar: Hermann Böhlaus Nachfolger, 1914.
Mouffe, Chantal. *On the Political*. London: Routledge, 2005.

Nancy, Jean-Luc. *Being Singular Plural*. Palo Alto: Stanford University Press, 2000.
Origen. *Prologue to the Commentary on the Song of Songs*. Introduction by Rowan A. Greer. In *An Exhortation to Martydom, Prayer and Selected Works*. Classics of Western Spirituality, edited by Rowan Greer. London: SPCK, 1979.
Rubenson, Samuel. "Himmelsk åtrå. Höga Visan i tidigkristen tolkning." In *Eros och Agape. Barmhärtighet, kärlek och mystik i den tidiga kyrkan*, edited by Henrik Rydell Johnsén and Per Rönnegård, 105-27. SIDOR Skellefteå: Artos, 2009.
Ruether, Rosemarie Radford. *Sexism and God-Talk: Towards a Feminist Theology*. Boston: Beacon, 1983.
Schneider, Laurel. "Crib notes from Bethlehem." In *Polydoxy. Theology of Multiplicity and Relation*, edited by Catherine Keller and Laurel C. Schneider, 19-35. New York: Routledge, 2011.
Stolt, Birgit. *Luther själv, Hjärtats och glädjens teolog*. Skellefteå: Artos, 2004.
Wendte, Martin. "This is my body, which is for you. Exploring the significance of Luther's theology of the Eucharist in a technological age." In *The Body Unbound, Philosophical Perspectives on Politics, Embodiment and Religion*, edited by Ola Sigurdson et al., 89-105. Newcastle: Cambridge Scholars, 2010.
Wiberg Pedersen, Else Marie. *Bernhard af Clairvaux. Teolog eller mystiker?* Köpenhamn: Anis, 2008.
———. "A Man Caught Between Bad Anthropology and Good Theology? Martin Luther's view of women generally and of Mary specifically." In *Dialog* 49.3 (2010) 191-201.
———. "One body in Christ? Ecclesiology and Ministry between Good Theology and Bad Anthropology." In *Like Living Stones. Lutheran Reflections on the One, Holy, Catholic, and Apostolic Church*, edited by Hans-Peter Grosshans and Martin L. Sinaga, 59-82. Geneva: LWF Studies, 2011.
Wingren, Gustaf. *Creation and Gospel. The New Situation on European Theology*. Eugene: Wipf & Stock, 2004.
———. *Creation and Law*. Eugene: Wipf & Stock, 2003.
———. *Man and the Incarnation. A Study in the Biblical Theology of Irenaeus*. Eugene: Wipf & Stock, 2004.

www.ingramcontent.com/pod-product-compliance
Lightning Source LLC
Chambersburg PA
CBHW050440240426
43661CB00055B/2457